Please return or renew by

D0946895

The Allocation of Economic Resources

The Allocation of
Economic Resources

by

MOSES ABRAMOVITZ   GEORGE W. HILTON

ARMEN ALCHIAN   H. S. HOUTHAKKER

KENNETH J. ARROW   CHARLES E. LINDBLOM

PAUL A. BARAN   MELVIN W. REDER

PHILIP W. CARTWRIGHT   TIBOR SCITOVSKY

HOLLIS B. CHENERY   E. S. SHAW

LORIE TARSHIS

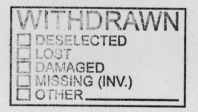

WITHDRAWN
☐ DESELECTED
☐ LOST
☐ DAMAGED
☐ MISSING (INV.)
☐ OTHER_____

STANFORD UNIVERSITY PRESS

STANFORD, CALIFORNIA

HB
601
A454
1968

STANFORD UNIVERSITY PRESS
STANFORD, CALIFORNIA
LONDON: OXFORD UNIVERSITY PRESS
© 1959 BY THE BOARD OF TRUSTEES OF THE
LELAND STANFORD JUNIOR UNIVERSITY
PRINTED IN THE UNITED STATES OF AMERICA

ORIGINAL EDITION 1959
REPRINTED 1961, 1964, 1965, 1968

WARD CHIPMAN LIBRARY
U.N.B. IN SAINT JOHN

Preface

This collection of essays has to do primarily with allocation and distribution of economic resources. As colleagues and students of Professor Haley, the authors of these papers have greatly benefited from his learning and spirit of critical inquiry in this large and important field of economic research. It is with a deep sense of gratitude, admiration, and affection that the contributors dedicate the present volume to Bernard Francis Haley on the occasion of his sixtieth birthday.

PAUL A. BARAN
TIBOR SCITOVSKY
EDWARD S. SHAW

Stanford and Berkeley, California
August 26, 1958

Contents

The Allocation of Economic Resources

The Welfare Interpretation of Secular Trends In National Income and Product[1]

MOSES ABRAMOVITZ

It is commonly said that, since national product is our most nearly comprehensive measure of economic achievement, we may best define economic growth as a sustained increase of either *per capita* or aggregate national product or income. Few scholars, it is true, are unaware of the fact that national income is not an utterly comprehensive measure, and few fail to recognize that its meaning is uncertain. Studies of economic growth, nevertheless, almost invariably treat long-term change in national product as the most basic index of national economic achievement and seek to associate other variables with it as causes, concomitants, and effects.

This fact makes it useful to raise anew the much-discussed questions of the measurement of national product and income over time and the interpretation of the resulting tables, for these questions have been examined in the past with an eye chiefly to other problems. These have had to do either with tests of the desirability of economic reforms or policies or with the measurement of short-term fluctuations of aggregate output. In either event, the tables of national income generally refer to particular countries, and the comparisons of interest relate to adjacent years or to quite short periods of the order of duration of business cycles. The problems of achieving consistent and meaningful results take their character from this relatively short-term focus and from the stability in the nature and organization of the economy and of the society at large, on which we generally have a right to count for short periods within single nations.

Within comparatively recent years, however, the phenomena and problems of long-term growth have again come to occupy a place in the front

[1] An earlier draft of this paper was presented to the Conference on Research in Income and Wealth which met in Williamstown, Mass. in September, 1957. The present revision has benefited from the advice of several generous readers, especially from Professor Abram Bergson's comments read to the conference and from discussions with Professors Richard Easterlin and Tibor Scitovsky.

rank of economic studies, coordinate with questions of resource allocation and short-term fluctuations. For growth studies, we are, as stated,
interested in sustained movements, changes which, in Professor Kuznets'
definition, "extend beyond a period so short that they might be confused
with transient disturbances, either roughly recurrent and associated with
business cycles or more irregular and often associated with calamities,
natural or man-made. For practical purposes a period not much shorter
than half a century is desirable" (1). Further, since we are inevitably
concerned with comparisons of rates of growth in different periods, measurements stretching over several half-centuries are necessary. Accordingly,
we have seen efforts to extend the span of national product tables over
periods of one hundred or one hundred and fifty years, or even longer. It
is now not uncommon to compare levels of national income in periods
separated by a century or more in time and by radical changes in the
structure of economic life and to make judgments about differences in
levels of output and in rates of growth.[2] In these circumstances, it is appropriate that we ask ourselves whether comprehensive and consistent
measures of national income and product covering such long periods of
time can be achieved and what meaning can be attached to them.

II

In order to make some contribution to the renewal of this discussion
and also to help indicate what place this single essay can hope to have

[2] Simon Kuznets' well-known tables for the United States now extend from
1869 to 1953, a span of 84 years, and he has assembled estimates in constant prices
for ten other countries extending back to various years from 1841 to 1878 ("Quantitative Aspects of the Economic Growth of Nations," *Economic Development and
Cultural Changes*, October 1956). The Conference on Income and Wealth devoted
its 1958 meetings to the consideration of an attempt to extend the various components of a national product table for the United States back to the beginning of
the 19th century. Phyllis Deane has recently devoted two articles to a review of
contemporary estimates of British national income in the nineteenth century, "the
object being to extract their implications for a study of the long-term growth of
the economy" (*Economic History Review*, April 1956; April 1957). Kuznets has
used long-term estimates of national product in numerous countries in an attempt
to establish a tendency toward retardation in the rate of economic growth (*ibid.*).
At the same time, Colin Clark, Kuznets, and many other scholars have employed
national product figures to compare levels of output and income in all or virtually
all the nations of the world from the economically most advanced to the most primitive. Such comparisons obviously raise problems that parallel those raised by long-
range inter-temporal comparisons for a single country, since the differences in economic organization and spirit which separate Liberia or Thailand from Great Britain
or the United States today are surely no less profound than those that separate contemporary Great Britain and America from their early periods of industrialization
or their pre-industrial past. Although the problems are largely parallel, I shall,
for convenience in exposition, confine myself to a discussion of the interpretation
of national income figures in studies of the economic growth of individual countries.

within the broad limits of the problem, we must go back to the beginning. Economic growth takes its meaning from a conception of the interest of society. Conventionally, the view taken by economists is the utilitarian view that the interest of society lies in satisfying the wants of the society's individual members. Such satisfactions are the content of *welfare*. Since Pigou, further, economists have generally distinguished between social welfare, or welfare at large, and the narrower concept of economic welfare which refers to "that part of social welfare that can be brought directly or indirectly into relation with the measuring rod of money" (2). National product, in turn, is taken to be the objective, measurable counterpart of economic welfare, and that is why sustained change in national product is commonly accepted as the basic index of economic growth.

When economists explicitly or implicitly accept the identification of economic welfare with the supply of goods and services, they are not unaware of the difference between economic and social welfare or of the fact that causes which affect economic welfare favorably may conceivably affect social welfare unfavorably. Pigou himself pointed to such matters as the impact of urbanization on family life, the influence of industrialization on the character of work and on the status and dignity of workers, and the relation between the character of consumption and the development or frustration of people's latent talents. The importance of these matters, and of others that might be added, for the satisfaction of human wants in economic life can hardly be contested. Economists have, nevertheless, normally disregarded possible divergences between the effects of identical causes upon economic and social welfare. In part, perhaps, this has been a matter of expediency reflecting our feeling about a sensible division of labor between economics and the other social sciences. More fundamentally, however, the practice rests upon an empirical judgment. Pigou expressed it in his dictum that there is a clear presumption that changes in economic welfare indicate changes in social welfare in the same direction, if not in the same degree. We may rephrase this by saying that we have normally operated on the view that the dominant effect of economic causes is on the quantity of output and that satisfactions from changes in output overshadow those from concomitant changes in the organization, structure, and location of industry and population and in other aspects of life.

If we now reconsider Pigou's dictum, it must be clear that its authority rests heavily on the fact that we have been preoccupied in the past with short-term problems in single countries. Production is subject to marked short-term fluctuations, while the structure and manner of economic life change only slowly. It is natural and right, in such circumstances, to attend to the former while disregarding the latter. But when we compare generations and half-centuries, we cannot escape the fact that the causes which produce large differences in output also shape the nature and organization of work and modify the substance of our material opportunities, liberties, and security, and, therefore, the satisfaction we can obtain from these aspects or consequences of economic activity and organization. We should also recognize that the relative importance of the manner in which things are produced and incomes earned tends to become larger as the level of output per head increases. For at low levels of income, physical survival itself is a matter of additional output, while at high levels of income, increments to output satisfy far less urgent needs. As income increases, the additional satisfactions we can obtain from economic activity come to depend more and more on the ways we earn our living rather than on how much more we earn.

The somewhat obvious moral of this section, therefore, is that, for studies of economic growth, the association between social welfare and national income as the measurable counterpart of economic welfare breaks down. Over long periods of time, the satisfactions from other aspects of economic life change concomitantly with output, but not necessarily in the same direction as do those from output, surely not in the same proportion. Changes in national product as a measure of output are, therefore, at best a measure of one aspect of economic growth. They cannot be its sovereign index.[3]

III

In line with this argument, I regard economic growth in this essay as a sustained change in the contribution of economic activity to social welfare, and I propose to consider how far national product measures can be treated as indexes of the contribution of *output* (which is one important aspect of economic activity) to social welfare. These are the most significant meanings we can attribute to economic growth and to national product as an index of growth, and also the senses in which these terms are most commonly used (4). It is important to notice, however, that national product figures have been interpreted in another, more restricted sense, simply as indexes of change in the productive capacity or production potential of an economy. The professed aim of national product measures on this second view is to obtain an indication of change in an economy's capacity to produce alternative collections of goods without regard to its relative capacity to satisfy the wants of individuals. Whether these two apparently distinct lines of approach—the Welfare Approach and the Production Potential Approach—can be treated as fundamentally independent, or whether, at bottom, capacity to produce goods and capacity to satisfy wants are conceptually identical is an important question. It becomes all the more important as we discover basic difficulties with the

---

[3] Cf. Simon Kuznets' statement: "National income . . . gauges the net positive contribution to consumers' satisfaction in the form of commodities and services; the burden of work and discomfort are ignored . . ." [*National Income: A Summary of Findings* (5), p. 127].

Welfare Approach. But this is a question I must leave to one side. This essay is concerned with national product as a welfare measure over long periods.

In this discussion, my intention is to confine myself to some questions of principle, disregarding all the practical problems of statistical estimation. Such questions of principle may be said to be of two sorts. One arises from the need to achieve a comprehensive and consistent catalogue of the physical output of commodities and services over long periods of time. Under this heading there is, first, the question of maintaining a consistent distinction between "goods" and "nongoods" or between productive and nonproductive activities, having in mind the welfare objective of the estimates. It is a vexing question because, in the course of industrialization, certain goods that once were free have become scarce, or vice versa, because the sphere of household and other unpaid production has shrunk in favor of commercial production, because output includes capital formation as well as goods consumed immediately by individuals, and because of the great rise in government output for which the test of consumer demand in the market place is not available.

Under the same heading, secondly, is the question of distinguishing consistently between final goods and intermediate goods in a fashion which properly reflects the welfare goal of the index. The normal procedure of assuming that consumer outlays are made for final products, while business spending is either for capital goods or intermediate goods is unsatisfactory. Significant segments of consumer outlays are spent to raise or support the individual's capacity to earn income, and these segments have been of variable importance principally because the urbanization of industry, the growing complexity of economic life, and the changing role of education have imposed serious "business" expenses upon households and individuals. The provision of consumer services under the guise of corporate business expense has also grown, less rapidly perhaps, but still notably.

The goods and services provided by the government, of substantial importance in recent decades, must also be separated into final and intermediate categories. While some government services are clearly of aid to individuals and some clearly support particular industries, a large segment of government services provides diffused utilities which help support the social or economic organization of the nation. There appears to be no secure way to divide these services into those flowing to consumers (final goods) and those which merely support other production (intermediate goods). Estimates made on alternative bases are presumably indicated.

Important as this first sort of problem is, I shall, nevertheless, disregard it, partly because it has already been discussed at length (5), partly because the questions that arise under it seem to me to be less critical. Choices must be made concerning the treatment of certain free goods, concerning household production, concerning government services, and so on. But there seems to be no fundamental difficulty in the way of making reasonable choices or, at worst, of providing alternative estimates.

The second sort of problem, however, is less tractable. To arrive at a measure of the contribution of output to welfare, the individual categories of final goods must be combined into a significant value total whose changes have a clear and relevant meaning. Here the difficulties are of an entirely different order when we consider them in the context of long-term growth. I shall try to state the nature of these difficulties in the following sections.

IV

When one has catalogued the final goods and services that are relevant to the satisfaction of the wants of individuals, the physical quantities must be weighted in such a fashion as to produce a value aggregate which can be interpreted as a welfare index. The current view of this matter rests on Pigou's formulation in the fourth edition of the *Economics of Welfare* (2). This has been restated and further refined by Hicks and others (6–8). I start with a very brief exposition following Hicks.

If we have valued the physical components of national product at their market prices, we may imagine two situations, I and II, for each of which we have a collection of two goods Q_1 (composed of q_1 and q_1') and Q_2 (q_2 and q_2') and corresponding prices, p_1 and p_1' and p_2 and p_2'. Let this information refer to a single individual, and let us represent the information on an indifference diagram (see Figure 1).

$P_1 P_1$ and $P_2 P_2$ are price lines and indicate the individual's opportunities to purchase in the two situations. Q_1 and Q_2 are the collections of goods chosen. The actual shapes of the indifference curves through these points are unknown. But consumer equilibrium implies that the indifference curves through Q_1 and Q_2 are tangent to the price lines at those points. Consumer equilibrium also implies that indifference curves are convex to the axes at those points and do not intersect their corresponding price lines. Finally—if the individual has a rational and consistent body of preferences, and if these do not change—the indifference curves will not intersect.

It follows from these considerations that points to the left of the price line through Q_2 are inferior to Q_2. Points to the right are not necessarily superior; the answer depends on the curvature of the indifference curve through Q_2 about which we know nothing. In the Hicks diagram Q_2 is preferred to Q_1.

Still following Hicks, we can express the meaning of this comparison substantively. We note that the price lines tell not only the terms on which one commodity can be exchanged for another, but that they also represent the various aggregate collections of goods available to the individual in each year, given his income and the prices. The price line through Q_1

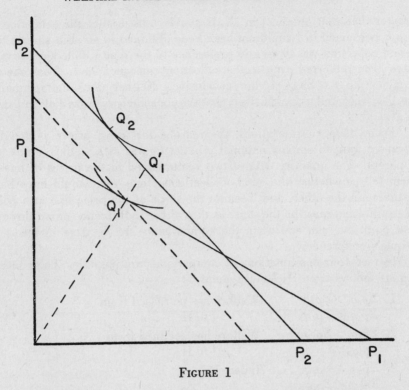

FIGURE 1

parallel to P_2P_2 (the dotted line in the figure), therefore, tells us what are the various collections of goods open to a man confronted with the prices of situation II, but with an income just sufficient to purchase the collection Q_1. And if Q_1 lies to the left of P_2P_2, the price line through Q_1 parallel to P_2P_2 will lie to the left of the latter and represent a lower income in the following important sense (as the diagram makes evident): that the collection of goods available in situation I could also be purchased in situation II, and in larger quantity (Q_1'). Since a different collection is, in fact, chosen and presumably preferred, we may infer that the collection consumed in II is preferred to that consumed in I.

In terms of income in constant prices, a preferred position in II compared with I is indicated by the inequality, $\Sigma p_2q_2 > \Sigma p_2q_1$, that is, by a comparison in which physical quantities are valued at year II prices. Similarly, a preferred position in I is indicated by the inequality $\Sigma p_1q_1 > \Sigma p_1q_2$, that is, by a comparison in which physical quantities are valued at year I prices. These, of course, are the comparisons which the deflation of national product by price indexes of the Laspeyre and Paasche types are supposed to approximate.

It should be noted, however, that the opposite of the first inequality (i.e., $\Sigma p_2q_2 < \Sigma p_2q_1$) does *not* mean that real value obtainable in I is greater than that obtained in II. It merely tells us that the collection of goods consumed in I could not have been obtained in II. But since a different collection was chosen in preference to the type I collection, it may have been preferred even to the collection consumed in I. Thus the inequality $\Sigma p_2 q_2 < \Sigma p_2 q_1$ is not conclusive. Neither does the inequality $\Sigma p_1 q_1 < \Sigma p_1 q_2$ tell us conclusively that the consumer was worse off in I than in II.

From these considerations, the reasons for using prices as weights when we want to employ national product figures as a welfare index are apparent. The quantity data of two years valued in the prices of one of them tell us whether the goods collection of one year would have been available in the other, and, because the slope of the price line at a point of equilibrium must be the same as that of the indifference curve through that point, we can say when the comparisons are decisive in terms of people's preferences.

In fact, four combinations of comparisons are possible. Their meaning, as follows from Hicks' argument, is

1. $\Sigma p_2 q_2 > \Sigma p_2 q_1$ Welfare has increased from
   $\Sigma p_1 q_1 < \Sigma p_1 q_2$ I to II

2. $\Sigma p_1 q_1 > \Sigma p_1 q_2$ Welfare has declined from
   $\Sigma p_2 q_2 < \Sigma p_2 q_1$ I to II

3. $\Sigma p_2 q_2 < \Sigma p_2 q_1$ Indecisive
   $\Sigma p_1 q_1 < \Sigma p_1 q_2$

4. $\Sigma p_2 q_2 > \Sigma p_2 q_1$ A contradiction. Either the assumption of con-
   $\Sigma p_1 q_1 > \Sigma p_1 q_2$ stant tastes is invalid or our observations do
                       not refer to equilibrium positions.

These criteria tell us when, under certain assumptions about the character and constancy of tastes, we can infer from income data that an individual will deem himself better or worse off and when we can infer nothing. If the criteria can be extended from the individual to the economy at large, it is clear that at least limited welfare implications could be drawn from national product figures. The extension of the Hicks criteria to the group of individuals composing a society has, therefore, been the main concern of the recent literature on the subject. The complications of the argument make it necessary to treat it very cursorily, and I confine myself to indicating the character of the results.

The problem may be posed by recognizing that, in the case of a nation, the inequality $\Sigma p_2 q_2 > \Sigma p_2 q_1$ still tells us that the bundle of goods obtained in Year II was preferred to a bundle of Year I composition but larger in size than that obtained in Year I.[4] *A fortiori*, from the point of view of

---

[4] The index numbers cannot tell us that a bundle of goods of Year I type could actually have been obtained in Year II in larger quantity. They could do this only

Year II tastes, the bundle obtained in Year II was preferred to the bundle obtained in Year I. But the index numbers can tell us nothing about the distributions of the goods enjoyed in the two periods among the numbers of the society.

In this situation, the modern welfare theory, seeking very wide generalizations, forces itself to operate under highly restrictive rules. It assumes that the satisfaction of individuals is incomparable. Hence, if there has been a shift in distribution which leaves any single person in II less well off than he was in I, the theory proposes to say nothing about an actual increase in welfare.

Hicks attempted to bypass this difficulty by making the index number comparison signify a change, not in the actual but in the *potential* welfare afforded by the bundles of goods acquired. He argued that if the bundle of goods acquired in II were larger than that in I, there must be some distribution of the bundle enjoyed in I which would make everyone worse off than in II. And he goes on:

As compared with this particular distribution, every other distribution of the q_1's would make some people better off and some worse off. Consequently, if there is one distribution of the q_1's in which every member of the group is worse off than he actually is in the II situation, there can be no distribution in which everyone is better off, or even as well off. Thus if we start from any actual distribution of wealth in the I situation, what the condition $\Sigma p_2 q_2 > \Sigma p_2 q_1$ tells us is that it is impossible to reach, by redistribution, a position in which everyone is as well off as he is in the II situation.

This would seem to be quite acceptable as a definition of increase in real social income. [(6), p. 111.]

The general acceptability of this conclusion has been challenged by Samuelson (8), and Scitovsky (9) has attempted to define again the limited conditions under which a change in national income may be interpreted as change of potential welfare in the same direction. I bypass the details of this argument in order to explore some difficulties with which the Hicks approach and the subsequent discussion does not grapple.

The practical importance of these difficulties depends largely, although not exclusively, upon the fact that the question to which the Hicks criteria are directed is not a sufficiently far-reaching question for studies of economic growth. The question Hicks tries to answer is, "Has welfare risen or declined between two dates?" For studies of economic growth, however, we clearly want something more. We want to be able to say not only that welfare in II is greater than in I, but also that the improvement from

---

if prices represented marginal costs and if the latter were constant. But this is immaterial to a welfare judgment which depends solely on the proposition that the indifference curve tangent to a price line stands ordinally higher than any other indifference curve touching the price line. Hence (in terms of Fig. 1) if $\Sigma p_2 q_2 > \Sigma p_2 q_1$, Q_2 is preferred to Q_1', which is preferred to Q_1.

II to III is greater or less than that between I and II, and so on. The Hicks question is one that is appropriate for problems having to do with the effects of some possible or proposed change in economic organization, or of taxes, subsidies, or the like, upon the current level of output. Will the effect be to raise or lower welfare? In growth studies, however, we are continually attempting to determine whether the rate of increase of output was larger or smaller in one long period than in another. Indeed, unless such differences between rates of growth in different long periods can be established and connected with other variables as cause or effect, the core of growth studies would disappear. When the question is posed in this way, the welfare interpretation of national product becomes far more difficult, at the present time surely impossible. Two sorts of problems appear. One concerns the price data by which physical quantities are combined, or value aggregates deflated. The other concerns the character and stability of utility functions, that is, the psychological presuppositions of the welfare interpretation.

V

I start with prices. The welfare approach to national product calls for the construction of national product series in which physical quantities are weighted by market prices. The reason is that market prices in equilibrium are supposed to be indexes of relative marginal utilities or of marginal rates of substitution. It is this assumption which, in terms of Figure 1, enables us to say that Q_2 lies on a higher indifference curve than does Q_1' and so is a preferred position. A number of difficulties, however, arise.

First, when we consider the problem of a society rather than an individual, the inference we should like to draw from price-weighted output indexes is strictly permissible only if the choices of one individual do not affect the satisfactions obtained by others—only if private marginal utility does not differ from social marginal utility. But if, to use a hackneyed illustration, a wholesale decision to abandon trains in favor of automobiles causes a traffic and parking problem, the attempt by individuals to maximize their private satisfactions may cause group welfare to decline. Q_2 may lie on a lower indifference curve than Q_1'. We are, therefore, no longer able to say unambiguously that Q_2 lies on a higher indifference curve than Q_1, even if output potential has risen. This obviously aggravates the difficulty of interpreting rates of growth of output in terms of welfare.

If we consider this problem in the context of the long-term development of the economy, what must stand out, I believe, is the fact that the growth of large cities and the radical improvements in transportation and communication have greatly increased the dependence of each person's satisfaction on the consumption choices of others. There is no way to say, on the basis of general considerations, whether private marginal utility commonly exceeds social marginal utility or the reverse; but it does seem right to think that the index number criteria become less reliable instruments of welfare analysis as the interdependence of people's lives increases.

The argument so far refers only to satisfactions obtained from consumer goods proper, but national product is a broader entity. Like the goods and services which flow to consumers directly and immediately, the portions of final product offset by savings and government outlay ought to be valued according to their relative marginal utility to consumers. During the last century in the United States these categories of output have risen, in orders of magnitude, from perhaps 10 per cent to 20 or 30 per cent of net national product, depending on the portion of government expenditure treated as final. Yet it seems doubtful that the goods in question are valued at figures we can take to be even approximations of relative marginal utility. Moreover, no one can say whether the weights at which they enter into the national product accounts on the whole overstate their relative marginal utility or understate it, or whether they have done one or the other consistently. Thus a bias of unknown size and possibly changing direction is injected into the national accounts considered as an index of welfare.

Ideally, the capital formation element in national product in any period ought to be assigned a value equal to the discounted worth of the expected future proceeds of real new capital to its present beneficial owners. In the course of the last 150 years, it is clear that a growing proportion of private investment has come to be made by managers of firms who are not the beneficial owners of the capital and that, at present, the bulk of private investment is so made. At best, this portion of investment enters the national product at values equal to the discounted worth of the expected future yields as these are assessed by the managers of corporate enterprises. These are, no doubt, better evaluators of future yields than are most of the beneficial owners. The development of the capital market has meant that, on the whole, a growing share of the flow of investment funds has come into the hands of better informed and more skillful evaluators of future possibilities. So far as that goes, the contribution of investment to welfare presumably has been growing more rapidly than the deflated value of new capital goods. But it is also clear that the rates at which corporate managers discount future possibilities for futurity and risk are not equal to the rates which beneficial owners would apply against the same set of possibilities. The function of the capital market, from one point of view, is to move investible funds into the hands of people who discount the future more optimistically and at a lower rate of time preference than do the savers themselves. So far as this is accomplished, the output of the future is made greater, but riskier, than savers would think it worth while to do. By the same token, the value of new capital to its ultimate beneficiaries is something other than the value assigned to it in

the accounts, and, considering the elaborate and indirect processes of
security trading and speculation by which savings are channeled to investors and securities to intermediate credit institutions and thence, in
changed form, to savers, it is not at all clear what the relation between
these values is.

The difficulty with the valuation of government output is of somewhat
the same sort. We should want to enter final goods and services provided
by government at values proportionate to their marginal utility to consumers. We are forced to value this category at the cost to the government. Since the quantities provided are determined by a nonmarket process, value to consumers must, in general, be different from cost.

This is inevitable. Most things provided by government have been
brought into the government sphere because the market process would
itself be inefficient. The value of such things to consumers at large is
deemed greater than individuals would assign to them in their household
budgets. But when the government does act, there is no reason to think
that its decisions are wise, certainly no reason to think that marginal social
utility is equated with cost. The political process is manifestly different
from that by which individuals make market choices and test results
against experience. Phrases like "the government output consists of goods
and services we choose to provide collectively rather than privately" have
their uses in certain spheres; but they do not help us assimilate government
and private output into a single set of accounts consistently valued over
time in such fashion as to express the contribution of output to welfare.

VI

I turn, finally, to the psychological implications of the welfare interpretation of secular trends in national product. The commitments we must
make in this connection are much more far-reaching than we are required
to make when we attempt simply to say whether welfare is higher or
lower in one period than it is in another. For the latter purpose, a simple
ordinal proposition about the relation between output and welfare is
enough. We need only agree that—apart from changes in distribution—
if the supply of goods is larger, the level of welfare is higher. But when
we shift our sights to national product as a measure of growth, the welfare
interpretation demands that we be able to make judgments about the implications of differences between the rates of growth of output in different
periods for rates of increase in welfare. For this purpose, simple, ordinal
propositions about the relation between level of output and level of welfare are not enough; for, if we are to say that an increase in the rate of
growth of output implies an increase in the rate of growth of welfare, we
must be able to say more than that a measured rise of output during a
period means some rise in welfare. We must be able to say how much.
Thus a stable and measurable relation between changes in output and

changes in amounts of welfare is required. The difficulty of specifying and describing such a stable relation is the basic trouble with national product as an index of secular trend in welfare. Let us see what the problems are.

It is sometimes argued that, since market prices are a measure of the relative importance of the marginal increments of different commodities, an output index in which quantities are weighted by market prices in a base year can serve as an index of the value or significance of output increments to consumers. This, however, is a mistake. Market prices are, at best, only indexes of the relative marginal utility of different commodities at a given level of income. They can help us in the construction of output indexes where the problem is to transform, for purposes of comparison, the actual bundle of goods produced in a given period into a hypothetical bundle with a composition similar to that produced in another period. From this, with the help of ordinal propositions about utility, we can judge whether potential welfare has increased or declined between two dates; but relative marginal valuations cannot help us gauge the importance to consumers of changes in the level of output. The nature of the real problem can be exposed starkly by considering a case in which no questions of index number construction arise. Let there be but one commodity and one consumer. What is now the relation between the trend of output and the trend of welfare? Prices—which do not exist—can give us no help in the one-commodity case. Neither can they help in the many-commodity real world. To answer our question, it is clear, we need to specify a utility function and combine it with an index of output. No measure of output alone can serve our purpose.

There is, of course, nothing new in this. Modern welfare theory specifies a relation between output and welfare, but it is a very limited relation in terms of better or worse. For growth studies, we need a relation which tells us something useful about how much better or how much worse. Can we find it? Is it even there to be found?

If we have any notion about the shape of a utility function at the present time, it is the idea that utility of increments of income diminishes as the level of income increases. There is, indeed, some empirical evidence in favor of this theory. For example, it appears to be true that people, on the whole, prefer to work fewer hours per week when incomes rise. Under the same conditions, young people do not enter the labor force so early, and old people retire when they are younger. Of course, such evidence is not conclusive, and not all of it points in the same direction. The participation of married women in work in the United States, for example, is markedly greater today than it was half a century ago when incomes were much lower.

It is still the case, therefore, that the strongest support for the theory of the diminishing marginal utility of income is intuitional. We have a

strong feeling that it is so. Conceiving ourselves to be in some degree
rational beings with some understanding of our needs, which we feel to
be in some degree stable, we naturally think of ourselves as tending to
satisfy our more urgent and important wants first. This intuition is further
supported by additional psychological insights.

In the first place, our feeling that increments of income tend to satisfy
wants of diminishing urgency is less strong than, in a sense, it ought to be—
for some of our apparent satisfaction from additional goods is, in a long-
term view, transitory or *self-defeating*, subject to erosion by habituation,
creating, therefore, an exaggerated notion of the importance of additional
goods. Pigou (10), for example, argues, as follows:

. . . consider two undergraduates precisely alike in temperament and constitution. One is poor and goes on a cheap Continental holiday, stopping the
night at youth hostels: the other does an exactly similar tour at much greater
expense and stopping at luxury hotels. Each of them is conditioned by habit
and experience to his circumstances. Is there any reason to suppose that the
rich undergraduate has a better time—achieves more utility—than the poor
one? Yet again in prewar days well-to-do people had elaborate meals and
had a number of servants to work for them. Now they have simpler meals
and do their own work. After they have become accustomed to the new conditions, are they less happy than before? It is very doubtful whether a mod-
erately well-to-do man is appreciably happier now than he would be if trans-
planted back to the pre-railway age and attuned to the conditions of that
age . . . From a long-run standpoint, after incomes in excess of a certain
moderate level have been attained, further increases in it may well not be
significant for economic welfare.

In the second place, we normally suppose that our satisfactions are
independent of the levels of income and consumption enjoyed by others
and, indeed, build our analyses of welfare on this assumption. On closer
examination, however, the idea becomes implausible. Our wants for goods
are, to some degree, *competitive,* and few would deny that a considerable
part of our drive for income is derived from a desire for distinction. It
follows that, to this extent, extra income cannot provide additional satisfaction to the community at large.

Third, there is the fact that, to some extent, our desires for goods are
irrational. We tend to judge our needs by our desires, but our desires do
not correspond in any stable way to the capacity of goods to satisfy wants.
Pigou (10) saw and stated the problem clearly.

It might seem that when [a person's] desire attitude is given, his satisfaction depends straightforwardly on the extent to which his desires are fulfilled. But the satisfaction yielded when a desire is satisfied does not always
bear the same proportion to the intensity of the desire. Not only may people
make mistakes, desiring certain objects in the hope of satisfactions which they
do not in fact yield, but also, as Sedgwick observed, 'I do not judge pleasures
to be greater or less exactly in proportion as they exercise more or less in-

fluence in stimulating the will to actions likely to sustain or produce them.' Some economists, neglecting this point, have employed the term 'utility' indifferently for satisfactions and for desiredness. I shall employ it here to mean satisfactions . . .

As Pigou says, the problem is not simply one of "mistakes," a term which suggests the possibility of correction through a process of comparing experience with expectation. The problem is the deeper one of the correspondence of people's desires with their physical and psychic needs or, as we might say, of the rationality of their desires. Rationality is concerned with the relation between means and ends. But if the ends of action are unconscious, realistic appraisal of the appropriateness of means to ends is difficult.

The utilitarian psychology on which both the "old" and the "new" welfare analysis is based views human beings as rational individuals. They possess a consistent set of wants known to themselves and are able to compare the capacity of different kinds and quantities of goods to satisfy their needs. Modern psychology, however, runs in terms that are quite at variance with this view. It regards individuals as bundles of needs that are partly conscious and partly unconscious. The psyche, in Freud's metaphor, is an iceberg, seven-eighths submerged. Yet the wants that we may not acknowledge influence our actions, all the more because they are not subject to realistic or rational appraisal. It is difficult to speak of the welfare significance of income for people whose personalities are, to a greater or less extent, a compound of repressions, addictions, compulsions, and obsessions.

From the viewpoint of long-term comparisons of welfare, the competitive, self-defeating, and irrational elements in consumption appear to have at least one important thing in common. Their scope of action becomes larger the higher the level of per capita income. This conclusion is virtually contained in the very notion that consumption may be self-defeating after a point, for this idea implies that the urgency of additional goods for satisfying solid needs becomes smaller and smaller, until at last the sole significance of increments is to avoid disappointing the established expectations which they themselves create. It is also plausible to suppose that, so long as consumption levels are barely sufficient to provide for survival and minimum comfort, the competitive and irrational drives of individuals are held in check, at least to a greater extent than they are when food, clothing, and shelter are more abundant. Thus, the significance of additional income for welfare becomes progressively weaker as industrialization proceeds, as per capita income rises, as the options in consumption become greater, and as goods come more and more to have symbolic rather than material significance.

If arguments such as these lead us to entertain the hypothesis of the diminishing marginal utility of income, we can proceed a short distance, but only a short distance; for the theory implies no more than that given percentage increments of income will correspond to successively smaller percentage increments of utility. This enables us to say that, if national product indexes give evidence of retardation in the rate of growth of income, then, *a fortiori,* they provide *prima facie* evidence of retardation in the rate of growth of welfare (unless, indeed, the rate of decline of marginal utility were itself declining at a sufficiently rapid rate). But if national product indexes suggest that the rate of growth of income has been increasing, we can say only that the rate of growth of welfare was growing less rapidly than income. There may well have been retardation in the growth of welfare. It is hard to see how much further we could stretch our intuitions about utility functions, if, indeed, we are willing to stretch them so far. One should not, of course, disdain limited conclusions. Very rapid acceleration in growth of income creates at least a presumption of some acceleration in growth of welfare. Even such qualified inferences about growth of welfare could be of use in helping us understand the course of economic development.[5]

These statements assume that the quantity which is of interest to us is the relative rate of growth of welfare. It may be argued, however, that we are really concerned with absolute increments of welfare. In that case, it is perhaps still more difficult to draw clear inferences about changes in the growth of welfare from changes in the rate of growth of output. To do so, we must assume that marginal utility declines at a particular rate as income rises. If it were true that marginal utility declined at the same rate as the level of income rose, it would follow that when income grew at a constant percentage rate, welfare would increase by constant absolute amounts. And if income grew at increasing or declining percentage rates, welfare would rise by increasing or diminishing amounts, as the case might be.

It may be contended that the assumption about the form of the utility function just stated is exactly what is implied by the common practice of measuring the rate of economic growth by percentage changes in output. And it might be argued that the prevalence of this practice is evidence of a widespread feeling that the assumption is an acceptable approximation to reality. Such intuitions do, indeed, lend some support to the assumption

---

[5] Notice that, as a practical matter, the difficulties raised in this paragraph apply only to the large changes in income which are of interest in studies of economic growth. We may very well be willing to say—making a plausible judgment —that a 2 per cent rise in national income per capita during (say) 1957 increased welfare more than a 1 per cent rise during 1956. But few people would be confident that a 100 per cent increase during the second quarter of the twentieth century implied a larger increase in welfare than did 50 per cent increase during the last quarter of the nineteenth century. The point is simply that the marginal utility of income may be presumed to be nearly constant over the small range of incomes with which we are concerned in short periods. But we cannot easily assume substantially constant marginal utility over the large range of incomes of concern in long periods.

implied in common practice. Further, insofar as income taxes are assessed at equal proportional rates, we have further indirect evidence of the acceptability of the assumption.[6] But it is also important to realize that this is the sum total of the evidence. When it is exposed to critical reason, it is hard to accept this unique assumption about the rate of decline of marginal utility for the purpose of drawing inferences about changes in growth of welfare from changes in the percentage rate of growth of income.

We are, therefore, faced with a wide range of possibilities. If marginal utility declines fast enough, acceleration in the relative rate of growth of output is consistent with diminishing absolute increments of utility. If marginal utility declines very slowly, relative retardation in growth of income is consistent with rising absolute increments of welfare so long as the absolute increments of income are not themselves declining.

This argument runs to the conclusion that judgments about changes in the contribution of output to long term changes in the growth of welfare must at present be vague and uncertain. But whatever inferences we may be inclined to draw can be valid only so far as we can suppose that the power of income to satisfy wants remains substantially unchanged. This is only too obvious,[7] and on this issue, a student of economic growth must

[6] The assessment of income taxes as proportions of income is, of course, in part a social judgment that marginal utility declines with income. But the use of equiproportional rates is far from universal. The Federal income tax rates in the USA and in many foreign countries are steeply progressive, and so are those in some individual states of the USA. On the other hand, many other elements of the tax structure are regressive, and the total tax structure in the USA is much less progressive than the structure of direct taxes alone. It is clear, moreover, that principles other than equality of sacrifice are also influential. So it is hard to say what weight should be given to the structure of direct taxes and what to the structure of total taxes in determining society's judgment about the form of utility functions. Moreover, it is apparent that there is much disagreement about the degree of progressiveness that would produce equality of sacrifice and that if tax practice is to be taken as evidence of a social consensus, this practice has changed drastically over time.

[7] To avoid confusion, however, it is well to be clear that the difficulty would not disappear even if we could be sure that, though want systems change from period to period, the relation between output and utility appropriate to a given period could always be described by a curve in which marginal utility diminishes with income. This assumption allows us to say that, *from the point of view of either period*, retardation in income growth implies retardation in growth of welfare. But it does not permit us to judge how the rates of growth of welfare actually compared in two periods so long as we cannot measure shifts in a cardinal utility function. The same difficulty, indeed, makes it impossible to say whether welfare has even risen between two dates—an ordinal question—though it may appear to have done so from the point of view of either one. Unless we may assume constant and consistent indifference maps for individuals, the Hicks criteria must fail, as he has clearly stated [p. 107 in (7)]. But for marginal changes in economic institutions or policies and for short periods, we are entitled to assume substantial constancy of want systems. So the Hicks criteria remain of interest in such contexts.

be prepared to declare and, if possible, to justify his faith. Witness Kuznets:

It is as realistic to assume constancy of individuals' wants as it is to assume constancy of human nature. Despite substantial differences in wants and modes of living among different social classes, or among people at different periods, the basic wants and the broad categories of goods used to satisfy them—which account for most of social product—are much the same. [(4), p. 119.]

I think we must regard this statement as unsatisfactory. The broad categories of goods used to satisfy wants have remained the same during the period of industrialization only in the irrelevant sense that a place could, no doubt, be found for every commodity now used under the same broad classes of product we might have distinguished a century and a half ago. It is quite clear, however, that there have been significant changes in the relative importance of the various broad categories, as these are usually defined, and still more in their detailed content. This, however, is not basic. For the chief problem of welfare analysis has been precisely that of making welfare judgments in the face of changes in the composition of output.

The basic problem concerns the constancy of wants, and for this Kuznets relies on a presumed constancy of human nature. This, however, is inadequate. One might readily suppose that, placed in identical circumstances, a represenative individual today would feel and act in much the same way, and derive much the same satisfaction from the consumption of identical goods as did a representative individual a hundred years ago. Circumstances have changed in many ways, however, and it is implausible to suppose that these changed circumstances have made no substantial difference to our desire attitudes and our more basic needs as these concern consumption goods. Social-psychological literature, for example, is deeply concerned with the problem of the changing attitudes of people toward consumption (11). One may well reserve judgment about the validity of the particular characterizations of the changes which social psychologists have so far provided, but it is difficult not to accept the fact that the representative consumer views consumption and consumption goods from an angle which is different from that of his grandfather and great-grandfather.

The matter must be tackled on at least two levels. On the first we need merely recognize that the satisfaction individuals derive from various kinds and quantities of goods is influenced by the character of their work and by the extent to which they have gained freedom from work, by their social and economic status and the aspirations and standards which go with them, and by the level of their education. We should, therefore, expect to find that attitudes towards consumption in the United States, for example, have changed in the course of industrialization along with changes in such population characteristics as place of residence (farm or city; village or suburb), type of work (physically exhausting or light; concerned with physical production or with people), amount of leisure (approximately one-half working hours a century ago or twice working hours today), employment status (small proprietor or salaried official of a large corporation), educational level (usually lacking a full primary school education a century ago; today, a high school graduate and often a college graduate), and, no doubt, with changes in other characteristics of work, life, and formal training. In all these ways, the representative consumer is a different man today than he was 100 to 150 years ago, and this in itself makes the assumption of a constant set of desire attitudes or a constant system of wants inappropriate so far as the population at large is concerned.

On the second level, we must recognize that a more subtle process has been under way which has, to some significant extent, altered the personalities of representative individuals in ways which the changes in population characteristics cited above could not by themselves explain. The socio-psychological literature referred to above proceeds upon the hypothesis that character is, not entirely, but to a marked degree, a social product which is connected with the operating requirements of the society within which it emerges [cf. (11) and (12)]. We need not, at this point, enter into such questions as the mechanisms by which socio-economic conditions help to form character; nor need we be concerned with the specific personality changes which students of the question are persuaded have occurred, though it may be remarked that what I have referred to as the irrational, competitive, and self-defeating aspects of consumer psychology figure prominently. The essential points are that social-psychology and social-anthropology rest upon assumptions of personality variation over time and among countries, that such changes are associated with the process or degree of industrialization, and that they manifest themselves in attitudes towards consumption as well as in every other significant aspect of life. The hypothesis of a stable relation between consumption and satisfaction would not appeal to the social-psychologists.[8]

[8] It is perfectly clear that study of personality change is still in its early stages, the operational definitions of personality characteristics are only beginning to be developed, and that quantitive study is only starting. For what it is worth, however, social-psychological studies postulate numerous changes in attitudes toward consumption. They refer to such matters as a decline in the sense of attachment to possessions and property and a corresponding love of newness; to a growth of passivity and receptiveness, especially in the use of leisure time which reflects among other things a new hostility to work; to an increased tendency to base value upon price; to a greater emphasis upon conformity to group taste rather than upon a search for competitive distinction in consumption; to the widespread acceptance of the notion that consumption desires must be satisfied without delay.

VII

The attempt to use national product estimates as indexes of secular changes in economic welfare clearly runs into serious problems. Some are merely difficult, but others seem beyond solution. The standard problems of national product estimation—to define productive activity, to distinguish final from intermediate product, and to apply these distinctions consistently—appear in aggravated form when estimates must be carried back over many decades which have witnessed radical alterations in the composition of output, the methods and places of production, the role of the household and commercial economies, and the rise of government as an economic agent. These, however, are problems of measurement of quite an ordinary sort. They require clear definitions and the compilation of figures not now available. True, some of these figures will be hard to come by. The line between production and consumption must be followed through many strange twists and turns to maintain an adequately consistent measure of final product. But in all these matters we may at least hope, not only to reach agreement about what we are after, but also to achieve useful estimates in practice.

The goal seems to fade quite out of reach, however, when we face the the problems of valuation and interpreation. Again, some of the difficulties, troublesome though they are, can be viewed as questions about the degree of inaccuracy we can accept. We have no proper value weights, analogous to market prices, for capital formation and government product, and it seems impossible—not only practically but conceptually—that we should ever find any. But these categories, for long periods, were of limited importance. War outlay aside, they are still not of dominating importance. We must be prepared also to bypass the problems raised by changes in income distribution, by relying on the assumption that people who differ only with respect to income, may, at least in the large, and after a period of adjustment, be treated as equivalent in their capacity to derive satisfactions from different kinds and quantities of goods. If we have pushed our tolerance so far, however, there are still basic difficulties. For national income estimates as indexes of secular trends in welfare stand on very different ground than they do as tests of the desirability of some change in policy or institutions—particularly a marginal change—or as indexes of short-term changes in welfare. Three obdurate considerations chiefly account for the difference in principle.

First, when changes in output involve profound changes in social and economic organization, we can no longer plausibly presume that satisfactions from increased output overshadow those that flow from accompanying changes in work and life. Moreover, it seems right to think that, as incomes rise, the manner in which we earn and use our incomes increases in importance compared with changes in the amount of income at our disposal.

Second, the information we need about the relation between increments to output and increments to utility is much greater when we are concerned with growth questions. The answers to many policy questions hinge simply on whether welfare will rise or fall. An ordinal utility function is sufficient. But cardinal measures of the relation between output and utility are needed if we are to draw inferences about acceleration or retardation in growth of welfare from evidence about the trend of output. For short-term movements, we may perhaps rely on the assumption that marginal utility of income is nearly constant over the small range of incomes involved. But the marginal utility of income must be presumed to vary over the large range of incomes with which we are concerned in developing economies. Hence, we need to know the values of the parameters of a social utility function. If we could only describe its form by saying, for example, that marginal utility diminishes with income, we could draw limited inferences from output trends. We could, for example, infer secular retardation in relative growth of welfare from secular retardation in growth of income. But we could not say more.

Third, even this limited possibility is foreclosed if we cannot assume that a social utility function remains stable. In the course of economic development, however, want systems must be supposed to change, partly because wants and needs differ among social and economic classes and the relative importance of such classes changes in the course of economic development, partly because changes in the organization of society produce changes in personality which control the significance of income to people.

VIII

What may we conclude? National income at market prices is a general index of output constructed as consistently as possible to reflect the significance of output for welfare. If the argument of this essay is sound, however, we must be highly skeptical of the view that long-term changes in the rate of growth of welfare can be gauged even roughly from changes in the rate of growth of output.

This is, of course, no ground for abandoning the study of secular trends in national income at market prices. It is *an* index of output. No more logically constructed general index has yet been contrived. Study of secular trends in national income may well show—as, indeed, it already has—that the rate of growth of output is related in a more or less stable way to the growth of many other aspects of economic life and to various aspects of noneconomic life. It remains to be determined, however, whether these more or less stable relations emerge because national product is an index of secular trends in welfare or an index of secular trends in something else, or sometimes of one thing and sometimes of another. If and when we can discover what it is for which, in different contexts, the national product index is a proxy, we shall presumably be able to design general indexes of output which will reveal more stable relations between production and other activities than we now find. And, incidentally, we shall learn something about the significance of income changes for welfare. Although the burden of this essay is distressingly and regrettably negative, its more basic purpose is to encourage further thought about the meaning of secular changes in the rate of growth of national income and empirical studies that can fortify and lend substance to analysis.

References

1. Simon S. Kuznets, "Toward a Theory of Economic Growth," in Robert Lekachman (ed.), National Policy for Economic Welfare at Home and Abroad. Doubleday, Garden City, New York, 1955, p. 16.

2. A. C. Pigou, Economics of Welfare, 4th ed. Macmillan, London, 1932. Chap. I.

3. Simon S. Kuznets, "On the Valuation of Social Income—Reflections on Professor Hicks' Article," Economica, XV (February 1948), Part I.

4. Simon S. Kuznets, "On the Valuation of Social Income—Reflections on Professor Hicks' Article," Economica, XV (May 1948), Part II.

5. Simon S. Kuznets, National Income: A Summary of Findings (National Bureau of Economic Research, New York, 1946), Part IV; "National Income and Industrial Structure," Proceedings of the International Statistical Conferences, 1947 (Calcutta, 1951), V, 205–39; "National Income and Economic Welfare," Boletin del Banco Central de Venezuela, Nos. 53 and 54 (July–August, 1949). Both articles reprinted in S. S. Kuznets, Economic Change (Norton, New York, 1953).

6. F. C. Hicks, "The Valuation of Social Income," Economica, VII (May 1940).

7. I. M. D. Little, "The Valuation of Social Income," Economica, XVI (February 1949).

8. P. A. Samuelson, "Evaluation of Real National Income," Oxford Economic papers, n.s. II (January 1950).

9. Tibor Scitovsky, Welfare and Competition: The Economics of a Fully Employed Economy. Irwin, Homewood, Illinois, 1951, pp. 70–81.

10. A. C. Pigou, "Some Aspects of Welfare Economics," American Economic Review, XLI (June 1951), 294.

11. D. Riesman, N. Glazer, and R. Denney, The Lonely Crowd. Yale University Press, New Haven, 1950.

12. Erich Fromm, The Sane Society. Rinehart, New York, 1955, esp. pp. 152–65.

Costs and Outputs

ARMEN ALCHIAN[1]

Obscurities, ambiguities, and errors exist in cost and supply analysis despite, or because of, the immense literature on the subject. Especially obscure are the relationships between cost and output, both in the long run and in the short run. Propositions designed to eliminate some of these ambiguities and errors are presented in this paper. More important, these suggested propositions seem to be empirically valid.

COSTS

Costs will be defined initially as the change in equity caused by the performance of some specified operation, where, for simplicity of exposition, the attendant change in income is not included in the computation of the change in equity. Suppose that according to one's balance sheet the present value of his assets were $100, and suppose that at the end of the operation one year later the value of his assets were expected to be $80, not counting the sale value of the product of the operation. The present value of $80 a year hence (at 6 per cent) is $75.47, which yields a cost in present capital value (equity) of $24.53. Because of logical difficulties in converting this present value concept into a satisfactory rate (per unit of time) concept, we defer a discussion of this problem and, for convenience, measure costs in units of present value or equity. Hereafter, the unmodified expression "costs" will always mean the present worth, capital value concept of cost, i.e., the change in equity.

OUTPUT

All the characteristics of a production operation can affect its cost. In this paper we want to direct attention to three characteristics:

1. The rate of output is typically regarded in economic analysis as the

[1] University of California, Los Angeles, and the RAND Corporation. Indebtedness to William Meckling of the RAND Corporation, who gave many long hours to discussion of the points raised herein, even before the first of several drafts, is very great. Although my egoism prevents sharing the authorship with him, I cannot absolve him from responsibility for any errors that still remain and likewise for any merit the paper may have.

crucial feature. But it is only one feature, and concentration on it alone has led to serious error, as we shall see.

2. Total contemplated volume of output is another characteristic. Is a cumulated output volume of 10,000 or 100 or 1,000,000 units being contemplated? Whatever may be the rate of output, the total volume to be produced is a distinct feature with important effects on cost. Of course, for any rate of output, the larger the total cumulated volume to be produced, the longer the operation will continue. Hence, incorporated in this description of total output is the total time length of the programmed production. Will it span one month or one year, or (at the other extreme) is the contemplated total volume so large that at the rate of output an indefinitely long time is allowed to the production run?

3. The programmed time schedule of availability of output is a further characteristic. For a point output, the programmed date of the output availability is sufficient, but for outputs which continue over time, the time profile (delivery schedule) of the output replaces a single date. We shall call these three distinct aspects the output *rate*, the contemplated *total volume*, and the programmed delivery *dates*.

These three characteristics can be summarized in the following definition, which also defines a fourth characteristic, m, the total length of the programmed schedule of outputs:

$$V = \sum_{T}^{T+m} x(t)dt.$$

In this expression V is the total contemplated volume of output, $x(t)$ the output rate at moment t, T the moment at which the first unit of output is to be completed, and m the length of the interval over which the output is made available. Of these four features, only three are independently assignable; the fourth is then constrained. Unless specific exception is made, in the following we shall always discuss changes in only one of the features, V, $x(t)$, and T, assuming the other two to be constant and letting the full compensatory adjustment be made in m.[2]

PROPOSITIONS ABOUT COSTS AND OUTPUT

Our task is now to make some propositions about the way costs are affected by changes in these variables. Letting C denote costs (i.e., the change in equity), we have

$$C = F\ (V, x, T, m)$$

[2] We note that time or dating enters in a multitude of ways: there is the date at which the delivery of output is to begin; there is the period of time used as a basis for the measure of the rate of output, i.e., so many units per day, per week, or per year; and there is the total time over which the output is to be made available.

subject to the definition of V, which constrains us to three degrees of freedom among the four variables.

PROPOSITION 1:

$$\left. \frac{\partial C}{\partial x(t)} \right|_{\substack{T = T_0 \\ V = V_0}} > 0 \qquad (1)$$

The left-hand expression is the derivative of the costs with respect to x, when T and V are held constant, letting m make up the adjustment. It shows the change in costs when the rate of output is increased without increasing V and without changing the delivery date, but with an appropriate reduction of m. Proposition 1 states that the faster the rate at which a given volume of output is produced, the higher its cost. We emphasize that cost means the change in equity, not the *rate* of costs.

PROPOSITION 2:

$$\left. \frac{\partial^2 C}{\partial x^2} \right|_{\substack{V = V_0 \\ T = T_0}} > 0 \qquad (2)$$

The increment in C is an increasing function of the output rate. This is a proposition about increasing marginal cost in present value measure, and is usually derived as an implication of efficient allocation of scarce heterogeneous resources among alternative uses.

Its validity, however, does not depend upon the validity of the premises of the classical model. For example, inventories need not increase in proportion to the rate of output if the variance of random deviations in output rates does not increase more than proportionally to the expected output rate. In this event, a sufficient condition for Proposition 2 as derived by the classical model would be upset. But destruction of sufficient conditions does not eliminate the possibility of all necessary conditions being fulfilled; thus, even if the classical model's assumptions are upset, the proposition could still be true. Whether or not it is, in fact, true cannot be settled by an examination of the model from which it is derived. For present purposes, Proposition 2 can be regarded, if one wishes, as a postu-lated proposition.[3]

PROPOSITION 3:

$$\left. \frac{\partial C}{\partial V} \right|_{\substack{x\,=\,x_0 \\ T\,=\,T_0}} > 0 \tag{3}$$

C increases with V for given x and date of initial output, T. At a constant output rate, for example, this will require a longer program of production, a larger m.

PROPOSITION 4:

$$\left. \frac{\partial^2 C}{\partial V^2} \right|_{\substack{x\,=\,x_0 \\ T\,=\,T_0}} < 0 \tag{4}$$

Increments in C diminish as V increases, for any rate of output, x, and initial output date, T. Thus, for any constant rate of output, as the total planned output is increased by uniform increments, costs (changes in equity) will increase by diminishing increments. The "reasons" for this proposition will be given later.

Proposition 4 also implies decreasing cost *per unit* of total volume, V. We shall state this as a separate proposition.

PROPOSITION 5:

$$\left. \frac{\partial C/V}{\partial V} \right|_{\substack{x\,=\,x_0 \\ T\,=\,T_0}} < 0 \tag{4a}$$

[3] See T. M. Whitin and M. H. Peston, "Random Variations, Risk and Returns to Scale," *Quarterly Journal of Economics*, LXVIII (November 1954), 603–14, for a longer discussion of some forces that could reverse the inequality of Proposition 2. Some of their suggested forces, e.g., relation between stocks of repairmen and number of machines, are circumvented by the ability to buy services instead of the agents themselves. Another weakness is the association of size of output with the number of independent random forces.

1. *Graphic Illustration*

The above properties are shown by the cost surface in Figure 1. Proposition 1 describes the slope of a slice on the cost surface where the slice is parallel to the Cx plane. Proposition 2 states that the slope of the path

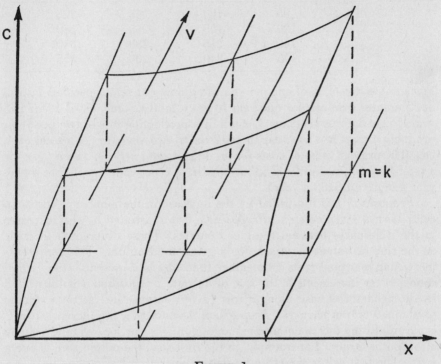

FIGURE 1

Cost Surface as Function of x and V

of such a slice on the cost surface increases with x. Proposition 3 is portrayed by the slope of a slice along the surface parallel to the CV plane—going back into the page. The slope of this slice decreases as V increases. Proposition 4 describes the decreasing rate at which this surface of costs increases along this slice. Movements in other directions can be visualized. For example, one possible path is to start from the origin and move out some ray. This gives costs as a function of proportional increase in both the rate and the total output for a fixed interval of production, m, but the behavior of the cost slope of this slice, except for the fact that it is positive, cannot be derived from these propositions.

2. *Tabular, Arithmetic Illustration*

TABLE I
COSTS, VOLUME OF OUTPUT, AND RATES OF OUTPUT

Rate of Output, x (per year)	Volume of Output			
	1	2	3	4
1..........	100	180	255	325
2..........	120	195	265	330
3..........	145	215	280	340
4..........	175	240	300	355

For an output rate, x, of one per year, beginning at some specified T, production must continue for one year to get a total volume, V, of 1, for two years to get 2, three years for 3, etc. For a production rate of two per year, production must last one year to get 2 units, two years to get a total of 4, etc. The present value of costs for an output rate, $x(t)$, of two a year for a total V of 4 in two years is $330 (which, at 6 per cent, is equal to a two-year annuity of $180 a year).

Proposition 1 is illustrated by the increase in the numbers (costs) in cells down a given column. *Proposition 2* is illustrated by the increases in the differences between these cell entries. These differences increase as the rate of output increases, for a given total output. This represents increasing marginal costs (remember that cost is a present value capital concept) for increments in the rate of output. *Proposition 3* is illustrated by the behavior of costs along a row (given output rate) as total volume of planned output changes. *Proposition 4* states that the increment in C is a diminishing increment as one moves across a row, i.e., as total volume of output is larger. For example, in the first row, the output *rate* is one a year. The first cell is therefore an output operation lasting one year, because only one is produced, at the rate of one a year. The total cost is $100. For a total contemplated output of two units, at a rate of one per year, the operation will take two years and the cost is $180. The marginal cost of one more unit of total volume of output—not of one unit higher *rate* of output—is $80. For a total output of three units in three years the cost is $255, an increment of $75, which is less than the previous increment of $80. Here the increments in cost are associated not with increments in rates of output, but with increments in total volume of output. *Proposition 5* is illustrated by dividing the cell entries in a row by the output quantities at the head of each column. The quotient, cost per unit of output quantity, decreases as V increases.

3. *Economic Illustration*

A comparison that could be made is the following: Imagine a person to contemplate a total volume of output of one unit at the rate of one a year. But he subsequently revises his plans and produces one more in the next year at the rate of one a year, again planning to produce a total volume of just one unit. Compare the total costs of that operation with an operation in which two units of total output were initially planned at the rate of one a year. Both take two years, but the cost of the latter is $180 while the former's present value is $100 plus $100 discounted back one year at 6 per cent, or a total of $194. Thus it is cheaper to produce from a *plan* for a two-year output of two units at the rate of one a year than to produce two by repetition of methods which contemplate only one total unit of output at the same rate of one a year.

From this example it would appear that a reason for Proposition 4 is that better foresight enables one to see farther into the future and make more accurate forecasts; but this is not the reason, however helpful better foresight may be. A larger planned V is produced in a different way from that of a smaller planned V. A classic example is the printing press. To get three hundred copies of a letter in one day may be cheaper with mimeograph than with either typewriter or offset printing. The mimeograph method may be so much superior that, even if the rate of output were stepped up to 300 in an hour (instead of in a day), mimeographing might still be cheaper than typing. This does not deny that higher rates of output imply higher costs, as for example that 300 in an hour will cost more than 300 in two hours. The method of production is a function of the volume of output, especially when output is produced from basic dies—and there are few, if any, methods of production that do not involve "dies." Why increased expenditures on more durable dies should result in more than proportional increase of output potential is a question that cannot be answered, except to say that the physical principles of the world are not all linear (which may or may not be the same thing as "indivisible").[4] Different methods of tooling, parts design, and assembly is the usual explanation given in the production engineering literature.

Proposition 4 seems not to be part of current economic principles. Yet it may be the key to seeing the error in some attempts to refute Proposition 2, which applies to increased *rates* of output for constant total volume of output (or, as we shall see later, for perpetuity durations of output). Propositions 2 and 4 refer to two counterforces, rate of output and total planned volume of output. What would be the net effect of increases in both cannot be deduced from the present propositions. All that can be said is that if the rate of output is increased for a given total contemplated volume of output, the increment in cost will be an increasing function of the rate of output. Proposition 4, on the other hand, implies diminishing increments as V increases, and it implies a lower per-unit cost for a larger

[4] Could it be that the term "indivisibility" has been meant to cover this phenomenon? A yes or no answer to that question is impossible because of the extreme vagueness and ambiguity with which the term has been used. Furthermore, the question is probably of little, if any, significance.

total volume of output. Thus, we have the possibility that higher rates of production might be available at lower unit costs if they are associated with a larger volume of output, because this latter factor may be sufficient to overcome the effects of the higher output rate.

A larger volume of output could, of course, be obtained by both longer time and faster rates of production, but the relationship between time and volume should not be allowed to mask the fact that it is total contemplated volume of output—not the longer duration of output—that is here asserted (maybe erroneously) to be the factor at work in Propositions 3 and 4.

If both the *volume* and the *rate* of output change in the same direction, the two effects on costs are not in the same direction, and neither the net effect on the rate of change of *increments* in the cost nor even the effect on the costs per unit of total volume of output is implied by these or any other accepted postulates. It has been said, for example, that if some automobile manufacturer were to cut V, the volume of cars produced of a given year's model, from one million to a half-million, costs per car would increase. This statement could refer either to a reduction in V achieved by producing for half the number of months at an unchanged monthly rate of output or to a simultaneous and parallel reduction in both V, the volume, and x, the monthly rate of output. If it refers to the former, it is a restatement of Proposition 5; if it refers to the latter, it is a statement that cannot be deduced from our propositions, which imply merely that costs would be lower if both V and x were reduced than if V alone were lowered.

Even returns to scale seem to have been confused with the effect of size of output. It is conjectured that a substantial portion of the alleged cases of increasing returns to scale in industries or firms is the result of ignoring the relation of costs to volume (rather than to rate) of output. The earlier discussions of automobile production and printing costs are simple illustrations of how this confusion can occur.

How many of the cases of alleged decreasing costs to *rates* of output are really decreasing costs to *volume* of output is an open question. Is it too much to expect that all of them can be so explained? Or that the realm of such cases can be greatly reduced by allowing for V, instead of letting x be the only variable? But that dirty empirical task is left for later and more ambitious efforts.

The observed concentration on a standardized model, e.g., four or five different sizes of tractors as distinct from a much greater possible range, is explained by the effect of volume of output on cost. Although an infinite range is possible, the concentration on a smaller set of fewer alternatives is more economical for most problems. The only way economic theory heretofore could explain this apparent anomaly was to invoke a falling cost curve for small output rates, in turn dependent upon some kind of unidentified indivisibility or returns to scale. Now the explanation may be contained in Propositions 4 and 9.

MORE PROPOSITIONS

Four more propositions remain. Proposition 6 is given in a footnote because its implications will not be suggested in this paper.[5] Propositions 7 and 8 concern the effects of changes in T, the time between the decision to produce and the delivery of output.

PROPOSITION 7:

$$\left. \frac{\partial C}{\partial T} \right|_{\substack{x = x_0 \\ V = V_0}} < 0 \tag{7}$$

---

[5] PROPOSITION 6:

$$\left. \frac{\partial^2 C}{\partial x \partial V} \right|_{T = T_0} < 0 \tag{5}$$

This says that the marginal present value-cost with respect to increased rates of output decreases as the total contemplated output increases. This can be regarded as a conjectural proposition, whose implications will not be developed in this paper. And the same proposition can be re-expressed as

$$\left. \frac{\partial^2 C}{\partial V \partial x} \right|_{T = T_0} < 0 \tag{6}$$

This states that marginal present-value costs of increased quantity of output decrease as the rate of output increases.

Of interest is the relationship between these postulates and the implied shape of the production possibility function, where the rate and the volume of output are the two output alternatives. The cost isoquant with x and V as the arguments can be convex or concave. Usually a concave function is implied when rates of output of two different products are the arguments. However, J. Hirshleifer, "Quality vs. Quantity: Cost Isoquant and Equilibrium," *Quarterly Journal of Economics*, LXIV (November 1955), 596–606, has pointed out that convex production possibilities are implicit in many engineering cost functions when quality and quantity are the alternative outputs. Hirshleifer, as it seems from his context, is really discussing cases where his quantity variable refers to volume and not to rate of output. Had he really meant rate of output rather than volume, his results might not have been so "reasonable." The convexity or concavity of the cost isoquant, it may be recalled, is given by the sign of

$$\frac{d^2x}{dV^2} = \frac{F_{xx}F_v^2 - 2\,F_{xv}F_xF_v + F_{vv}F_x^2}{F_v^3}$$

Substituting our postulated conditions shows that the expression may be of any sign, hence the indeterminacy of the concavity or convexity property. However, concavity of the cost isoquant where the two arguments are rates of production for two different products is still implied.

This is not shown in the graph or in the table, but it says that the longer the time between decision to produce and delivery of output, the less the cost.

If we think of a single output point, then T is relatively unambiguous. If the output is to be made available over a period of time, then T could be defined as the beginning moment of output. But many different output programs are possible, even when they all extend over the same interval. One might be tempted to use some sort of average T, say, the date of output weighted by the rate of output. However, such an average T cannot be used for our purposes, because any particular value of T can be identified with an infinite variety of output patterns. Since we are talking about partial derivatives, the whole problem is easily avoided. All we need do is to state that, if one moves any output program or schedule closer to the present (or farther into the future) by a simple time shift, T will have decreased (or increased). Whatever the shape of the output schedule, a reduction of the interval between the present moment and the beginning of the output date (a sort of uniform time-wise shifting) will increase cost. A more deferred output schedule (whatever its unchanged shape) will mean a lower cost.

Proposition 7 is really a corollary of Proposition 2. The slower the rate at which inputs are purchased, the lower their price because the lower are the costs to the seller, when Proposition 2 is applied to the seller.

Not only do the supply curves of inputs fall (or shift to the right) as more time is allowed, but the rates of shifting differ among inputs. The supply curves of some inputs are more elastic than those of others; and the rate at which the price elasticity of supply increases with T differs among inputs. Thus, while in an immediate period the price elasticity of supply of input x may be low relative to that of input y (and it may always be lower than that of y), the *ratio* of the costs of increments in y to the costs of increments in x may change with deferred purchase. If the ratio decreases, deferred purchases of y relative to purchases of x will be economical. In other words, it is not merely the slope of the supply curve or the price elasticity of supply that determines which inputs are going to be increased earliest. Rather, it is the rate at which these price elasticities *change* with deferred purchase that is critical. Thus, as stated earlier, the input x with a very low price elasticity of supply will vary more in the immediate period than the input of y with a higher price elasticity if the deferment of purchases by, say, a month would lower the cost of y more than that of x. As an extreme, if the supply curves of two inputs, x and y, were both horizontal, the input of one of them would be increased less if with deferred purchase the price or supply curve would become lower—though still horizontal. That input whose price would become lower with a deferred purchase would be increased in quantity later, with the relatively heavy present increase concentrated on that input whose deferred purchase price would not be as much lower.

PROPOSITION 8:

All the derivatives in Propositions 1–5 are diminishing functions of T, but not all diminish at the same rate. This proposition asserts a difference in the extent to which inputs will be varied in the immediate, the short, and the longer period.

Short and long run. Statements to the effect that certain inputs are fixed in the short run are frequent and characteristic. In fact, there is no such fixed factor in any interval other than the immediate moment *when all are fixed.* Such statements may represent a confusion between revealed choice and technological constraints. There are no technological or legal restraints preventing one from varying any of his inputs. Even in Viner's classic statement of the short- and long-run cost curves, the short run is defined in terms of some *fixed* inputs and other inputs which can be varied as desired.[6] He stated that the long run is the situation in which all the inputs are "freely" variable. One need only ask, "What do the desires to adjust depend upon in the short run?" and, "What does 'freely' variable mean?" The first is answered by "costs" and potential receipts of the variations, and the second by noting that "freely" does not mean that costs of changes are zero. The fact is that the costs of varying the inputs differ among inputs, and the ratios of these costs vary with the time interval within which the variation is to be made. At any *calendar* moment, T, the producer will choose which input to vary according to *economic costs* and not because of technical or legal fixities that prevent the changing of some inputs.[7]

Debate over definitions or postulates is pertinent only in the light of their purpose. The purpose of the short- and long-run distinction is, presumably, to explain the path of prices or output (x or V?) over time in response to some change in demand or supply. The postulate of fixed inputs, and others more variable with the passing of time, does imply a pattern of responses that seems to be verified by observable evidence. On that count, the falsity of the postulate is immaterial. But if there are other implications of such a postulate that are invalidated by observable evidence, the postulate becomes costly. The question arises, therefore, whether it is more convenient and useful to replace the fixity postulate by

[6] J. Viner, "Cost Curves and Supply Curves," *Zeitschrift fur Nationalökonomie,* III (1931), No. 1, 23–46.

[7] The nearest, but still different, presentation of the immediate, short run, and long run found by the author is that contained in Friedman's unpublished lecture notes. Other statements may exist; an exhausting search of the literature failed to clarify exactly what is meant by the long run and short run.

a more general one that yields all the valid implications that the former one did and more besides, while at the same time avoiding the empirically false implications. It appears that the proposed alternative is cheaper in terms of logical convenience, more general, and more valid in its implications. But that is a judgment which is perhaps best left to the reader.

The differences between a short-run (near T) and a long-run (distant T) operation imply differences in costs, and these costs are pertinent to an explanation of the path of prices or costs over time in response to a lasting change in demand or factor availabilities. For example, for a lasting increase in demand, the output made available at more distant dates is produceable at a lower cost; this means that the supply at a given cost will be larger and the price lower in the more distant future as the longer-run operations begin to yield their output. These outputs, having been planned for a later T date, are lower in cost. Output will be larger for a given price, thus reducing price in the market. This longer-run lower cost is the phenomenon whose explanation has usually been sought by resort to fixity of some particular inputs in the short run. The above argument suggests that this phenomenon can be explained without the fixity assumption that in turn leads to other, empirically wrong, implications.

The implication of our proposition is worth emphasizing here. It is that we define a "short run" and a "long run" not as differing in the fixity of some inputs; instead, we use T as the length of the run, and then from Proposition 8 derive the implications that were sought by the fixity assumption.

Most important, however, Proposition 8 makes it clear that there is not both a "long-run" and "short-run" cost for any given output program. For any given output program there is only *one* pertinent cost, *not* two. Unambiguous specification of the output or action to be costed makes the cost definition unambiguous and destroys the illusion that there are two costs to consider, a short- and a long-run cost for any given output. There is only one, and that is the *cheapest* cost of doing whatever the operation is specified to be. To produce a house in three months is one thing, to produce it in a year is something else. By uniquely identifying the operation to be charged there results one cost, not a range of costs from immediate to short- to longer-run costs. There is a range of operations to be considered, but to each there is only *one* cost. The question is not, "What are the long-run or short-run costs of some operation?" but instead, "How do total, average, and marginal costs vary as the T of the operation is changed?" Answer: "They decrease as T increases, according to Propositions 7 and 8."

The significance of this should be evident in the debate about marginal cost pricing policies for "optimal" output. Also the use of short-run and long-run costs as alternatives in public utility pricing appears to be a ripe area for clarification of concepts.

What the relationship is between the presently suggested effects of T, which we have just called a short- or long-run effect, and the common short run or long run in the standard literature is not entirely clear. Rather vague and imprecise implications about short and long run are available. Hence, rather than assert that the T effect is here being proposed as a substitute for the standard short-run analysis, the reader is left free to supply his own interpretation of the conventional "run" and to supplement or replace it, however he chooses, with the present proposition.

PROPOSITION 9:

The preceding propositions refer to costs of outputs for a given distribution of knowledge, F, at the present moment, to situations where technology is held constant.[8]

Proposition 9 is "As the total quantity of units produced increases, the cost of *future* output declines." The cost per unit may be either the average cost of a given number of incremental units of output or the cost of a specific unit. This is not identical with the earlier Proposition 4 referring to the effects of the larger planned V. There the effect was a result of varying *techniques* of production, not of changes in technology. Here we are asserting that knowledge increases as a result of production —that the cost function is lowered. It is not simply a matter of a larger V, but rather a lower cost for any subsequent V, consequent to improved knowledge. This distinction should not be attributed necessarily to all the explanations of the learning curve. Some describers of the learning curve bring in the effect of different techniques consequent to different-sized V. Others also mention that, as output is produced and experience acquired, improved knowledge is acquired. Thus, even if one continually planned to produce small batches of output, so the V was constant but repeated, the costs would nevertheless be falling. In the present presentation we have chosen to separate these two effects in logic and principle, attributing the first effect, that of technique, to changes in planned V but with a given state of knowledge (as in Proposition 4), while the second effect, that of increased knowledge consequent to accumulated production experience, is isolated in Proposition 9. A review of industrial and production management literature will show that both effects are adduced and incorporated in the learning curve discussion, contrary to our decision to separate them. This proposition about the rate of change in technology is accepted in industrial engineering. Usually the proposition is known as the "learning curve" or "progress curve."[9]

Several factors have been advanced as a rationale for this proposition:

[8] Technology, the state of distribution of knowledge, is different from techniques of production, which can be changed at any time, even with a constant technology.

[9] Sometimes the curve is called an 80 per cent progress curve, because it is sometimes asserted that the cost of the $2n$th item is 80 per cent of the cost of the nth item. Thus the fortieth plane would involve only 80 per cent of the direct man hours and materials that the twentieth plane did.

job familiarization, general improvement in coordination, shop organization and engineering liaison, more efficient subassembly production, and more efficient tools. An extensive literature on this proposition has been developed, but it seems to have escaped integration with the rest of cost theory in economics.[10]

Nevertheless, the proposition is a well-validated proposition and is widely used in industrial engineering. The significant implication of this proposition is that, in addition to rate of output, an important variable in determining total costs is the total planned output, for two reasons: first, because of changes in technique via Proposition 4, and, second, because the larger is the planned and ultimately realized output, the greater is the accumulated experience (technology) and knowledge at any point in the future via Proposition 9. Thus, the average cost per unit of output will be lower, the greater is the planned and ultimately experienced output. A more complete discussion of the evidence for this proposition would require a separate paper.

ON THE ADVANTAGES OF THE CAPITAL VALUE MEASURE

Use of capital values enables one to avoid misleading statements like "We are going to operate at a loss in the near future, but operations will be profitable later," "In the short run the firm may operate at a loss so long as receipts exceed variable costs," "A firm operates with long-run rather than short-run objectives." All of these statements are incorrect if liabilities or assets (other than money) are owned by the enterprise. What seems to be meant when a person talks about expecting to have losses for a while before getting profits is that cash flows will be negative for a while, but it is difficult to see how this is in any relevant sense a situation of losses. And, similarly, when a person talks about expecting losses it appears that he means he expects future events to occur which are unfavorable; and in this case the change belief about the future is immediately reflected in current values if not in current money flows—as many a stockholder has learned. Any periods during which expectation about future events becomes more favorable are periods of increasing equity (i.e., of profits), even though the period in which the more favorable events will occur is in the future. When a firm reports that it operated during the past quarter at a loss, it means simply that the net present value of assets decreased during that period, even though the future cash receipts and outlays have not yet been realized. The profits are in the present moment—the increase

[10] See W. Hirsch, "Manufacturing Progress Functions," *Review of Economics and Statistics*, XXXIV (May 1952), 143–55. A less accessible, but more complete, reference to the published material is given in H. Asher, *Cost-Quantity Relationship in the Airframe Industry* (The RAND Corporation, Santa Monica, California), July 1956. But see P. A. Samuelson, *Economics* (McGraw-Hill, New York, 1948), p. 473, where it is mentioned but left unincorporated.

in equity—as some stockholders have joyously learned. The presently anticipated increase in *future* receipts relative to future outlays means an increase in *present* equity values, profits.

Statements to the effect that a firm would willingly and knowingly operate at a loss in the short run are consistent only with an identification of costs with money flows, and are certainly inconsistent with the postulates of seeking increased wealth (or utility) as a goal or survival attribute. Such identification of costs with money flows eliminates capital theory from the theory of the firm and from much of price theory. There is no cause to pay this price since it is just as easy not to abandon capital theory, and if one retains it more useful implications will be derived.

Yet, in economic texts costs are almost always measured as *time-rates*, and only rarely as capital values. At first blush this would seem to be an irrelevant or trivial distinction, since capital values are merely the present values of *receipt* or *outlay* streams. But what about going from capital values to time rates of *cost* streams? New problems arise in this effort. Suppose that the outlay stream for some operation is used as the basis for cost calculations. If, and only if, *no* other assets or liabilities are involved can money flows be identified with costs; otherwise they represent, in part, accumulations of assets or liabilities. As soon as assets and liabilities are admitted, money flows are not synonymous with costs, and changes in values of assets or liabilities must now be included. With the break between money outlays and costs, the measure of costs becomes the change in present value of net equity consequent to some action (ignoring receipts, for present purposes).

If a firm signed a contract and committed itself to produce some quantity of output, then the cost it has incurred in signing the contract and obligating itself to produce the output is its decrease in equity, say $E_a - E_b$. At moment a, prior to the contract, the equity or net wealth of the firm is E_a. At this moment the firm considers entering into some production plan. If it does so, what will happen to its equity at the end of the plan, or how will the equity change over that interval? If, for the moment, we ignore the receipts or income from that plan, the decrease of equity by moment b would be the measure of cost of the output operation which it is obligated to perform. The difference, $E_a - E_b$, between the equity (E_a) at the beginning and the *present* value (E_b) of the equity (E_t) at the end of the operation, is the total cost, C, of the operation.

The *time-rate* of costs (of change in equity) is given by dE/dt, the slope of the line from E_a to E_t, which is quite different from C. The former, dE/dt, is a derivative, a time rate of change. The latter, C, is the integral of the former. It is a finite difference, $E_a - E_t$, obtained from two different points on the E curve, while the former is the slope of the E curve and can be obtained only after an E curve is obtained. What is the meaning of the E curve in such a case? Presumably it means that, if the firm decided at any moment to stop further output, under this contract it would find itself with an equity indicated by the height of the line E_aE_t. Ignoring the contractual liability for obligation to produce according to the contract, the equity declines along the E line; but if one does regard the contract performance liability, the equity does not change as output is produced because there is an exactly offsetting reduction in contractual liability as output is produced. The equity of the firm stays constant over the interval if the outlays and asset values initially forecast were forecast correctly.

If the *rate* of cost, dE/dt, or if the E curve is plotted not against time, but against the *output rate*, we do not get a curve similar in interpretation to the usual total cost curve in standard cost curve analysis. The *rate* of cost, dE/dt can be converted to average cost per unit of rate of output by dividing the rate of cost, dE/dt, by the associated rate of output at that moment, and the marginal time-rate of cost is obtained by asking how the slope of the equity curve dE/dt is affected by changes in x, i.e., $(d^2E/dt\,dx)$.

The difference between this curve, where dE/dt is plotted against x, and the usual time rate of cost curve analysis is that our current analysis is based on a larger set of variables, $x(t)$ and V, and hence dE/dt cannot be drawn uniquely merely against the rate of output, $x(t)$. A new curve must be drawn for each output operation contemplated; even worse, there is no assurance that such a curve of dE/dt drawn against the rate of output on the horizontal axis would have only one vertical height for each output rate. The curve might fold back on itself and be multivalued because one value of dE/dt might be associated with a particular rate of output early in the operation and another different value later in the operation, even though at both moments the output rate were the same.

The number of cost curves that could be drawn is greater by at least an extra factor, V. In fact, we have at least two families of curves, one for different values of V and one for different time profiles of $x(t)$, and it is not clear what is usually assumed about these in the standard cost curve analysis. One possibility is to assume that the length of the production run, m, or the contemplated total output, V, does not affect the rate at which equity changes for any given output rate. The difficulty with this position is not merely that it is logically wrong but that it leads to implications that are refuted by everyday events.

A kind of average or marginal cost can be defined on the basis of the approach suggested earlier. For any given contemplated operation, the change in equity implied can be computed and evaluated in present worths. If this cost is divided by the total contemplated volume of output, V, the result is present value cost per unit of product (not time rate per unit *rate* of output). If the same total output were to be produced at a higher output rate, x, and thus within a shorter time interval, m, the total cost (change in equity) would be greater, and so the cost per unit of total volume of output would be higher. As noted in the first part of this paper, the increase in total present value cost, $\partial C/x$ (not $d^2E/dt\,dx$), is the marginal cost, consequent to an increased rate of output. By varying the contemplated rates of output x for any given total output plan (V and T), one can get different total capital costs. These changes in total capital costs can be called the marginal capital costs. But it is important to note again that there are as many such marginal capital value cost functions as there are different possible total output patterns that can be contemplated, and these marginal capital costs are not time rates of costs.

CONCLUSION

Four features have been emphasized in the foregoing pages. First, the distinction between rate and quantity of output; second, changes in technology as distinct from changes in technique; third, the use of calendar time dates of output instead of technical fixity for distinguishing output operations; fourth, the use of capital value concepts instead of rates of costs.

The first and second features (and the ones that are emphasized in this paper) enable us to capture within our theory the lower costs attendant on larger quantities of output—not rates of output. Everyday experience where large rates of output are available at lower prices could be explained as a movement down the buyer's demand curve as the seller, in order to sell a larger amount, lowers price. But this seems to be incapable of explaining all such situations. Another explanation usually advanced is the economies of scale, where scale is related to *rate* of output. However, an alternative explanation suggested here is the lower cost resulting, not from higher *rates* of output per unit time, but from larger planned volume of total output quantities. An examination of the production management and engineering literature reveals much greater emphasis on batch or lot size as contrasted to the rate of output. Frequently the latter is not much of a variable in each particular firm's decision. This means that the extent to which rate of output *is* varied may be slight—not that it can't be varied or that its significance is slight. That there has been confusion between the rate of output and the batch size or quantity planned is sure. How much cannot be known.

The third feature—that of identifying each output operation with a calendar date and then postulating that the more distant the date the smaller the change in equity (the smaller the cost)—provides a way to escape the unnecessary bind imposed by the definition of short-run costs as that which results from fixed inputs. The ambiguous idea of two different costs, a short-run and a long-run cost for a given output, disappears and is replaced by one cost for each different program of output.

What must have been assumed in our present literature about the factors mentioned here? Was the rate of output profile assumed to be a constant rate extending into perpetuity? The answer could not be ascertained from an exhausting reading of the literature nor from analogically implied conditions. Certainly the standard cost curve analysis does not envisage a perpetuity output at some given rate, nor does it seem to specify the effects of shorter-length runs at any output. For example, Stigler, in his well-known paper on the effects of planning for variations in the rate of output, imagines one to be moving along a given cost curve appropriate to the case in which output varies. This desirable attempt to modify the cost curve analysis would have been more successful if the output had been further specified or identified in terms of V and T. Then the conventional curves would have disappeared, and many logical inconsistencies and ambiguities could have been removed from the standard analysis. But merely drawing the curve flatter and higher does not avoid the problems of appropriate interpretation of costs for unspecified values of the pertinent variables.

Finally, introduction of a new variable, V, complicates the equilibrium of demand and supply, for now there must be a similar element in demand which will determine the equilibrium size of V, if such there be. Suffice it to say here that even though consumers may not act or plan consciously in terms of V, their actions can be interpreted in terms of a resultant aggregative V. Producers, in contemplating the demand for their products, will be required to think of capital value or present value of income with the rate of output integrated into a V—possibly a break-even V—on the basis of which they may make production plans. A simple rate of output, price relationships, will not be sufficient. But this remains to be developed later, only if the present propositions prove valid and useful.

Toward a Theory of Price Adjustment

KENNETH J. ARROW

THE ROLE OF PRICE ADJUSTMENT EQUATIONS IN
ECONOMIC THEORY

In this essay, it is argued that there exists a logical gap in the usual formulations of the theory of the perfectly competitive economy, namely, that there is no place for a rational decision with respect to prices as there is with respect to quantities. A suggestion is made for filling this gap. The proposal implies that perfect competition can really prevail only at equilibrium. It is hoped that the line of development proposed will lead to a better understanding of the behavior of the economy in disequilibrium conditions.

In the traditional development of economic theory, the usual starting point is the construction for each individual (firm or household) of a pattern of reactions to events outside it (examples of elements of a reaction pattern: supply and demand curves, propensity to consume, liquidity preference, interindustrial movements of capital and labor in response to differential profit and wage rates). This point of view is explicit in the neoclassicists (Cournot, Jevons, Menger, and successors) and strongly implicit in the classicists (from Smith through Cairnes) in their discussion of the motivations of capitalists, workers, and landlords which lead to establishment of the equilibrium price levels for commodities, labor, and the use of land. The basic logic of Marx's system brings it, I believe, into the same category, although some writers have referred to his theories as being "class" economics rather than "individual" economics.[1] Although the dialectical discussion of value in the opening sections of Volume I of *Capital*[2] lend some credence to this view, it is already clear in Marx's discussion of relative surplus value (Volume I, Part IV) that the introduc-

---

[1] See, e.g., Klein [(1) page 118]: "Instead of studying the behavior of individuals, Marx studied the behavior of classes directly."

[2] K. Marx (2): Chap. I, and especially the discussion of surplus value in Chaps. VI, VII, VIII, and IX.

tion of new production processes is based on the profit-maximizing behavior of the individual entrepreneur;[3] and the role of the individual behavior reaction is basic in Marx's discussion of the equalization of profit rates in different industries in Volume III (especially Chapter X). In the opinion of most contemporary Marxist economists, such as Dobb (3) and Sweezy (4) and of sympathetic critics such as Lange (5),[4] the value theory of Volume I is to be regarded only as a first approximation to that of Volume III, so that the latter must be regarded as the basic part of Marx's price theory.[5]

There remains one school which might be interpreted as objecting to the development of economics from the viewpoint of individual reaction patterns. These are the institutionalists, such as Veblen (8), who attacked the behavior patterns hypothesized by contemporary economists for stressing the passive reacting character of individual behavior; but this argument seems partly a terminological question and partly an attack on the limited, excessively hedonistic expositions of the marginal utility theory current about 1900. Elsewhere both Veblen (9) and Mitchell (10) have emphasized the importance for the course of economic activity of the behavior of individuals, especially profit-making by firms.

In this individualistic framework, every relevant variable, except those classified as exogenous for the whole economic system, is the result of a decision on the part of some one individual unit of the economy. This paper considers the theoretical analysis of the decisions as to prices.

The standard development of the theory of behavior under competitive conditions has made both sides of any market take prices as given by some outside agency. Thus, for a single market,

$$D = f(p), \ S = g(p) \tag{1}$$

where D is the demand for the commodity, S its supply, and p its price. The functions $f(p)$ and $g(p)$ represent the behavior of consumers and producers, respectively. But relation 1 constitutes only two equations in the three unknowns D, S, and p.

The theoretical structure is usually completed by adding the condition of equality of supply and demand,

$$S = D. \tag{2}$$

[3] See especially Vol. I, pp. 347–53.

[4] The same view has been expressed by at least one Soviet textbook, Lapidus and Ostrovityanov, *Outlines of Political Economy*, referred to by H. Smith in "Marx and the Trade Cycle" (6).

[5] An alternative interpretation sometimes adopted is that there is a basic contradiction between the two price theories. This position has been adopted by numerous critics of Marxism, following E. Böhm von Bawerk, *Karl Marx and the Close of His System* (7). The same view has been taken by the ultra-Marxist, Daniel de Leon, who rejected Volume III as Engels' misinterpretation.

What is the rationale of relation 2? In the usual treatise on economics, a great deal of attention is paid to the derivation of the functions entering into relation 1, but equation 2 is usually taken pretty much for granted. If we look further into the reasoning given by such writers as do not regard equation 2 as completely self-evident, it is clear that it is regarded as the limit of a trial-and-error process describable by an equation of the general type

$$dp/dt = h(S-D) \tag{3}$$

where

$$h' < 0, h(0) = 0. \tag{4}$$

(Here and below, primes denote differentiation, so that h' is the rate of change of the function h with respect to an increase in the excess supply.)

Relation 3 is, of course, the well-known "Law of Supply and Demand." It asserts that price rises when demand exceeds supply and falls in the contrary case. Equations 1 and 3 together define a dynamic process in which supply, demand, and price vary in a prescribed way over time. If the process is stable, these three magnitudes approach limits. At the limiting values, there can be no pressure for any of the variables to change. In view of equations 3 and 4, price will remain stationary if and only if equation 2 holds; but if price remains stationary, demand and supply will do so also, by relation 1. [See Samuelson (11) and Arrow and Hurwicz (12).]

The Law of Supply and Demand may be a useful basis for interpreting some empirical phenomena, particularly the course of prices in markets subject to rapid changes in supply or demand conditions, although in fact few such applications have been made; however, the Law is not on the same logical level as the hypotheses underlying equation 1. It is not explained whose decision it is to change prices in accordance with equation 3. Each individual participant in the economy is supposed to take prices as given and determine his choices as to purchases and sales accordingly; there is no one left over whose job it is to make a decision on price.[6]

PRICE ADJUSTMENT UNDER MONOPOLY

Before discussing the mechanics of price adjustment under competitive conditions, we may consider the determination of price under monopoly. Here, there is no question of the locus of price decisions. In the standard theory (essentially unchanged from Cournot's original presentation), the monopolist fixes his price and output to maximize $R(x)-C(x)$, where x is output, $R(x)$ the total revenue curve, and $C(x)$ the total cost

---

[6] This problem has not gone unnoticed in the literature; thus T. Scitovsky observes, "The difficulty lies in visualizing a price that everybody on both sides of the market regards as given and that is determined by the 'impersonal forces of the market'" (13).

curve. Price and output are related by the demand curve, and the firm's output will, therefore, always equal demand. This theory clearly presupposes that the monopolist knows the true demand curve confronting him.

Lange (14) has sought to develop a theory of price adjustment for monopolies analogous to the Law of Supply and Demand under competition. Let $U(p)$ be the profit of the entrepreneur if he sets price p, assuming that the output has been fixed in accordance with the demand curve. Then Lange suggests

$$dp/dt = F(U') \qquad (5)$$

where

$$F' > 0, F(0) = 0. \qquad (6)$$

Rules 5 and 6 amount to saying that the entrepreneur varies his price in that direction which leads to an increased profit. The rules are of the type referred to in mathematics as gradient methods of maximization.

These rules have concealed in them implicit assumptions about the monopolist's knowledge of the demand curve facing him (I assume he has complete knowledge of his cost curve). Since Lange assumes that output equals sales, the monopolist must know the demand at the price chosen, and, to make equation 5 operationally meaningful, he must know the elasticity of demand at that price. On the other hand, the monopolist presumably does not know the entire demand curve, for otherwise he would jump immediately to the optimal position. Further, his knowledge must be changing over time. To see this, let p_0 be the price set at some time t_0 and p_1 the price at some later time t_1. Since the monopolist is increasing his profit by his successive trial prices, the profit $U(p_1)$ at time t_1 must be greater than $U(p_0)$, the profit at time t_0. If, at time t_0, the monopolist had known the demand at price p_1, he would have known that p_0 was not the point of maximum profit and would have chosen p_1 or, possibly, some price which yielded a still higher profit. Thus the value of demand at p_1 is knowledge which is available to the monopolist at time t_1 but not at time t_0.

Uncertainty, then, is a crucial consideration in the theory of monopolistic price adjustment. We cannot completely follow Lange in assuming that the monopolist never wets his toes in the cold waters of uncertainty as to the demand curve. It may be that, without knowing the exact value of demand at p_1, the monopolist knows that even under the worst possible conditions the profit will be greater than at p_0, where the demand is known. Indeed, it suffices that the expected profit corresponding to p_1 be sufficiently greater than the known profit at p_0 to overcome the entrepreneur's distaste for the greater uncertainty. Hence we must admit the possibility of a discrepancy between output and demand for a monopolist. The discrepancy once observed has a twofold significance for price adjustment.

On the one hand, it informs the monopolist of the extent to which he is in error and yields knowledge to estimate better his demand curve; on the other hand, the discrepancy alters his stock of inventories, which may in turn affect his cost situation in the next period.[7] The latter effect would, of course, not apply to cases where either no inventories can be accumulated, as with services, or where the carrying costs (including storage, depreciation, and foregone liquidity) are very high. It seems reasonable to conclude that price adjustment will be slower in the last-mentioned case than where inventories can be accumulated or decumulated more readily.

Thus, if demand is higher than anticipated, the monopolist will, in general, raise his price because both his marginal cost and anticipated marginal revenue curves have shifted upwards, and conversely for demands lower than anticipated. If the true demand and cost curves remain unchanged in the process, the monopolist will gradually converge towards his optimal price-quantity position. If, however, the demand and cost curves are shifting over time in response to influences exogenous to the market under consideration, the monopolist's price adjustment relations become part of a general dynamic system which is not necessarily stable. I will not elaborate here a more complete model, which can become very complicated.[8]

COMPETITIVE PRICE ADJUSTMENT

The above sketch of monopolistic price adjustment theory has been introduced here not only for its own sake, but for the purpose of laying the foundations for a theory of price adjustment under competitive circumstances. As has been understood since the days of Cournot and emphasized in more recent times by Chamberlain and Joan Robinson, the competitive firm is a monopolist with a special environment.

Ordinarily, the firm acting under competitive conditions is pictured as a monopolist confronted with a perfectly elastic demand curve. More explicitly, it is assumed that there exists a price, which we may refer to as the market price, such that the firm can sell any output it desires at a price not exceeding the market price, but can sell nothing at a higher price.

Triffin (16) has criticized this criterion of perfect elasticity of demand as a definition of pure competition, arguing that such a demand situation is itself a consequence of the fundamental technological and test factors

---

[7] If the total cost of producing x units is $C(x)$, the carrying cost is c per unit, and the amount carried forward is x_0, the cost associated with delivering x units in the next period is $C(x - x_0) + c x_0$. For low values of c, this cost will be less than $C(x)$, so that the cost curve for the next period has shifted downward.

[8] Such models are closely related to those which have been developed in inventory theory over the last twelve years. See, for example, Arrow, Karlin, and Scarf (15).

involved. He defines perfect competition instead in terms of certain cross-elasticities of supply and demand as between different firms.

Indeed, suppose we have a situation which conforms in all the aspects of homogeneity of output and multiplicity of firms to the usual concept of perfect competition, but in which the aggregate supply forthcoming at the "market" price exceeds the demand at that price. Then the individual firm cannot sell all it wishes to at the market price; i.e., when supply and demand do not balance, even in an objectively competitive market, the individual firms are in the position of monopolists as far as the imperfect elasticity of demand for their products is concerned.

What is the meaning of market price in such a situation? We are always told by the textbooks that there is one price in a competitive market at a given time. But what determines this one price? The answer has been given clearly by Reder. Under conditions of disequilibrium, there is no reason that there should be a single market price, and we may very well expect that each firm will charge a different price (17). The law that there is only one price on a competitive market (Jevons' Law of Indifference) is derived on the basis of profit- or utility-maximizing behavior on the part of both sides of the market; but there is no reason for such behavior to lead to unique price except in equilibrium, or possibly under conditions of perfect knowledge.

Let us consider in somewhat more detail the case in which demand exceeds supply. Assume that no firm can increase supply in a very short period. Then any individual entrepreneur knows that he can raise the price, even if his competitors do not raise theirs, because they cannot satisfy any more of the demand than they do already. The entrepreneur is faced with a sloping demand curve and raises his price in accordance with the profit-maximizing tactics of a monopolist, as sketched in the previous section. If none of the other sellers do in fact raise their prices, the entrepreneur will gradually approach his point of maximum profit, where the market will be cleared. But, under the conditions specified, it is equally to the profit of all other entrepreneurs to raise their prices also, although, if not subject to the same cost conditions, not necessarily by the same amount. The demand curve for the particular entrepreneur under consideration is thus shifting upward at the same time that he is exploring it. Thus supply will still not be in balance with demand, and the process continues.

It must also be stresesd that the amount of uncertainty during this process is apt to be very considerable. Any estimate of the demand curve to a single entrepreneur involves a guess as to both the supply conditions and the prices of other sellers, as well as some idea of the demand curve to the industry as a whole. Under competitive conditions none of these is likely to be known very well. Thus the whole adjustment process is apt to be very irregular. Although the broad tendency will be for prices to rise when demand exceed supply, there can easily be a considerable dispersion of prices among different sellers of the same commodity, as well as considerable variability over time in the rate of change of prices.

The uncertainty, in turn, puts a premium on information. Traditional economic theory stresses the sufficiency of the price system as a source of information for guiding economic behavior, and this is correct enough at equilibrium. But the monopolist in general has stricter informational requirements than the competitor, since he needs to know his whole demand curve, not merely a single price. In conditions of disequilibrium, the demand curve is shifting as a result of forces outside the private market of the monopolist, and a premium is placed on the acquisition of information from sources other than the prices and quantities of the firm's own sales.

So far, our detailed analysis has covered the case of a firm acting as a monopolist because demand exceeds supply for the industry of which the firm is a part. We have already seen that, on a market where supply exceeds demand, each firm can also be regarded as a monopolist, though for different reasons. By a parallel argument each buyer on a market with an inequality between supply and demand can be regarded as a monopsonist. The behavior of each firm as a buyer can be described in the same manner as that of the seller, and we forebear from detailed repetition.

However, this further remark requires some revision of our previous picture of the market. In disequilibrium, the market consists of a number of monopolists facing a number of monopsonists. The most general picture is that of a shifting set of bilateral monopolies. The range of indeterminacy in each bargaining situation is limited but not completely eliminated by the possibilities of other bargains. In general, though, it is reasonable to suppose that if the selling side of the market is much more concentrated than the buying side, the main force in changing prices will be the monopolistic behavior of the sellers. The buyers would find little possibility of exerting their individual monopsonistic powers because there are so many of them for each seller. Similarly, if the buying side of the market is the more concentrated, as in nonunionized labor markets, the dynamics will come from that side. It is perhaps for reasons such as these that the immediate location of price decisions is usually vested in the more concentrated side of the market, in sellers in the case of most commodities, in buyers in the case of unorganized labor. (In organized labor markets, bilateral monopoly prevails.) Thus the dynamics of prices may be affected by the structure of the market even in cases where there are sufficient numbers in the market to insure reasonably competitive behavior at equilibrium.

IMPLICATIONS FOR THE SPEED OF ADJUSTMENT

The preceding shows, of course, that the difference between supply and demand is a major factor in explaining the movement of prices, so that the Law of Supply and Demand, as expressed in equations 3 and 4, can be

thought of as a useful approximation. However, the "price" whose movements are explained by the Law must be thought of as the average price.
The model presented in this paper has some implications for the speed of
adjustment in different markets, as represented by the function h.

Consider, as before, the case where demand exceeds supply and sellers
are led to behave as monopolists. The existence of this excess both for the
particular seller under consideration and for his competitors enters into
the determination of the seller's anticipated demand curve. Given this, he
sets his price so as to equate anticipated marginal revenue (possibly discounted in some form for uncertainty) to marginal cost. The price increase
will thus depend on the shape of the marginal cost curve. It will be greater
if the marginal cost is rising sharply than if it is flat. In particular, then,
the speed of adjustment will be greater during a period of full utilization
of capacity than in a situation of excess capacity.

A second consideration affecting the speed of adjustment, already remarked in passing, is the possibility of accumulating and decumulating
inventories. An accumulation of inventories is both a signal to revise downward the anticipated demand curve and a cause of a downward shift in the
marginal cost curve in the next period. A decumulation of inventories has
the opposite effects. Hence, price adjustment will be more rapid in industries where inventories play a significant role.

A third factor suggested by the preceding analysis is the degree of information available to the individual entrepreneur. Relative absence of
information about the behavior of others in the market increases the degree
of uncertainty. Even in the absence of an aversion to risk-bearing, the
chances that the entrepreneur will misread the signals are greater than if
more information were available; we would therefore expect on the average
that the responsiveness of prices to supply–demand differences would be
less in the absence of information. An aversion to risk-bearing would
increase the entrepreneur's unwillingness to venture on price changes in
the absence of information. We would expect, therefore, that well-organized exchanges would display the greatest degree of price flexibility.

One special case in which information would be expected to be relatively scarce is that where the products are poorly standardized. Then
knowledge of prices and availabilities of supply for other firms will not
have a clear meaning for a particular firm, since its product may not be
a perfect substitute, and therefore an excess of demand over supply elsewhere in the market may not be due to an upward shift in demand for all
products on the market but to a shift away from its product to that of its
competitors.

THE COMPETITIVENESS OF THE ECONOMY

In any state of disequilibrium, i.e., any situation in which supply does
not equal demand, it follows from the above model that the economy will
show evidences of monopoly and monopsony. These evidences will be the

more intense, the greater the disequilibrium. We can understand from this point of view the feeling of the businessman that, contrary to economic theory, sales are by no means unlimited at the current market price. The demand for advertising and other forms of nonprice competition thus makes more sense than under the model of perfect competition at all times.

The model casts some light on the much-discussed problem of administered prices.[9] It was brought out by Gardiner Means and others in the 1930's that the quoted prices of some commodities produced by industries in which there was a high degree of concentration tended to be rigid, that is, insensitive to inequalities of demand and supply. Against this point of view it has been objected that the prices at which transactions actually take place differ from the quoted prices and are, for example, lower in conditions of excess capacity. Thus, the actual prices would be more nearly consistent with those of the competitive model. But it remains to be explained why the sellers resort to a fictitious price and secret undercutting instead of openly reducing prices. Explanations, such as Bailey's (18), which run in terms of informal social pressures within the industry, do not seem very satisfactory and, in any case, merely push the problem back one step.

If, however, it is accepted that an inequality of supply and demand leads to a condition of partial monopoly, then the most likely explanation for a divergence between quoted and actual prices is that it is a cloak for price discrimination. Not all buyers receive equal discounts, because they are not informed as to the prices actually paid. Such discrimination, if it can be shown to exist, would, of course, be incompatible with a purely competitive model.

The present model also suggests that the measurement of competitiveness by the concentration ratio has to be interpreted carefully. A degree of concentration which would be perfectly compatible with a reasonable degree of competition if the market were in equilibrium might easily fail to be so compatible in the event of serious inequality between supply and demand. There has been a position strongly held in recent years that the American economy is basically competitive, in that neither firms nor labor unions have, in fact, much control over prices, despite superficial appearances.[10] The present model suggests that the evidence, to the extent that it is valid, relates only to equilibrium and, therefore, to long-run situations. Such long-run competitiveness is not incompatible, on the present view, with considerable short-run monopoly powers in transitory situations.

The incomplete competitiveness of the economy under disequilibrium conditions implies a departure from the maximum of possible efficiency in the use of resources. To be sure, it does not necessarily follow that

[9] See M. J. Bailey, "Administered Prices in the American Economy," pp. 89–106, and earlier references cited there (18).
[10] For firms, this view has been held by Stigler (19), Nutter (20), and Harberger (21). For trade unions, see Friedman (22).

greater efficiency is necessarily achievable under feasible alternative rules. Any method of resource allocation requires a process for equating supply and demand (or some equivalent), and such a process may be in itself costly, though such costs are not considered in the usual formal analysis of welfare economics. Thus, a completely centralized system will incur high computational and informational costs. The monopolistic and monopsonistic misallocations implied by the model of the present paper may be thought of as costs alternative to those associated with centralization.

In particular, one would expect considerable departures from maximum efficiency in conditions of severe disequilibrium, such as inflations and depressions, despite Keynes's well-known remark to the contrary.[11] Under conditions of unemployment, the mobility of resources in response to price differences is seriously impaired. Thus, in a depression workers will not move from the farm to the city, despite considerable wage differences, because they are aware of the difficulty of getting a job; the individual worker faces a falling demand curve.

A REMARK ON INFLATION

The above model casts some light on the concept of cost inflation. Such a doctrine requires that there be important elements of unregulated monopoly in the economy. There is at least some doubt that such elements are significant in the long run. However, the model of this paper suggests that in a certain sense all inflationary processes are cost inflations in that it is the monopoly power resulting from excess demand which is their proximate cause. This may explain why acute observers differ so sharply in their evaluation of the same phenomenon. Those who see cost inflation may be looking at an immediate causal factor, while those who speak of demand inflation have their eye on a more ultimate stimulus.

In view of this, this paper would suggest caution in treating cost inflations by direct regulation.[12] They may be transitory phenomena which are necessary to achieve equilibrium, in which case regulation may simply lead to the replacement of overt by suppressed inflation.

References

1. L. R. Klein, "Theories of Effective Demand and Employment," *Journal of Political Economy*, LV (April 1947), 108–31.

2. K. Marx, Capital. Charles H. Kerr, Chicago, 1906, Vol. I.

3. M. Dobb, Marx as an Economist. International Publishers, New York, 1945, pp. 19–20.

[11] "I see no reason to suppose that the existing system seriously misemploys the factors of production which are in use. . . . When 9,000,000 men are employed out of 10,000,000 willing and able to work, there is no evidence that the labor of the 9,000,000 men is misdirected" (23).

[12] See the proposals of Lerner (24).

4. P. M. Sweezy, The Theory of Capitalist Development. Oxford, New York, 1942, Chap. VII.

5. O. Lange, "Marxian Economics and Modern Economic Theory," *Review of Economic Studies*, II (1934–35), 189–201; especially pp. 194, 195.

6. H. Smith, "Marx and the Trade Cycle," *Review of Economic Studies*, IV (June 1937), 197.

7. E. Böhm von Bawerk, Karl Marx and the Close of His System. Unwin, London, 1898.

8. T. Veblen, "Limitations of Marginal Utility" and "Professor Clark's Economics," reprinted in The Place of Science in Modern Civilization and Other Essays. Huebsch, New York, 1919, pp. 180–251.

9. T. Veblen, The Theory of Business Enterprise. Scribner's, New York, 1904.

10. W. C. Mitchell, Business Cycles: The Problem and Its Setting. National Bureau of Economic Research, New York, 1927, pp. 105–7.

11. P. A. Samuelson, Foundations of Economic Analysis. Harvard University Press, Cambridge, 1947, Chap. IX.

12. K. J. Arrow and L. Hurwicz, "On the Stability of the Competitive Equilibrium, I," *Econometrica* (to be published).

13. T. Scitovsky, Welfare and Competition. Allen and Unwin, London, 1952, p. 16.

14. O. Lange, Price Flexibility and Employment. Cowles Commission Monograph No. 8. Principia Press, Bloomington, Indiana, 1944, pp. 35–37, 107–9.

15. K. J. Arrow, S. Karlin, and H. Scarf, Studies in the Mathematical Theory of Inventory and Production. Stanford University Press, Stanford, California, 1958.

16. R. M. Triffin, Monopolistic Competition and General Equilibrium Theory. Harvard University Press, Cambridge, 1940, pp. 137–41.

17. M. W. Reder, Studies in the Theory of Welfare Economics. Columbia University Press, New York, 1947, pp. 126–51.

18. M. J. Bailey, "Administered Prices in the American Economy," in The Relationship of Prices to Economic Stability and Growth. Joint Economic Committee, U.S. Congress, Washington, D.C., 1958, pp. 89–106.

19. G. J. Stigler, Five Lectures on Economic Problems. Longmans, Green, New York, London, and Toronto, 1949. Lecture 5, pp. 44–65.

20. G. Warren Nutter, The Extent of Enterprise Monopoly in the United States, 1899–1939. University of Chicago Press, Chicago, 1951.

21. A. C. Harberger, "Monopoly and Resource Allocation," *American Economic Review*, XLIV, No. 2 (May 1954), 77–87.

22. M. Friedman, "Some Comments on the Significance of Labor Unions for Economic Policy," in D. M. Wright (ed.), The Impact of the Union. Harcourt, Brace, NewYork, 1951, Chap. X, pp. 204–34.

23. J. M. Keynes, The General Theory of Employment, Interest and Money. Harcourt, Brace, New York, 1936, p. 379.

24. A. P. Lerner, "Inflationary Depression and the Regulation of Administered Prices," in The Relationship of Prices to Economic Stability and Growth. Joint Economic Committee, U.S. Congress, Washington, D.C., 1958, pp. 267–68.

Reflections on Underconsumption[1]

PAUL A. BARAN

At a time when many distinguished writers in the fields of economics and social comment are devoting increasing attention to waste and excessive consumption in our society, theorizing in terms of underconsumption may be deemed bizarre and anachronistic.[2] Yet, without attempting to review the extensive literature on underconsumption, it will be argued in what follows not only that the basic concepts developed in underconsumption theory are of paramount importance to any attempt to understand the working principles of the capitalist system, but that ignoring them constitutes an insuperable obstacle to the comprehension of the very phenomena of waste and excessive consumption that have been moving into the center of current preoccupation.

I

To be sure, the theory of underconsumption has never had much standing among reputable economists. The reasons—apart from those that need to be dealt with in terms of sociology of knowledge—for this conspicuous lack of esteem for a theoretical position that dates back to the very beginnings of modern economics are twofold. In the first place, there has been a general sense, best expressed perhaps by Professor Gottfried Haberler, that the scientific standard of the underconsumption theories is unduly low (3). Secondly, it has been held that the actual course of capitalist development was to such an extent at variance with what was taken to be the factual presuppositions of the underconsumption theory as to render that theory entirely baseless.

[1] This essay reflects work carried on jointly with Paul M. Sweezy the preliminary results of which we hope to submit in the none too distant future in a book on American capitalism. The responsibility for the specific formulations contained in this paper is, however, mine.

[2] Cf. *Problems of United States Economic Development* (1), in particular the contributions of Moses Abramovitz, Roy F. Harrod, Ralph Hawtrey, David Riesman; also Galbraith (2).

The first objection undoubtedly has some force; even the expression "underconsumption" has been used very loosely, with different writers attaching widely different meanings to it. Although it is self-evident that for this expression to be usefully employed it is necessary to state unambiguously *with regard to what* consumption is considered to be deficient, this elementary rule has by no means always been observed. Thus, to a number of writers "underconsumption" spelled simply an insufficiency of consumption for the maintenance of health and efficiency of the population. Others, in speaking of underconsumption, have referred to an apportionment of aggregate output between consumption and investment (or between consumption and other "nonconsumption" purposes, such as construction of fortifications or of monuments) which they considered to be inadequate in terms of what they took to be the proper allocation of resources either in the present or as between the present and the future. Still others treated underconsumption as a condition in which the share of output absorbed by current consumption is such as to give rise to a volume of investment exceeding that which would be warranted by the prevailing level of output (and income), with the result that aggregate effective demand would be insufficient for the maintenance of full employment of resources.

While the first mentioned variants of the underconsumption concept are hardly useful for analytical purposes, the last one represents a most promising point of departure for further inquiry. In fact, all that is required to turn it into a powerful tool for the study of capitalist development is its refinement and reformulation. The needed refinement calls primarily for a qualitative and quantitative differentiation of consumption into its *useful* and *wasteful* components, for it is only along these lines that we can hope to clarify both the dynamic of consumption itself and its impact on socioeconomic development as a whole. The required reformulation should state clearly that "underconsumption" is not necessarily a description of achieved results but, rather, refers to an important *tendency* operative in the capitalist process and co-determining its outcome at any given time. This tendency obviously is neither the *only* tendency at work, nor even necessarily the dominant one. In any particular situation, its effect may be modified and indeed completely offset by other tendencies, with the resulting parallelogram of forces responsible for the actually evolving historical constellation.

These considerations must be taken into account when we turn to the second objection to the underconsumption theory: its alleged lack of correspondence with observed historical events. This point, frequently made, was reiterated most recently by Nicholas Kaldor, who dismisses the proposition that as a result of increasing monopoly "the share of profits would go on rising beyond the point where it covers investment needs and the consumption of capitalists" and, therefore, that "the system will cease to be capable of generating sufficient purchasing power to keep the mechanism of growth in operation" with the flat statement: "the plain answer to this is that so far, at any rate, this has not happened"(4). It should be obvious, however, that this argument, far from disposing of the problem, fails even to reach the theoretical level on which it arises. What would we think of a theorist in the field of international economics who would deal with the issue of balance of payments' disequilibrium by enunciating the profound wisdom that international payments "so far, at any rate" have always been in balance? It surely does not require prolonged reflection to realize that what matters with regard to international payments is not the surface phenomenon of their always being in balance, but the truly significant questions concerning the structure of output, the level of income, and the volume of employment with which any given balance is associated, and the process by which such balance as may exist is actually attained. Similarly, in a theoretical analysis of the generation of "sufficient purchasing power to keep the mechanism of growth in operation," little is gained by registering whatever volume of purchasing power happened to enter the market resulting in such a level of income and employment (and unemployment) as happened to prevail, if no effort is made to pierce the obvious and to comprehend the forces which gave rise to that volume of purchasing power and which determined the nature and the rate of growth of the output related thereto.

II

Nor is it necessary in this particular case to depart far from the immediately observable, measurable *fact*, that Moloch which is always seeking to devour analytic thought in contemporary social science. For, if the available and currently forthcoming statistical evidence were based on categories calculated to reveal rather than conceal what might be called the basal metabolism of the capitalist system, the relevant relations would become apparent even to the naked eye. While the confines of this essay preclude anything like a comprehensive discussion of this problem, its barest outline may be drawn with reference to American experience.

The most conspicuous feature of the evolution of American capitalism, particularly since about 1870, is the enormous growth of the forces of production. Between 1869 and 1956, output per man-hour in the commodity-producing industries (agriculture, mining, and manufacturing) multiplied approximately eight times.[3] There is to my knowledge no estimate of the per man-hour productivity increase during the same period of *production workers*, i.e., of labor engaged in the process of *production*, rather than

[3] For the increase of man-hour productivity from 1869 to 1949 cf. Barger (5), pp. 37 ff.; the change from 1949 to 1956 is estimated on the basis of *Economic Growth in the United States, Its Past and Future* (6), p. 31.

in that of administration, selling, financing, advertising, etc.[4] That increase must have been very much larger, since the proportion of production workers in the total labor force has markedly declined, and since the growth of "productivity" of the nonproduction workers has proceeded very slowly.[5] The importance of the magnitude of the productivity increase of production workers can hardly be exaggerated. The relation between the productivity of production workers and their real wages has not been studied systematically for a period comparable to that covered by Professor Barger's investigation of distribution. Yet, according to statistics available for the years 1909 to 1956, there has been a considerable gap between the growth of productivity and the rise of real wages of production workers. While the output per man-hour of production workers has risen in the course of that half-century by 277.1 per cent, their real average hourly earnings increased by 230.0 per cent so that the real earnings of production workers per unit of output declined by 13.5 per cent.[6] As a result, the *economic surplus* produced by society has grown considerably larger, not merely in absolute terms, but in the only relevant sense: as a share of aggregate output.

[4] "The Bureau of Labor Statistics includes in its definition of *production workers* all nonsupervisory workers (including working foremen) engaged in fabricating, processing, assembling, inspecting, receiving, storing, handling, packing, warehousing, and shipping; also workers engaged in maintenance, repair, janitorial and watchman services, product development and auxiliary production for a plant's own use (e.g., powerplant) and record-keeping, and other services immediately associated with these production operations. In this group is found the bulk of all factory machinists, mechanics, toolmakers and other craftsmen, welders, filers, grinders, and other operatives, janitors, charwomen, guards, and similar service workers (except, for example, plant cafeteria personnel), and most of the unskilled laborers employed in manufacturing. *Nonproduction workers,* defined by process of exclusion from the production worker category, are those engaged in executive, purchasing, finance, accounting, legal, personnel, cafeteria, medical, professional, and technical activities; sales delivery, advertising, credit, collection, installation and servicing of the firm's own products; routine office functions, factory supervision, and force-account construction. The bulk of factory management and personnel employees, engineers, scientists, bookkeepers, typists, clerks, salesmen, payroll workers, and employees engaged in similar activities are included in this group." "Nonproduction Workers in Factories, 1919-56" (italics added) (7). To be sure, the distinction made by the Bureau of Labor Statistics is not the same as the distinction suggested by our analysis, i.e., between those engaged in contributing to the creation of useful goods and services, the production and distribution of which would be required also in a more rational social order and those whose activities are determined by the composition of output enforced by the capitalist system and by selling operations characteristic of the capitalist market. The BLS distinction is useful, nevertheless, since it provides at least an idea of orders of magnitudes and trends which aggregative data entirely obscure.

[5] Cf. Barger (5), p. 39.

[6] *Productivity, Prices and Incomes* (8), Table 54, p. 148, and Table 57, p. 151.

What is perhaps even more significant is that, while this spectacular increase of output per man-hour of production workers was achieved to some extent by a marked improvement of health and efficiency of the working population, its mainspring was a vast expansion of the volume of capital equipment. The dimensions of this expansion are suggested by a comparison over time of capital (except land and improvements) employed per worker. Measured in 1929 prices and adjusted for standard hours, it increased from $1860 in 1879 to $3760 in 1909, and to $6260 in 1944 (9). Since these statistics are calculated by taking into account the *entire* labor force, they undoubtedly underestimate the extent of the mechanization of the work of production workers. This may be more adequately assessed if it is considered that manufacturing establishments use now approximately 10 horsepower of energy per production worker as compared with 1.25 horsepower in 1879 [(6), p. 32]. This sweeping mechanization was propelled by massive capital accumulation, by extensive exploitation of "economies of scale," and by a consequent general transition to mass production methods; and this in turn has led to the emergence and growth of large-scale industrial enterprise and to a concentration of the bulk of industrial output in the hands of a relatively small number of giant concerns. These concerns, controlling large (and growing[7]) shares of their industries' output, are, as regards the purpose of capitalist enterprise (i.e., returns on invested capital) in a position that is much more powerful than that of either their small competitive ancestors or their small competitive contemporaries. Able to gauge the impact of their own business policies on the prices prevailing in their markets, they need not be content with the rates of profit that used to be earned in the competitive markets of old and that are still being earned in the competitive sectors of the present capitalist system. Far from being less single-minded in their pursuit of profits

---

[7] The advance of concentration between 1909 and 1947 is shown in Paolo Sylos Labini, *Oligopolio e Progresso Tecnico* (Milano, 1957), Appendix to Chapter I; on the development during the postwar decade information is provided in the following table:

SHARE OF TOTAL VALUE ADDED BY MANUFACTURE ACCOUNTED FOR BY
LARGEST COMPANIES IN 1954 COMPARED WITH 1947

	Per Cent of Value Added in 1954	Per Cent of Value Added in 1947
Largest 50 companies	23	17
Largest 100 companies	30	23
Largest 150 companies	34	27
Largest 200 companies	37	30

Source: 85th Congress, 1st Session, *Concentration in American Industry*, Report of the Subcommittee on Antitrust and Monopoly to the Committee on the Judiciary, U.S. Senate (Washington, D.C., 1957), p. 11.

than capitalists used to be in the past—all assertions to the contrary on the part of the now so fashionable apologists of Big Business notwithstanding—the modern monopolistic and oligopolistic corporations find themselves in objective circumstances most favorable to highest returns, and, in exploiting these circumstances to the hilt, have developed what used to be the art of making a lot of money into what is rapidly becoming a science of profit maximization in the long run [cf. 10)].

Thus the increase of the productivity of labor (and the mechanism by which it is attained), combined with the mode of apportionment of its fruits as between wages of production workers and profits of capitalists, which is an inherent characteristic of the capitalist system,[8] has a double-pronged effect; the economic surplus generated by the economy *tends* to become an ever-increasing proportion of aggregate output, and this economic surplus *tends* to be continually redistributed in favor of a steadily decreasing number of giant capitalist enterprises.[9]

If these were the only tendencies operating in the capitalist system, there would be no need to argue the theoretic relevance of the underconsumption concept as previously formulated. The capitalist system would be choking in a flood of economic surplus, for neither capitalists' consumption nor investment in capitalist enterprise would be able singly or jointly to absorb the rising tide. The former is not only physically limited—particularly since the bulk of the surplus accrues to a small number of giant corporations and wealthy stockholders—but also runs counter to the capitalists' basic urge to accumulate. The latter is circumscribed by the profit maximization requirements of monopolistic and oligopolistic business and tends under normal conditions to fall considerably short of the volume of the desired capital accumulation.[10] Under such circumstances, chronic depression would be capitalism's permanent condition, and increasing unemployment its permanent accompaniment.

III

Yet, as most diseases of organic entities call forth some remedial forces, so economic tendencies are usually counteracted—at least to some extent—by opposing developments. Both the plethora of surplus and the ascent of monopolistic and oligopolistic enterprise have drastically changed the nature and strategy of modern business. Price-cutting, which during the earlier, competitive phase of capitalism was the principal method by which individual firms sought to maintain and to expand their sales, now ranks

[8] It has been well observed by Levinson (11) that "The potentialities of redistribution out of profits are very slight as long as producers remain free to adjust their prices, techniques and employment so as to protect their profit position."

[9] Some statistics illustrating this process of profit redistribution are presented in Baran (12), p. 59.

[10] This is more fully explained in Baran (12), Chap. III.

very low among the strategies of the competitive struggle.[11] Its place has been taken over by tremendously expanded (and expensive) sales organizations, advertising campaigns, public relations programs, lobbying schemes, and by a continuous, relentless effort at product differentiation, model variation, and the invention and promotion of fancier, more elaborate, more sumptuous, and more expensive consumer goods. In the euphemistic words of Professor Arthur F. Burns: "The rivalries of the business world are nowadays as keen or keener than ever. Competition with respect to the quality of products and the services associated with them has increased. However, less stress is being placed by many of our larger businesses on price competition" [(13), p. 83].

The results of this development are a rampant growth of the system's unproductive sector and a striking multiplication of waste. The proportion of nonproduction workers in the labor force of manufacturing industries has increased from 19.4 per cent in 1919 to 23.1 per cent in 1957.[12] To be sure, a part of this increase is attributable to the expansion of research activities on the part of industrial concerns. It should be clear, however, that in areas other than those related to the production of armaments much of what goes under the name of research is merely a glorified form of merchandising [cf. (15)]. At the same time these statistics fail to reflect the full extent of the increase of the unproductive component in manufacturing. For, as pointed out earlier, the definitions of the Bureau of Labor Statistics referred to above classify as production workers those whose assignment is actually undistinguishable from that of salesmen, advertising men, and the like. This category of labor affixing chrome and fins on automobiles, producing different wrappings for identical products, turning and twisting perfectly functional articles in order to create artificial obsolescence of earlier models, all merely with the view to sales promotion, belongs undoubtedly to the unproductive segment of the labor force. Not that the boundaries of this group are readily drawn or that its size is easily measured. Yet the difficulties of definition and measurement should not be allowed to obscure the existence of a phenomenon or to serve as an excuse for the refusal to exercise rational judgment in its analysis. While taking this into account may well bring up the estimate of the unproductive part of the manufacturing labor force to as much as one-third of the total, this is by no means the end of the story. A not insignificant part of the construction industry engaged in the erection of luxurious office buildings—the castles of the feudal barons of today—and of even more sumptuous hotels and golf clubs supported by the expense accounts of corporate

---

[11] *Business Week* (June 15, 1957) characterized this change succinctly by referring to the existing price system as to one "that works only one way—up."

[12] See (7), p. 436, and (14), p. 215. It is most important to realize that this ratio had declined in 1942–44 to around 14 per cent when wartime exigencies reduced the need for sales promotion and enforced a measure of rationalization in the conduct of capitalist enterprise.

executives, much of the catering trade owing its existence to the same source, and many other similar activities, all represent an important drain of the overflowing economic surplus.

But as the economic surplus grows and the process of its unproductive absorption assumes an increasing importance, activities providing for such relief tend to separate themselves from production proper and to become organized in establishments of their own. The pride of place in this group—which includes among others legal practice, finance, real estate, and insurance—belongs indisputably to monopoly capitalism's very own creation: the sprawling and still briskly expanding advertising industry. The economic importance of advertising is not even approximately measured by the volume of resources which it directly absorbs, although this is by no means negligible.[13] Its significance stems from its promoting a continual enlargement of the economy's unproductive sector, from its constituting one of the most powerful devices for the propagation of artificial obsolescence and irrational differentiation of consumer goods, from its representing an indispensable mechanism for the systematic molding of consumers' wants to suit the requirements of monopolistic and oligopolistic business.

Still the growth of the economic surplus tends to surpass the possibilities of its utilization, for a large part of the expenses of selling, advertising, model-changing, etc., etc., become necessary costs of doing business under monopoly capitalism and are shifted on to the consumer, thus replenishing the economic surplus. At the same time a large share of the sizable income accruing to corporate executives, salesmen, admen, public relations experts, market researchers, and fashion designers is *saved* rather than spent by their recipients and gives rise to what might be called "secondary accumulation of capital"—another category in which the economic surplus makes its statistical appearance.[14]

Nor are other more or less automatically functioning mechanisms of

[13] By 1880 advertising had increased threefold since the Civil War period. By 1900 it stood at 95 million dollars a year which marked a tenfold increase over the amount in 1865. By 1919 it exceeded half a billion dollars, by 1929 it reached 1.12 billion, and in 1957 it is estimated to have climbed to no less than 10.5 billion dollars. It rose from .59 per cent of National Income in 1890 to 1.27 per cent in 1929 and to 3.14 per cent in 1957. Cf. Borden (16), Potter (17), and the 1957 estimate presented in *Printer's Ink*, (February 8, 1957). If activities kindred to advertising are taken into account—public relations and market research—the size of the aggregate "influence" business would be in the neighborhood of 15 billion dollars or over 4 per cent of National Income.

[14] One of the foremost functions of advertising is to "fight" this "secondary accumulation of capital" by shaping the wants of the upper- and middle-income groups and thus raising their propensity to consume. This is illustrated by a recently undertaken survey of the market for new automobiles: "Nearly two thirds of the new-car buyers hold executive, professional or semi-professional positions. Much less than a third of the purchases are made by people in non-supervisory jobs. And probably only a fraction of these are in factory work" (18).

surplus absorption—capital exports, corporate outlays on research and development, and the like—powerful enough to solve the problem. A conscious effort at utilization of the economic surplus is indispensable if its congesting effects are to be kept within tolerable limits, if depression and unemployment are not to be allowed to assume major proportions and thus to endanger the stability of the economic and social order. Such a conscious effort can be undertaken only by the government. The government in capitalist society, however, is not constituted in a way to promote the purposeful and sustained employment of the economic surplus for the advancement of human welfare.[15] The powerful capitalist interests by which it is controlled, as well as its social and ideological make-up, render such a policy most difficult if not entirely impossible. It is unable to control the practices of Big Business, let alone invest directly in productive enterprise, since this would be manifestly in conflict with the dominant interests of monopolistic and oligopolistic corporations.[16] It is barred by the values and mores of a capitalist society from large-scale spending on welfare objectives (at home and abroad). Thus even a liberal, progressive administration tends to seek salvation in military spending, adding in this way deliberately organized waste in the government sector to automatically expanding waste in the business sector.

Waste, however, cannot expand smoothly and rapidly. For, although the very survival of monopoly capitalism becomes increasingly dependent on squandering of resources, *to the individual capitalist enterprise* waste represents a deplorable deduction from surplus, to be resisted as strongly as possible. Thus, no one firm, not even the largest, can squander more resources than is necessitated by prevailing business practices, so that increases in waste can only develop slowly and gradually, only as all the important firms enlarge their unproductive expenditures and thereby set new standards for the economy as a whole. Similarly, the snowballing of governmentally organized waste and skyrocketing military budgets, indispensable as they are to monopoly capitalism, spell to individual Congress-

[15] Hence the striking inadequancy of public services in the wealthiest country in the world deplored but not explained by J. K. Galbraith (2).

[16] "It [the public utility concept] originated as a system of public restraint designed primarily, or at least ostensibly, to protect consumers from the aggressions of monopolists, it has ended as a device to protect the property, *i.e.*, the capitalized expectancy, of these monopolists from the just demands of society, and to obstruct the development of socially superior institutions. This perversion of the public utility concept from its original purpose was perhaps inevitable under capitalism. Here, as in other areas of our economic and social life, the compelling sanctions of private property and private profit, working within a framework of special privilege, determined the direction and outlook of public policy. Just as in the days of the Empire all roads led to Rome so in a capitalistic society all forms of social control lead ultimately to state protection of the dominant interests, *i.e.*, property. The public utility concept has thus merely gone the way of all flesh" (19).

men and Senators (and to the majority of their constituents) nothing but higher taxes or a heavier national debt burden, and are permitted only reluctantly and only in an atmosphere of external danger (real or contrived).

Except during wars and their aftermaths, the interaction of all these forces creates a vast potential excess of economic surplus, which means underproduction, underconsumption, and underinvestment, or—what is the same—underemployment of men, underutilization of productive capacity, and depression.[17] The only remedy for this persistent malaise that is available to the capitalist system is further multiplication of waste both in the private and the public sectors of the economy.

IV

The process thus briefly sketched cannot be comprehended by even the most painstaking observation or statistical measurement of the economic and social surface, for that surface itself is not an elemental datum but is at any particular time the *outcome* of the interacting and interlocking tendencies which in their dynamic totality constitute historical development. This can be seen clearly in the case of the two categories that matter most in the present context. The magnitude of profits in any given year as reported by statistical agencies reflects only partly and tenuously the size of the economic surplus generated by the system during that period. Leaving aside taxation, there is an entire group of important factors accounting for the gap between the volume of reported profits and the amount of the economic surplus. The components of that gap can be readily identified, impossible as it may be to measure them even approximately with the help of the available statistical information. It includes land rent and interest and a large part of executive salaries and expense accounts. It comprises a considerable share of depreciation and depletion allowances and of the firms' nonproduction expenditures: on advertising, public relations, lobbying, legal departments, market studies, model changes, and the like. Thus the magnitude of profits that actually rises to the statistical surface is determined not only by the size of the economic surplus but also by the mode of its utilization, both of which depend in turn on the character of industrial organization, on the prevailing degree of monopoly, on the extent to which taxes, selling costs, etc., are shifted to the consumer, and so forth.

It could be objected that all of this is unimportant and that what is relevant is exclusively the *actual* share of statistically reported profits in national income, or even merely the relation of the proportion of the profits share which the profit recipients desire to accumulate to the volume of

[17] As Professor Arthur F. Burns remarks, "every sustained spending wave that occurred between 1939 and 1954 was heavily influenced, if not dominated, by war finance or its sequelae" (13), p. 12. This applies, however, not merely to the Second World War and the subsequent 12 years, but to nearly the entire life-span of monopoly capitalism.

aggregate intended investment. From the viewpoint of shortrun business analysis and forecasting this objection is undoubtedly justified, but if the problem be considered in terms of economic and social development in the longer run, or in terms of human welfare even in the short run, this objection falls to the ground. For surely both the present condition of society and its prospects in the future are greatly influenced by the mode of utilization not only of the statistically recorded part of the economic surplus (profits and individual saving) but also of its probably larger unrecorded part. It is surely not a negligible question how large that unrecorded part is, whether it finds its way into education, urban renewal, or aid to poverty-stricken peoples, or whether it is absorbed by advertising, merchandizing, or the military establishment. In other words, even if Mr. Kaldor's earlier referred to contention 'were true that the share of profits does *not* "go on rising beyond the point where it covers investment needs and the consumption of capitalists," (4) it would still remain decisively important, whether the absence of that rise had been caused by the constancy or decline of the share of economic surplus in aggregate output, or whether that rise has been merely hidden by the procedures of statistical reporting or the intricacies of tax regulations, or, finally, whether that rise has been prevented by the diversion of an increasing proportion of the economic surplus to some governmentally determined purposes. In the latter case, clearly, the nature of those purposes is of the utmost relevance.

Looking at the matter from the other side: what applies to profits also applies, *mutatis mutandis*, but with no less force, to consumption. The statistically recorded consumers' expenditure obviously covers *all* consumption, regardless of whether it is consumption of productive workers or of nonproductive workers, whether it is consumption of teachers or consumption of soldiers. It includes, in other words, not merely useful consumption but also consumption which merely wastes part of the economic surplus. Again, these distinctions may not matter much for the determination of the immediate business outlook, but they matter a great deal if what is at issue is the welfare of society, its economic, moral, and cultural condition. To the present and future of the American people (and of the world as a whole) it matters a great deal that (in 1956) $42 billion were spent on military purposes while $1.5 billion were found for economic aid to underdeveloped countries; that automobile transportation absorbed $27 billion, while education (private and public) commanded $15 billion; that $3 billion worth of resources were used for recreation goods of all kinds, while $.6 billion were devoted to books; that basic research was assigned $.5 billion, while the services of stockbrokers and investment counselors were valued at $.9 billion.

Once more, even if it were true (which it is not) that there has been no actual decline of consumption as a share of aggregate output, it would remain a problem of overriding importance what economic and social forces are keeping consumption on whatever level it happens to maintain, what are its composition and its distribution. Just as in the earlier-mentioned case of the balance of international payments, so also in regard to consumption what is decisive is the nature of the *balancing factor*, the morphology of the difference between what consumption would be in a rational social order and what it is under the impact of Madison Avenue, of the values and mores of monopoly capitalism. Without an analysis of that morphology there can be neither an understanding of the present nor a meaningful assessment of the developmental probabilities in the future.

As Marx remarked, "all science would be superfluous if the appearance of things coincided directly with their essence" (20). Ignoring this basic principle results inevitably in the descent of economics into shallow empiricism and in the abandonment of the great tradition of social thought in favor of what goes nowadays under the name of "behavioral sciences."

References

1. Committee for Economic Development, Problems of United States Economic Development. New York, 1958, Vol. I.
2. J. K. Galbraith, The Affluent Society. Houghton Mifflin, Boston, 1958.
3. Gottfried Haberler, Prosperity and Depression. Geneva, 1939, p. 119.
4. Nicholas Kaldor, "A Model of Economic Growth," *Economic Journal*, December 1957, p. 621.
5. Harold Barger, Distribution's Place in the American Economy since 1869. Princeton University Press, Princeton, 1955.
6. Committee for Economic Development, Economic Growth in the United States, Its Past and Future. New York, 1958.
7. "Nonproduction Workers in Factories, 1919–56," *Monthly Labor Review*, April 1957, pp. 435 ff.
8. Productivity, Prices and Incomes. Materials Prepared for the Joint Economic Committee by the Committee Staff, 85th Congress, 1st Session. Washington, D.C., 1957.
9. Simon S. Kuznets, "Long-Term Changes in the National Income of the United States of America Since 1870," in Simon S. Kuznets (ed.), Income and Wealth in the United States, Trends and Structure. Income and Wealth Series II. Bowes & Bowes, Cambridge, 1952, p. 78.
10. James S. Earley, "Marginal Policies of 'Excellently Managed' Companies," *American Economic Review*, March 1956.
11. Harold M. Levinson, "Collective Bargaining and Income Distribution," *American Economic Review*, May 1954, p. 316.
12. Paul A. Baran, The Political Economy of Growth. Monthly Review Press, New York, 1957.
13. Arthur F. Burns, Prosperity Without Inflation. Fordham University Press, New York, 1957.
14. *Fortune*, April 1958.
15. Eric Hodgins, "The Strange State of American Research," *Fortune*, April 1955.
16. Neil H. Borden, The Economic Effects of Advertising. Irwin, Chicago, 1942, p. 48.

17. David M. Potter, People of Plenty. University of Chicago Press, Chicago, 1954, p. 169.

18. "New Cars: Who Buys Them; How They're Paid For," *U.S. News and World Report*, March 14, 1958.

19. Horace M. Gray, "The Passing of the Public Utility Concept," *Journal of Land and Public Utility Economics*, February 1940. Reprinted in E. M. Hoover, Jr., and Joel Dean (eds.), Readings in the Social Control of Industry. Blakiston, Philadelphia, 1942, p. 294.

20. Karl Marx, Das Kapital, 6th ed. Hamburg, 1922. Cited and translated by Paul A. Baran. Vol. III, Part 2, p. 352.

Unemployment Compensation and the Allocation of Resources[1]

PHILIP W. CARTWRIGHT

In a private enterprise economy the price system allocates the available resources to alternative uses and determines the distribution of the total product among the members of society. The establishment of systems of unemployment compensation by governmental units, financed by payroll taxes and specifying certain distributions of benefits, superimposes on the price system an alternative mechanism for allocating resources and distributing product. The institution of unemployment compensation is likely, therefore, to interfere with the operation of a free price system. The question we wish to examine is whether the institution of unemployment compensation results in a more or less "efficient" allocation of resources.

We define an "efficient" allocation of resources, following Professor Scitovsky (1) and others in the field of welfare economics, as one which conforms to the community's preferences. These preferences are expressed on the one hand by consumers' marginal valuations of each product as compared with every other product, and on the other hand by workers' marginal valuation of leisure as against income. An efficient organization of economic activity from society's point of view "should be such as to balance correctly the satisfaction derived from its output and the burden of effort needed to produce this output" [p. 165 in (1)].

It is a well-known proposition in welfare economics that if pure competition exists among all buyers and sellers of both products and factors of production then the organization of economic activity will be "efficient", for then the marginal rate of substitution for all individuals between any two products (including leisure and income) will be equated to the ratio of their prices, which in turn will be equated to the marginal rate of transformation within and between all firms engaged in producing these prod-

[1] I am indebted to my colleagues, Professors Donald F. Gordon and Arnold Zellner, for helpful comments and criticisms of this paper and to Miss Freda Messerschmidt and Mr. Tomoji Kaya for the statistical computations.

ucts. Thus, the model of pure competition balances the marginal preference of workers for income against leisure in every alternative occupation with the consumers' preferences, at the margin for the use of workers in each alternative occupation, and may be said to be an "efficient organization of economic activity."

An assumption of the pure competition model as generally used in welfare economics is that there is always full employment of labor. We wish to relax this assumption in our model and assume, rather, that the total level of expenditures of consumers, investors, and government fluctuates over time. It has been demonstrated by Professor Reder (2) that, under certain assumptions, when there is unemployment of labor any employment to which this labor can be put (providing it is not a nuisance to society) will increase the welfare of society.[2] Under slightly altered assumptions, Professor Reder points out that a public policy to increase employment may result in inflation, which would redistribute income and (if compensations were not made) might reduce welfare. The proposition that welfare *might* be reduced is true, but it involves interpersonal comparisons of utility which cannot be made. However, we can argue, using Scitovsky's concepts, that on "equity" rather than "efficiency" criteria the government does not choose to maintain full employment constantly for fear of inflation.

It makes no difference for our purposes why full employment is not maintained; all we assume is that the total level of expenditures is variable through time, nor are we particularly concerned with whether the variation in total expenditures is caused by variation in government expenditure, investment spending, or a change in the preferences of consumers for consumption vis-à-vis saving. If the total level of expenditures is variable through time, the level of demand for the various products of society will be variable; but there is no reason to expect the rate of variation over time of expenditure for individual products to correspond to the rate of variation over time for all expenditures. On the contrary, we wish to assume (more realistically) that the time rate of variations is different for different products. This simply means that, given a decrease in total expenditures, unemployment will be greater in the production of some products than in others. We know from empirical observation, for example, that employment in automobiles is more variable than employment in paper products.

With this modification in the assumption of full employment in the pure competition model, we need to re-examine the notion of consumer preferences for income as against leisure, for if unemployment is more severe over time in some occupations than in others, this fact will affect the prefer-

[2] This must be qualified by the proposition that the real incomes of none of those laborers already employed are reduced by the employment of the unemployed. This is tantamount to saying that a policy which results in an increment to real output and does not redistribute the existing output will increase welfare.

ences of the worker in choosing alternative jobs. If other aspects of the job are equal, the worker must still consider the income/leisure relationship of an occupation in which leisure may be forced by unemployment. For simplicity's sake we will assume that the worker will have no alternative employment opportunity available while he is unemployed. The comparison of the desirability of alternative jobs now requires a specific time period long enough to include a complete cycle for each alternative employment which shows cyclical variation in employment. The same sort of comparison and choice must be made with respect to seasonality of employment. A time period long enough to include a cycle for an industry will be longer than a year and will include the seasonal instability.

A worker, in comparing two alternative employments, who is indifferent with respect to other dimensions of the job (i.e., length of work week, training and skill required, working conditions, general desirability of the type of work, etc.) will ordinarily favor that job which pays the higher income over the whole cycle.[3] This cyclical income will depend on the wage rate per hour, including overtime rates and fringes, and the continuity of employment. Consequently, if there is pure competition among workers for alternative jobs (which implies free entry into any occupation) the marginal valuation of each alternative employment, for the marginal worker, will be equal to the cyclical income (income over the whole cycle) for that employment. The cyclical income will be equal to or greater than the transfer price for each worker, and, at the margin, the marginal valuations of the different employments will be in proportion to the cyclical incomes for those employments.

The marginal valuation of an employment opportunity may be effected by the forced leisure created by unemployment, since leisure is not necessarily an inferior good. In other words, between two alternative employment opportunities which are equal in other respects and pay the same cyclical income, most workers would prefer the opportunity which provided more leisure, even though the leisure consisted of long periods of continuous layoff.[4] The marginal value of such leisure, however, is probably very low and in some cases even negative, since long periods of idleness are injurious to the worker's skill and morale.

The equality of the marginal valuation of work and cyclical incomes means, of course, that for two alternative employment opportunities which are equal in other respects but unequal with respect to stability of employ-

[3] An exception would exist for those who seek temporary employment and for whom the forced leisure of unemployment represents no loss of satisfaction. Since these individuals are exceptions and constitute a small part of the labor force, we will ignore them.

[4] This problem is analogous to the problem of how high a level of benefit can be made under unemployment compensation before the unemployed worker prefers the leisure of unemployment to working.

ment the wage rate must be higher in the relatively unstable employment opportunity. If the marginal valuation of forced leisure is zero, then the wage rate must be sufficiently greater in the unstable opportunity to yield the same cyclical income as in the more stable opportunity. Insofar as the forced leisure has a positive value, the cyclical income may be less, requiring less differential in the wage rate to leave marginal workers indifferent.

An arithmetic illustration may be of assistance in making this proposition clear. Suppose we have two alternative industries between which a new labor force entrant is choosing. Assume that in one industry 2000 persons are employed full time (2080 hours per year) for a five-year period. In the other industry employment is 2000 at full time the first year, 1000 at full time the second year, 2000 the third year, 1000 the fourth year, and 2000 the fifth year. The question is how much higher will the wage rate have to be in the unstable industry to leave the new entrant indifferent, if all other aspects of the employment are comparable. If the value of the additional leisure in the unstable industry is zero, and if the workers are homogeneous so that the likelihood of layoff in the unstable industry for one employee is no greater than for any other, the wage rate in the unstable industry must be in the same ratio to the wage rate in the stable industry as total (or average) employment for the five years in the stable industry is in ratio to total (or average) employment in the unstable industry. In our example, the wage rate for the unstable industry must be 1.25 times the wage for the stable industry. Such a wage differential would provide the same cyclical income (5 year) for the prospective entrant in either employment opportunity.[5]

If the value of leisure is greater than zero, the wage differential which would equalize the opportunities would be reduced. For example, if the value of the additional leisure is worth $1000 and the five-year income in the stable industry is $10,000 per worker, then a wage differential of 1.111 would equalize the opportunities. If the value of the leisure is negative, a differential greater than 1.25 would be required. If the worker, when he is unemployed, can produce income (goods) for his own use, the value of these goods would similarly reduce the required wage rate differential.

If there is a positive rate of interest in the economy, some adjustment should be made in our example of required wage rate differentials since the income flows over time are different. What we are really balancing is the present value of two streams of income, and the difference in the pattern of flow may affect this. In our example, this factor would have no effect, but had we assumed a pattern of employment in the unstable industry which

---

[5] We are, of course, concerned with income after taxes since a progressive income tax structure would alter the preference of the worker, since, although the five-year income is the same, the flow of income over the five years is not, with the result that the worker with the unstable flow of income would pay higher taxes.

was not symmetrical over the five years the interest factor would have changed the required wage rate differential.[6]

In our arithmetical example we assumed that workers were homogeneous with respect to layoff, which is consistent with our model of pure competition. If this assumption is relaxed, for the moment, to recognize the existence of seniority rules and other imperfections which reduce the uncertainty concerning the identity of the individuals who would be unemployed, then the required wage rate differential between stable and unstable opportunities becomes different, for we are concerned with equality at the margin. If a prospective entrant to an industry is certain that he will be laid off when employment declines, he will be interested not in a wage rate which equalizes the average income per worker in the two alternatives, but rather in a wage rate which equalizes his income. In our example this would require a wage rate differential of 1.67 rather than 1.25. This required differential would be modified by factors reducing the certainty of layoff.

In summary, we have said that under conditions of pure competition, but with variable levels of total employment and differential rates of unemployment among industries, workers will equate the marginal valuations of alternative employment to the income over time rather than the wage rate. Competition among workers as well as among employers will result in equality at the margin of the ratios of the marginal valuation of individual sellers of their productive effort to the cyclical income for each employment opportunity. Competition on both sides of product markets as well will result in an allocation of labor resources which will balance consumer (worker) preferences for cyclical income against leisure in every alternative employment with consumer preferences for the use of that labor in each alternative employment. In other words, if the allocation of labor resources is to be "efficient", it is cyclical income with which we are concerned, and not hourly or weekly rates or earnings.

With our assumption of variable employment through time, if labor resources are so allocated as to equate weekly or hourly wage rates as between industries that offer different degrees of employment stability, the allocation will be "inefficient". There will be too much labor devoted to producing products for which the demand is unstable, and too little devoted to producing products for which the demand is stable. With pure competition in the product markets, the ratios of product prices will be equal to the ratios of marginal costs of the products, but these costs will represent the current costs of production and not the "real burden effort," which

[6] It is interesting to note, however, that individuals are not always rational about these problems, even with a positive rate of interest. For example, there is a surprising number of faculty members who would prefer their nine-months' salaries to be paid in twelve installments starting at the beginning of the academic year. Their preference is to forego the interest in order to avoid the self-discipline required in saving—nor is this peculiar only to academicians.

must include the costs of providing income to the workers when they are unemployed. Given this sort of "inefficient" allocation, a shift in resources from unstable to stable industries will increase "efficiency". This would involve a re-ordering of preferences at the product level, with the marginal costs in the unstable industries rising and the marginal costs in the stable industries falling, and, in equilibrium, with the marginal rate of substitution between products for consumers being equal to the new ratios of marginal costs.

We are not arguing that such a re-allocation would increase the sum total of all consumer satisfactions. Since some product costs and prices would rise and others would fall, we believe it is impossible to say whether or not the sum of all satisfactions is increased. This would involve interpersonal comparisons which cannot be made. We are also aware of the difficulties pointed out by Professor Arrow (3) in constructing a social preference function at all. We can simply say that an allocation of resources which recognizes the relative instability of employment will balance consumer preferences with worker preferences at the margin, while any other allocation will not. To say that this is more desirable may involve making a dictatorial value judgment for society; but it is a judgment which is frequently made by economists in this field of inquiry.

Within the framework of our basic model we now wish to examine the effect of the imposition of an unemployment compensation system on the allocation of labor resources. Unemployment compensation is a procedure by which transfers of income are effected according to prescribed rules. There are basically two types of transfers which result from unemployment compensation: (1) a transfer of income through time, and (2) interpersonal transfers between workers, between stockholders or other factors and workers, or between certain consumers and workers.[7]

The basic features of these systems are, first, that a tax is levied on the individual firm, the base of the tax being the payroll of the firm. The tax rate varies from firm to firm in different state systems according to different sets of rules prescribed by the respective state systems under so-called experience-rating provisions. We shall return subsequently to a discussion of the rationality of the variability of the rates among various industries and firms. The second basic feature is that each employee acquires credits against a pool of funds during his period of employment. The credits enable the employee to draw funds from the pool during a period of unemployment, the amount and duration depending on the amount of credits accumulated and the rules prescribed by the system.

As long as some tax is levied on the firm, the cost of production of the firm's output will reflect this tax, since the tax is levied against the payroll and thus is variable with respect to output. We are not concerned with the

[7] For a discussion of transfers of this sort, see Cartwright (4).

incidence of such a tax, as this will be determined by our model of pure competition in all markets. The important feature is that the cost of production of the firm reflects a payment which eventually becomes income to the unemployed worker.

We have argued that workers' preferences for alternative employments *under pure competition* will reflect the instability of employment of the various alternatives, since this instability would represent different amounts and patterns of income flow to the workers over time. If we now impose a system of unemployment compensation on our model, we will alter this amount and pattern of income flow over time. For example, if a worker considering two alternative employment opportunities knew that because of the existence of an unemployment compensation system that he would receive an equivalent income in either occupation regardless of the instability of employment, he would be indifferent, with respect to the criterion of instability, to the alternatives. An equivalent income would not be an equal income, since the increased leisure of the unstable employment opportunity would have to be considered, as indicated earlier.

If workers receive unemployment compensation in an amount sufficient to compensate them for the loss in wages due to unemployment, and if they receive this for the total time period of seasonally or cyclically induced layoff, their marginal valuations of alternative employment opportunities will be equated at the margin to the wage rates, without regard to the instability of employment. The question now is whether this will alter the allocation of labor resources from that which resulted from pure competition without unemployment compensation.

The answer to this question depends upon how the costs of the unemployment compensation benefit payments are assigned to various firms and products. If the payroll taxes are levied in such a way that each firm pays (incurs costs) for the unemployment which results from its own instability, then the relative marginal costs of each product would be the same as if there were no unemployment compensation system and the wage rates reflected the relative instability between firms. If there is no reason to assume a different ordering of consumer preferences as between products,[8] the action of consumers equating their marginal rates of substitution between products to relative prices and marginal costs will result in the same "efficient" allocation of labor resources.[9]

[8] Interpersonal transfers of income between the workers of a given plant might occur, however, and this might alter consumer preferences in general since persons' tastes are different. This is primarily an "equity" rather than an "efficiency" problem, however.

[9] We ignore here the interest effect, mentioned earlier, that the pattern of income flow resulting from a lower wage rate plus unemployment benefits might be different from that of a higher wage rate without benefits. In the latter situation, a worker with a higher wage rate could achieve the same time pattern of income

If, on the other hand, the payroll taxes are levied in such a way that the costs of unemployment are not charged to each firm according to its instability, the marginal costs of alternative products will not reflect the real costs of the output in terms of worker preferences. The relative prices will in turn not reflect these preferences, and, although competition will insure that consumers' marginal rates of substitution will be equal to the ratio of prices, they will no longer balance the relative burden of effort or real cost of alternative products. The allocation of resources will be different from that obtained by pure competition and will be "inefficient" to the extent that the relative tax rates on different firms will impose arbitrary costs which do not reflect the income (benefit) payments to the firm's labor force.

If competition were pure in all markets and, implicitly, if workers had knowledge, not only of alternative wage rates but also of alternative employment patterns through time, there would be no need for unemployment compensation systems from the standpoint of "efficiency." A properly designed unemployment compensation system would not disturb this "efficiency," but it would not improve it. An improperly designed system (which, incidentally, all are) would only worsen the "efficiency" of allocation of resources. There may be a need for such systems, however, on "equity" grounds, since even with pure competition the incidence of unemployment and, hence, income is different among different workers. Even if workers were homogeneous with respect to layoff, some must bear the brunt of layoff without income. An unemployment compensation system transfers income from workers who are unemployed less to those who are unemployed more, thus reducing the risk attached to instability of employment. Like other programs of reduced hours, or work-sharing, such programs are redistributive and involve "equity" rather than "efficiency" considerations.

Up to now, the only qualification we have made to the model of "pure competition" as applied in welfare economics is that of variable unemployment through time. Let us now assume that workers have no knowledge of the relative degrees of instability of employment of alternative employment opportunities. They are aware of current rates of wages in different jobs but can only assume continuity of employment in the future. Under this assumption the allocation of resources would not be "efficient" (unless there were full employment continuously) since it would depend on balancing consumer- and worker-preferences on the basis of wage rates rather than of income. Let us now examine the effect of the imposition of an unemployment compensation system in this context.

---

as the worker with the lower rate plus unemployment benefits. But the reverse is not true. However, this consideration would appear to have negligible effects on the allocation of resources.

In this situation, the existence of the unemployment compensation system substitutes for knowledge on the part of the workers. In making a choice between two alternative employment opportunities, the worker need not be concerned about the instability of either if he knows that his income will continue at the same rate[10] even though he may be laid off. From the standpoint of the workers' preferences between income and leisure, the unemployment compensation system improves the ability of the workers to make a rational choice between the alternatives without the otherwise necessary knowledge. In order that this choice may result in an "efficient" allocation of labor, the cost of maintenance of income during the period of layoff must be charged to each firm in accordance with its relative instability, as in the earlier case.

If the stable firm is charged to pay the benefits to the unemployed of the unstable firm, the relative marginal costs of the firms will not reflect the worker preferences and will result in a mis-allocation of resources. The costs and prices of the output of stable firms will be too high, and, with free consumer choice, too little will be purchased with too few resources devoted to their production. The costs of the unstable firms would be too low and the output and allocation of resources too high. The argument usually made that the instability of production is due to the market and not the firm and that therefore the firm shouldn't be penalized is irrelevant. If the market creates differing degrees of instability, the market is responsible. If this instability is not reflected in costs, it means that consumers of stable firms are subsidizing consumers of unstable firms, with a resulting "inefficient" allocation of resources.

Thus, if workers are ignorant of the relative instability of different industries, and to the extent that unemployment compensation systems maintain workers' incomes during periods of layoff, these systems will result in a more "efficient" allocation of resources. This increase in "efficiency" depends on the results not being vitiated by an arbitrary and improper assignment of the costs of the program to the wrong firms.

Devising a program which will assign the costs of unemployment compensation in a manner which will maximize efficiency is not a simple task. Different states have tried different systems of "experience-rating,"[11] partly as an inducement to industries to stabilize and partly as a device to lower payroll taxes below the 3 per cent required under Federal law. Most writers in the field of social security would argue that the states have failed on the first objective of inducing stability, but that is obviously because either the market demand is unstable or the flow of other resources (including natural resources) is unstable. The costs (loss of profits) of stabilizing employ-

[10] Adjusted for the value of leisure.

[11] For an excellent discussion of the types of experience rating systems and their difficulties, see Burns (5, 6).

ment of labor are, in the face of instability of the demand or supply of other resources, too great to induce such action. The penalty of providing the necessary pool of funds to provide for unemployment compensation at the present benefit and duration rate is a smaller cost and hence more profitable.

The fact that they have failed in this first objective does not deter us from recommending some sort of experience-rating, for *our objective* accepts the instability of the market and the wish to allocate resources in accordance with it. The fact that states may have used experience rating to reduce taxes and, concurrent therewith, benefit payments, duration, or eligibility, is to be deplored. Insofar as our assumption is valid that workers are ignorant of the degree of stability of different employment opportunities, any tendency to reduce unemployment compensation benefits below the level necessary to equalize the opportunities (other aspects of the employment being equal) will result in a less "efficient" allocation of resources.

It is impossible to say how much knowledge workers have in our economy concerning alternative remunerations, stability of employment, and other perquisites of different employment opportunities. It seems safe to say, however, that knowledge of stability is likely to be very slight. Knowledge concerning seasonal instability is, of course, greater than that concerning cyclical instability, as the former is far more predictable. The economist can tell you that employment in durable goods is likely to be more unstable than in nondurable goods, but that is so general a classification as to be practically useless for our purposes. It is possible to find firms and even industries producing durables whose employment is more stable in a particular cycle than is the employment of other firms or industries producing nondurables. One of the major obstacles to knowing about the stability of employment opportunities is that different industries have different degrees of stability in different cyclical periods. These differences are even more pronounced for individual firms.

Although we cannot easily tell how much workers know about these things, we may be able to infer something about their knowledge from the behavior of wage rates and employment stability. If an examination of wage rates (earnings) in different industries reflected the degree of instability and showed them to be the higher, the more unstable the employment, we might infer that workers were able to make rational choices at the margin. If we could somehow determine that the wage rates entirely compensated for the instability of employment, we would then be able to say that unemployment compensation systems (properly financed) would neither increase nor decrease the "efficiency" of allocation of resources. The obvious difficulty in this problem lies in the fact that the wage rates must compensate for all other aspects of the employment opportunity as well as instability, and it is impossible to isolate the one factor. On the other hand, if we could determine that there was little or no relationship between wage rates and instability of employment, we could then argue that unemployment compensation systems (properly financed) would increase the "efficiency" of allocation of resources. Such a result would not be as handicapped by other aspects of the employment opportunity, since it seems unlikely that the wage rates would compensate for instability and yet show no relation to it. The following section of this paper will discuss an empirical attempt to determine whether wage rates compensate for instability.

In making our investigation of the relation between wage rates and instability, we have selected as our group of industries the three-digit classification of manufacturing industries of the Standard Industrial Classification (S.I.C.). The data consists of reports of the Bureau of Labor Statistics (B.L.S.) on monthly employment and average weekly earnings of production workers in manufacturing classified in accordance with the S.I.C. and revised in accordance with 1956 benchmarks. The period of time that was covered by these reports was from January 1948 to May 1957.

In order to determine whether wage rates for different industries reflect the degree of instability of these industries, it was necessary to construct an index of instability for each of the industries. This index was constructed as follows: The monthly series for each industry was examined and the peak level of employment for 1948 determined, as well as the peak employment for the year ending May 1957. A trend line connecting these two peaks was then established to determine what we shall refer to as the "full employment labor force" of the specific industry. The total employment (the sum of the monthly employment figures) subsumed by this trend line between the two peaks was calculated, this figure representing a hypothetical amount of employment which would have been offered by the industry if it had been perfectly stable at a full employment rate. The trend line enabled us to take account of the fact that some industries were growing and others declining over the approximately ten-year period.

The sum of the actual monthly employment figures was then calculated. This hypothetical full-employment total was then divided by the actual total to establish an index of instability. If the industry's employment did not deviate from its ten-year trend its index of instability was 1.00, while the greater the degree of deviation from the trend, the greater would be the index of instability.

The method is illustrated by Figure 1. Suppose that the figures for monthly employment of production workers for the period 1948–57 for Industry A were as described by the solid line in the diagram. The hypothetical trend line which represents the "full employment labor force" is thus given by the dotted line.

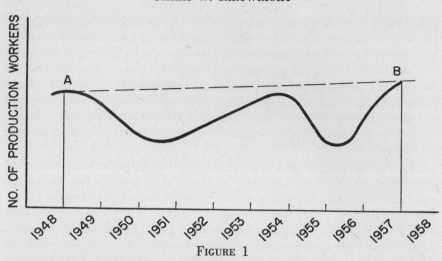

FIGURE 1

The index of instability is given by the ratio of the area subsumed under the dotted lines between the peaks A and B to the area subsumed under the solid line between the peaks A and B. If the industry were completely stable, the dotted and solid lines would coincide and the ratio would have been 1.

For most of the industries in the group studied, the period covered included two short cycles and hence three peaks as shown in the diagram. This was true also for the total of all employment in the United States. Of the total number of industries for which the B.L.S. reported employment of production workers in 1957, some had to be combined in order to obtain a comparable series over the whole ten-year period. In a few cases, industries were dropped from the group because of noncomparability of the data. The canning industry was omitted on the grounds that a very large percentage of its labor force consisted of temporary entrants to the labor force and that therefore it was not relevant to our problem. Three industries connected with military procurement were omitted because, over the time period covered, they had only one distinct peak, occurring during the Korean War, and a trend line could not be established. The cycle for these industries, if one exists, would be longer than the ten-year period covered by the study.

The remaining sample of industries consisted of 96 separate industrial classifications. In five of the 96 cases the peak employment in the 1953 period exceeded the peaks of both 1948 and 1956–57, so that a trend line connecting 1948 and 1956–57 would have given a lower index of instability than was warranted by the actual behavior of these industries. In each of these five industries, a separate index of instability was constructed for each of the two cycles covered by the period, and the mean of these two indexes was used as the index for the whole period of time.

The index for each industry represents a composite of seasonal and cyclical instability. Since we are concerned with the question of whether or not wage rates reflect instability of any sort, it is this composite index which is relevant. The number of months covered varies from one industry to another as the timing of the peaks varies, since we are concerned with the cyclical instability of each industry independently of the total level of activity. For the vast majority of the 96 industries this variation is limited to a few months at either end of the ten-year period.

The measure we used for wage rates was the average weekly earnings of production workers at the peak employment period in 1948 and 1956–57.

A number of different statistical tests was made to determine whether the earnings rate reflected the instability. Since, even in a competitive model, the earning rate would tend to reflect dimensions of the industrial occupation other than instability (such as skills required, capital-labor ratios, differential growth rates of industry demand, etc.), the first test made was that of rank correlation. The 96 industries were ranked according to the index of instability and according to the earnings rate, and a correlation computed for these rankings. If there were no other differences in the occupations and if the earnings rate reflected the instability, then the rank correlation should have been 1.00. Actually, the rank correlation between the 1948 earnings ratio and indexes of instability was .19772, which was not significant. The rank correlation between the 1957 earnings rates and the index of instability was .18759, which was similarly not significant.

The 96 industries were then divided into durable- and nondurable-goods classifications, using the S.I.C. definitions of these terms, and rank correlations were computed for the two groups separately. For the non-durable-goods classification (in which there were 48 industries) the rank correlations were .01289 using 1948 earnings and .01412 using 1957 earnings. In the durable-goods classification (in which there were also 48 industries) the rank correlations were .43618 using 1948 earnings and .35153 using 1957 earnings. Although these latter correlations did not appear to be very high in terms of our problem of whether the wage rates compensated for instability, they were statistically significant, indicating something more than a random relation between earnings and instability for the durable-goods industries.

It is an observation frequently made by economists, particularly those dealing with labor economics, that wage rates in durable-goods industries exceed those in nondurable-goods industries because of the instability of employment in the former as compared to the latter. If this causal relation were valid, one might have expected that the rank correlation for the 96 industries comprising both durables and nondurables would be higher than either of the rank correlations of the separate classifications. This was obviously not the case, which suggests that the differences between earnings in durables and nondurables is due to something other than stability.

A further test of this proposition consisted of an anlysis of variance of the 96 industries. The industries were segregated into three columns by the instability index and into two rows representing durables and non-durables. Analysis of the means of the earnings rate for each of the columns (the instability factor) showed no significant variance from the mean of the total, while analysis of the rows (durables and nondurables) showed a significant variance. This test provided some further evidence that the earnings differential between durables and nondurables was caused not by instability of employment but by some other factor.

One reason for examining the rank correlations for both 1948 earnings and 1957 earnings was to determine whether the pattern of instability of the ten post-war years might have caused the earnings rate more nearly to reflect instability at the end than at the beginning of the period. In other words, did workers become more knowledgeable concerning different degrees of instability among industries and change their preferences for alternative employments accordingly? In the only case where the rank correlation was statistically significant, that of durables, the correlation with 1957 earnings was lower than with 1948 earnings, suggesting a negative response to our question.

In order to determine whether the rank correlation for durables signified that earnings rates within this classification compensated for instability, two further tests were made. The first consisted in using a Lorenz-curve technique for measuring the dispersion of wage rates. The 48 industries were arrayed from lowest to highest earnings rate on the horizontal axis of the box diagram. The earnings for each industry were arrayed cumulatively on the vertical axis of the diagram. A curve was then plotted indicating the cumulative number of industries and the cumulative earnings of each number of industries. A diagonal line connecting the corners of the diagram as shown would reflect a situation in which the earnings of all industries were the same. The measure of dispersion or inequality in the distribution of earnings is given by the ratio of the area, A, described between the actual distribution and the diagonal line (the shaded area of the diagram) and the total area, $A + B$, subsumed under the diagonal line. This ratio, expressed as a percentage, was 7.81 per cent.

As has been indicated earlier, if the wage rates exactly compensated for instability, the income for the ten-year period for a randomly selected member of the "full employment labor force" of any industry would be the same as for any other industry. In this case, if the 48 industries were again arrayed on the Lorenz diagram on the basis of the ten-year income per average "full-employment" worker, and the income rather than wage rate were cumulatively arrayed on the vertical axis, the line relating the

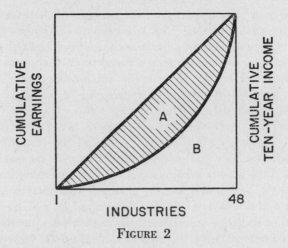

FIGURE 2

two would be the diagonal line representing zero dispersion of income. The extent to which the actual earnings rate compensates for instability is shown by the degree to which the measure of the dispersion-of-earnings rate among the 48 industries is reduced by the substitution of the ten-year income figure for the weekly earnings rate.

It was necessary to obtain a ten-year income figure per member of the full-employment labor force of each industry. This figure was calculated for each industry by multiplying average weekly earnings by actual employment for each month, summing this series, and then dividing this sum by the mean of the two peak employments. The mean of the two peak employments represents the "full employment labor force" attached to the industry. The income figure thus obtained is equivalent to the income an average or representative member of the industry's labor force would have received over the ten-year period.[12] (See Figure 2.)

When the vertical scale of the Lorenz diagram was changed from

---

[12] This analysis has ignored the fact that unemployment compensation payments were actually made during the period covered to unemployed members of the labor force. The treatment of both the earnings rate and the ten-year income figures are deficient in this regard. Information concerning the amount of unemployment benefit payments by industry was not available. However, studies of state unemployment compensation systems indicate that the ratio of the rate of benefit payments to regular earnings approximates 30 per cent, that many unemployed workers are ineligible, and that many exhaust their entitlement in a short time period. Consequently the deficiency in the data is not likely to qualify the results seriously. It is certainly safe to say that the present level of benefit payments does not adequately compensate for the periods of layoff of all workers. Consequently, earnings rates in the industries, exclusive of unemployment benefits, would still have to be correlated with instability if workers are to be indifferent at the margin with respect to alternative industrial employments.

weekly earnings to ten-year income, the measure of dispersion (the ratio of A to $A + B$) changed from 7.81 per cent to 7.35 per cent. In other words, the dispersion was not significantly reduced toward zero, so that the earnings ratio, though correlated with instability, did not significantly compensate for it. A similar test for the nondurable-goods industries resulted in the measure of dispersion *increasing* from 12.12 per cent to 12.42 per cent rather than moving toward zero.

The second test of whether the earnings rates for different industries in the durable-goods classification compensated for instability consisted of a rank correlation between the hypothetical ten-year income figure calculated above and the weekly earnings rate. If there were no unemployment benefit payments, and if the weekly earnings rate exactly compensated for instability and there were no other differences for which earnings must compensate, then this rank correlation between ten-year income and weekly earnings should be zero, since the incomes would be the same for all industries but the weekly earnings would vary. Since some unemployment benefits were paid, the weekly earnings diffentials could fall short of equalizing incomes of the various industries by the amount of unemployment benefits; and now the correlation between weekly earnings and ten-year income should be negative. The actual correlation between weekly earnings and the ten-year income figure for durable-goods industries was .80624, a high positive correlation. For the nondurable-goods industries this correlation was .92855. This test further suggests that the earnings differential between industries is caused by factors other than instability of employment.

One final test was made for the durable-goods industries. A hypothetical regression was computed between the weekly earnings and the index of instability, such that the slope of the regression would give equal ten-year incomes at any point. The regression was obtained by taking the mean instability index and the mean weekly-earnings rate which would compensate for instability. The mean instability index was approximately 1.08 and the mean weekly-earnings rate approximately $86.00, so that at an index of instability of 1.00, the minimum index, the earnings rate would have to be $79.63, and at an index of instability of 1.36, the maximum index observed, the earnings rate would have to be $108.30. The regression of actual weekly earnings in relation to instability was computed. The coefficient of correlation was quite low for this actual regression, and it differed distinctly in slope from the hypothetical regression. This suggested further that the earnings rate for various durable-goods industries was not affected by the varying degrees of instability.

All of the empirical evidence has suggested that wage rates in different industries do not reflect the instability of employment opportunity. Returning now to our theoretical model, the empirical evidence suggests that workers in general are not knowledgeable concerning the degrees of instability of alternative industrial opportunities and that they are, therefore, unable to make rational choices which would be consistent with their preferences as between alternative jobs of varying degrees of stability. Consequently, an unemployment compensation system which maintains workers' incomes at approximately the same level when unemployed as when employed, and which is properly financed, will substitute for workers' lack of knowledge. Wage rates among different industries, then, need not vary because of instability (although unemployment compensation taxes will vary). Workers' preferences with respect to other dimensions of the job might still be reflected in the wage differentials. The allocation of local resources between alternative industries will more closely approximate workers' preferences for income versus leisure, and will be more "efficient" than if the unemployment compensation system did not exist or were improperly financed.

References

1. Tibor Scitovsky, Welfare and Competition: The Economics of a Fully Employed Economy. Irwin, Homewood, Illinois, 1951.

2. Melvin Reder, Studies in the Theory of Welfare Economics. Columbia University Press, New York, 1947, Chap. XIV.

3. Kenneth J. Arrow, "A Difficulty in the Concept of Social Welfare," *Journal of Political Economy*, LVIII (August 1950), 328–46.

4. Philip W. Cartwright, "The Economics of the UAW-Ford Contract," *American Economic Review*, XLV (December 1955), 932.

5. Eveline M. Burns, The American Social Security System. Houghton Mifflin, Boston, 1949, Chap. VII.

6. Eveline M. Burns, Social Security and Public Policy. McGraw-Hill, New York, 1956, pp. 165–71, 184–88.

The Interdependence of Investment Decisions[1]

HOLLIS B. CHENERY

It is now widely recognized that the classical theory of resource allocation must be modified to take account of existing conditions in under-developed countries, particularly as regards investment decisions. In his celebrated article on the *Problems of Industrialization of Eastern and Southeastern Europe* (1) Professor Rosenstein-Rodan suggested that a group of investments which would be profitable if considered together may separately appear unprofitable and may not be undertaken by an individual investor who does not take advantage of external economies. Rosenstein-Rodan concluded that government coordination of investment would be necessary to make the best use of available resources and that the calculation of the profitability of a given investment should include the resulting increase in profitability of investment in other sectors.

A number of writers have followed Rosenstein-Rodan in suggesting limitations to the applicability of general equilibrium theory for the analysis of resource use in underdeveloped economies: Nurkse (2), Lewis (3), Singer (4), and Myrdal (5), to mention only a few. Although concerned with a variety of problems, they agree in doubting the existence of an automatic tendency toward equilibrium with optimal resource allocation in such economies.

In contrast to the general equilibrium system, which has been elaborated with increasing precision over a long period, the postulates of a model which would permit the analysis of the conditions thought to be characteristic of underdeveloped countries have not been stated with any accuracy. It is customary to list a number of ways in which the competi-

[1] I am indebted to Tibor Scitovsky, Kenneth Arrow, Robert Dorfman, John Haldi, and Louis Lefeber for helpful discussions of the theoretical problems analyzed here, and to the staff of the U.N. Economic Commission for Latin America for much useful background material on the steel-metalworking complex in Latin America, which provides the empirical core of the paper. My research in this field has been supported by a grant from the Ford Foundation to the Stanford Project for Quantitative Research in Economic Development.

tive mechanism does not function properly and then to draw general conclusions from them without concretely specifying the model which is
being used.[2] The efforts of more orthodox theorists to demolish these conclusions are generally unconvincing, however, because they stick too
closely to the classical assumptions.

One theoretical aspect of the problem has been clarified in recent
articles by Scitovsky (6), Fleming (7), Arndt (8), and Bator (9): the
difference between the Marshallian concept of "external economies" and
the meaning given to this term by Rosenstein-Rodan and other growth
theorists. In earlier usage it pertains to costs and benefits of production
not adequately reflected in the price mechanism; in growth theory it refers
to the effect of one investment on the profitability of another. The former
uses the assumptions of competitive equilibrium, while the latter acquires
its significance from the assumptions of dynamic disequilibrium.

In the present paper, I will take up one of the arguments advanced by
Rosenstein-Rodan for the coordination of investment decisions, which
accounts for part of his "external economies." My aim is to present a
model which will permit measurement of the importance of interdependence in production for investment decisions, and to work out a concrete
example in which they are thought to be significant. When this has been
done, I will return to the theoretical formulation of the phenomenon of
external economies and its practical implications.

THE PROBLEM

The problem may be stated as follows: To what extent and under what
circumstances do coordinated investment decisions lead to more efficient
resource use than do individual decisions based on existing market information? It has been shown that, if conditions of competitive equilibrium
are continuously maintained and economies of scale are excluded, then
external economies are limited to rather exceptional cases of nonmarket
(or technological) interdependence whose quantitative significance is
slight.[3]

The maintenance of competitive equilibrium over time requires that
present prices must accurately reflect future as well as present demand and
supply conditions and that investors should react in such a way that their
price expectations are continuously realized.[4] These are very strong conditions. Under these assumptions, the "pecuniary" or market effects of

---

[2] There are a number of exceptions to this generalization, such as Lewis' brilliant article (3) on the implications of surplus labor for development, but they have
not been concerned with the problem to be discussed here.

[3] See Scitovsky (6), Bator (9). The static case is analyzed most completely
by the latter.

[4] The conditions under which competitive equilibrium is maintained over time
are stated more precisely in Dorfman, Samuelson, and Solow (10), pp. 318 ff.

one investment on the profitability calculations of other investors are part of the mechanism by which the market coordinates action among investors and eliminates the difference between private and social profitability of the initial investment.

When the continuous adjustments needed to maintain competitive equilibrium are not assumed to take place, these market effects have quite a different significance. The resulting situation has been most precisely formulated by Scitovsky:[5]

"Investment in industry A will cheapen its product; and if this is used as a factor in industry B, the latter's profits will rise . . . The profits of industry B, created by the lower price of factor A, call for investment and expansion in industry B, one result of which will be an increase in industry B's demand for industry A's product . . . equilibrium is reached only when successive doses of investment and expansion in the two industries have led to the simultaneous elimination of profits in both. It is only at this stage, where equilibrium has been established, that the conclusions of equilibrium theory become applicable . . . We can conclude, therefore, that when an investment gives rise to pecuniary external economies, its private profitability understates its social desirability."

Furthermore, if the system does not start from a position of competitive equilibrium, it cannot be assumed that the investment that takes place will necessarily lead toward such an equilibrium.

The mechanism I propose to study is essentially that outlined by Scitovsky. Although included in the concept of external economies used by Rosenstein-Rodan and Nurkse, it is subordinate in their analysis to the effects of investment that are transmitted via the increase in consumers' income. This extension of the concept, however, seems undesirable to me because it combines production phenomena which are specific to individual investments with income effects that are produced by any investment. I will therefore adopt the following definitions of external economies as applied to the effects of investment:

(i) *For the whole economy*, external economies may be said to exist when the real cost of supplying a given set of demands is less with coordinated investment decisions than with individual decisions based on existing market information.

(ii) *With reference to particular industries*, it can be said that industries A, B, C, . . . , provide external economies to industries K, L, M, . . . , if investment in industries A, B, C, . . . , causes a decrease in the cost of supplying the demands for the products of K, L, M, . . .[6]

[5] Reference (6), p. 148.
[6] The earlier distinction between cost reduction via price changes (pecuniary) and cost reduction via a change in input requirements (technological) can also be made, but the second case is not of great significance for the analysis of investment decisions.

The following example suggests some of the situations in which external economies may be important for investment decisions. Consider two related industries, steel and metalworking. There are demands of 1000 for the products of each industry, which are currently supplied by imports in each case. The domestic production of metal products would require an input of .2 units of steel per unit of output but would not be profitable at existing prices. Steel production also has not been profitable heretofore.

Assume now, as Scitovsky does, an innovation leading to investment in steel production which "will cheapen its product." If the existing market demand for steel is taken as a guide to the scale of the investment, a capacity of 1000 units will be installed. But if the price of steel is lowered in accordance with its lower cost, investment in metalworking will now become profitable. Investment in capacity to produce 1000 units of metal products will lead to an additional demand for 200 units of steel, so that further investment in the steel industry will be needed.

In this case, external economies exist on the above definitions because coordinated investment decisions would result in simultaneous investment in steel and metalworking and a lower-cost supply of metal products. The difference in total cost between the coordinated and uncoordinated result is due to the timing of investment and will be wiped out by the working of market forces in the long run if (i) the price of steel is reduced and (ii) the demand for steel does not increase further in the meantime.

Under other assumptions, the external economies produced by coordinated investment may not be eliminated over time by market reactions. If there are internal economies of scale in the steel industry, it may be profitable to invest at a demand of 1200 units but not at 1000. In this event, the investments must be made in both sectors together if either is to be profitable.

Innovation is only one of a number of initiating factors which can lead to external economies of this type. The discovery of a new source of iron ore, the building of a railway, a rise in the cost of securing imports, or any other change which makes the initial investment in steel profitable may have similar repercussions. These examples all involve additional sectors of the economy, and to analyze them in any detail requires some sort of interindustry model. Such a model is suggested in the next section.

Since the significance of external economies depends largely on the magnitudes involved, I will work with a concrete example based on the present conditions in the steel and metalworking industries in Latin America. The number of sectors included is the minimum which appears necessary to take account of the more directly related investments. This example has been chosen because it contains practically all of the elements that have been suggested in the discussion of dynamic external economies. My procedure will be to compare the resource allocation resulting under the two extreme assumptions of perfect coordination and complete lack of coordination of investment decisions. Alternative assumptions will then be made with regard to the factor costs, size of the market, and degree of coordination in order to measure the importance of these several factors.

The interdependence of investment decisions will be discussed in the context of conditions prevailing in the less developed countries, for which it has greater significance than for more advanced countries. Interdependence is also more important for products sold to producers, and hence it occurs typically in sectors related to manufacturing. In the underdeveloped countries, manufacturing is initiated originally as a substitute for either handicraft production or imports. Either assumption could be made in the general case, but the latter is clearly more appropriate for the commodities discussed here.

The model to be proposed is intended to provide an explicit analysis of production and investment in a group of related sectors[7] within a simplified general-equilibrium framework. For the sectors in which the levels of production and investment are important to the result, it specifies a production function in the form of an "activity" or column of Leontief-type input coefficients. Demands for the outputs of these sectors in the rest of the economy are taken as given. Supplies of inputs from other sectors in the economy, of imports, and of labor and capital, are assumed to be available at fixed prices. The effects of relaxing these assumptions are considered later.

The model provides for the analysis of the following characteristics of underdeveloped countries, which may affect either the source of the initial incentive to invest or the extent of coordination which should be assumed:

(i) *Failure to use known lower-cost techniques of production* because of ignorance, scarcity of innovators, or lack of capital in large blocks.

(ii) *Small markets for manufactured goods* in relation to the size of a minimum-cost plant. The explanation may be found in relatively high transport costs and tariff barriers combined with low levels of income. Demands for these commodities are largely supplied from imports.

(iii) *Imperfection in factor markets* with a wide range of prices for labor, capital, and foreign exchange, caused by institutional and cultural obstacles to the movement of these factors between uses. The opportunity cost of labor is frequently lower than its cost to industry, while capital and foreign exchange are frequently rationed in various ways.

---

[7] Market interrelations can be classified in various ways, but the most important distinction is between *interdependence in production* (supplier-user, users of a common input, etc.) and *interdependence via increased consumer incomes*. I will be concerned mainly with the first type and will therefore take consumer demands as given for most of the analysis. Fleming [(7), p. 250] distinguishes between "vertical" and "horizontal" economies in approximately the same way.

(iv) *The absence of adequate overhead facilities*—transport, power, etc.

It is this set of factors, rather than the level of *per capita* income *per se*, that is important to the discussion of the effects of interdependence of investments.

The Analysis of Production

To take account of the structural factors listed above, the description of production in terms of activities has important advantages. The formulation used in mathematical programming permits the determination of the optimal allocation of resources when there are limitations on the quantities demanded and on factor supplies. Such a solution corresponds to the case of perfect coordination. In addition, it will be necessary to work out solutions to represent the results of uncoordinated individual decisions.

The model to be used is summarized in Table I as a set of 10 equations in activity analysis form. It has the following features:

(i) *Each equation corresponds to a commodity* or primary factor input. The first seven equations apply to the commodities produced within the part of the economy covered in detail by the model. The first six are the outputs of sectors most directly affected by the level of production in the steel industry, either as suppliers or users. Foreign exchange [equation 7] is also treated as a commodity, and exports are included within the model to show the resources used in obtaining imports. Equation 8 applies to commodities produced elsewhere in the economy and is included in the system to account for all production costs.

(ii) *The activities in the model* describe the alternative ways of supplying each commodity. The output of each activity is shown by a positive coefficient, 1.0. The activity level therefore indicates the net amount produced by the activity, there being no joint products. The use of a commodity in production is shown by a negative coefficient, a_{ij}, the amount of commodity i used in sector j being $a_{ij}X_j$. Production activities (X_j) require inputs from other sectors in the model and also from outside the system (inputs 8–10). Import activities (M_j) require an input of foreign exchange in the amount indicated by the coefficient in line 7 per unit of product supplied. Imports are possible for commodities 1, 2, 3, and 5. (For all activities, the commodity supplied is indicated by the subscript.)

(iii) *The first eight equations* in the model constitute a set of restrictions on the possible levels of production, imports, and exports. Each equation is formed by multiplying each coefficient in the row by the corresponding activity level $(X_j, M_j, \text{ or } E_j)$ and setting the total equal to the demand outside the system. For example, the equation for iron and steel reads:

$$- .22X_1 + M_2 + X_2 - .05X_3 - .01X_4 - .01X_5 - .02X_6 = 1000. \quad (2)$$

TABLE I
The Model of Production

Equation	Commodity	M_1	X_1	M_2	X_2	M_3	X_3	X_4	M_5	X_5	X_6	E_7	X_8	Outside Demand	Given Prices
(1)	Metal products†	1.0	1.0											1000	
(2)	Iron and steel		-.22	1.0	1.0		-.05	-.01		-.01	-.02			1000	
(3)	Iron ore				-.08	1.0	1.0							0	
(4)	Electric power		-.01		-.02		-.02	1.0		-.03				0	
(5)	Coal				-.10			-.25	1.0	1.0	-.07			0	
(6)	Transport		-.01		-.02		-.50			-.20	1.0			0	
(7a)	Foreign exchange (a)	-.85		-1.2		-1.1			-1.0			1.0		0	
(7b)	(b)	-.815		-1.05											
(8)	Other inputs		-.17		-.09		-.10			-.08	-.17	-.10	1.0	0	
(9)	Labor		-.7		-.2		-.3			-.4	-.7	-1.0	-1.0	–	1.5
(10)	Capital		-.7		-2.7		-.5			-.7	-2.5	-2.2	-1.5	–	1.0

Activities*

* All input coefficients are measured in value per unit of output except labor, which is in man-years. The value units for outside demand (and hence for labor) are arbitrary.

† "Metal products" refers to machinery, vehicles, and other products in the 36, 37, and 38 categories of the International Standard Industrial Classification.

The total supply is given by $(M_2 + X_2)$; the total use of iron and steel in the sectors within the system is $\Sigma_j a_{2j} X_j$; and the "outside" use in the rest of the economy is 1000. Outside demands are assumed only for the first two commodities, since the existence of outside demands for the remainder does not affect the nature of the solution.[8]

The equation for foreign exchange supplied and demanded has a similar form:

$$- .85M_1 - 1.2M_2 - 1.1M_3 - 1.0M_5 + 1.0E_7 = 0. \qquad (7a)$$

(For reasons explained below, alternative assumptions a and b will be made as to the magnitude of the coefficients specifying the cost of imports of commodities 1 and 2.)

(iv) *The use of primary factors*, capital and labor, is shown in equations 9 and 10. For these unproduced inputs, no restriction is placed on supply since only a small range of variation will be considered. Instead, prices are assumed to be given by conditions in the rest of the economy, with the price of capital arbitrarily set at 1.0. At a later stage, economies of scale will be introduced by making average capital and labor coefficients a declining function of the level of output. (The activity analysis model can readily handle supply limitations in a more general case.)

A solution to a programming model such as this consists of a set of nonnegative activity levels which satisfy equations 1–8. In linear programming, it is necessary to consider only "basic" solutions—those which have only as many positive activity levels as there are equations. A similar rule holds when there are economies of scale, so that almost all of the solutions with which I will be concerned are basic solutions. In the present model, a basic solution will contain one activity having a positive output for each commodity restriction. The total number of such combinations is 2^4, or 16, in the present example, since there are alternative sources for four commodities.[9] There are only six different solutions arising from these possible combinations, however; they are given in Table II.

The coefficients used in Table I are intended to be realistic, but in order to avoid local peculiarities I have not used the actual data of any one country. The selection of sectors and of the input-output data (apart from steel) was based on a comparison of interindustry structure in four countries.[10] Latin America data (13) were used for the steel industry, and

[8] Production or import levels calculated for the remaining commodities can be considered as increases above a given level, which is not affected by the investment choices in the sectors being analyzed.

[9] Although it would be quite simple to include alternative techniques of production in each sector, this was not necessary in the present case because exports and imports provide an alternative to local production. Since the more important choice in these sectors is between imports and the most efficient production technique, I have limited the possibilities to these two.

[10] Chenery and Watanabe (11).

TABLE II

Basic Solutions to the Model*

Solu-tion	Activity Level												Factor Use		
	M_1	M_2	X_1	X_2	M_3	X_3	X_4	M_5	X_5	X_6	E_7†	X_8	Labor‡	Capital‡	Total
0.......	1000	1000			0		0	0		0	1865	187	2052	4383	7461
1.......		1220	1000		0		10	3		10	1285	301	2296	4035	7479
2.......	1000			1001	80		20	106		20	1009	196	1425	5332	7470
3.......	1000			1007		80	25		113	83	815	206	1357	5231	7267
4.......			1000	1221	98		35	133		34	241	313	1532	5195	7493
5.......			1000	1229		98	41		141	112		324	1446	5065	7234

* The total of 16 possible combinations of imports and production in sectors 1, 2, 3, 5 is reduced to six because (i) when steel is imported, demands for ore and coal are zero and solutions 0 and 1 each represent four possible bases; and (ii) I have omitted the possibility of importing ore and producing coal or vice versa because it does not arise under my assumptions as to the extent of coordination.

† Exports under import assumption b.

‡ Labor and capital in case I.

Japanese labor and capital coefficients for the remaining sectors.[11] Import prices and export costs are hypothetical. The proportions of external demand for steel and metal products are initially fixed at arbitrary levels, but the effect of varying them is considered explicitly in a later section.

Prices and External Economies

Since I wish to isolate the effects of interdependence in production, I assume that income is increasing and investment is taking place at a given rate in the economy as a whole. The level of income at any time determines the specified demands for steel and metal products, while the investment opportunities in the remainder of the economy fix the marginal productivity of investment and the opportunity cost of labor. Prices of "other inputs" are determined by labor and capital costs, since the internal structures of the industries producing them are omitted from the model.

Except as specified, prices will be assumed to satisfy the conditions of marginal cost pricing.[12] An initial position is assumed in which each commodity is either produced or imported, which is a basic solution. I also assume a price of labor of 1.5, which is its opportunity cost. The commodity prices and the price of foreign exchange can then be calculated from the condition that price equals marginal cost. (In case I, with no economies of scale, marginal cost is also average cost.) This calculation involves solving eight simultaneous equations, one for each activity, of the following form:

$$a_{1j}P_1 + a_{2j}P_2 + a_{3j}P_3 + \ldots + a_{10j}P_{10} = 0 \ (j = 1 \ldots 8) \quad (11)$$

where a_{ij} is the (marginal) input coefficient for input 1 in activity j. Prices as thus defined are the same as the "shadow" or equilibrium prices of a programming system for the linear case except for the exogenous labor input, whose price is given.[13]

The relative prices with which the economy starts are determined by the source of supply—from domestic production or imports—of each commodity and the cost of securing foreign exchange. I will assume that initially all of the commodities that can be imported—metal products,

---

[11] From unpublished studies by T. Watanabe of the Stanford Project for Quantitative Research in Economic Development.

[12] For simplicity, I ignore differences in the durability of capital and risk among sectors and assume that the gross rate of return required by investors in each sector is the same. Variations in these factors could readily be introduced but would serve no useful purpose in the present context.

[13] The general formulation used in activity analysis and the economic interpretation of shadow prices are discussed in Dorfman, Samuelson, and Solow (10), especially Chaps. 6–8.

steel, iron ore, and coal—are imported.[14] Once the price of foreign exchange is determined, their prices will be given.

The price of "other inputs," P_8, is readily computed from the price of labor and capital to be 3.0. By substituting $P_8 - P_{10}$ into equation 11 for the export activity, the price of foreign exchange is determined to be 4.0. The price of each imported commodity is then found by multiplying its cost in foreign exchange by the price (opportunity cost) of foreign exchange. The same procedure is followed in later solutions.

The prices of the domestically produced commodities in this and subsequent solutions must be determined simultaneously, since each sector (except the first) sells to one or more of the others. To facilitate this solution, the matrix of coefficients has been arranged in order of maximum triangularity—i.e., the elements above the diagonal in the solution are reduced to a minimum.[15] The set of initial prices is shown in line (1) of Table III.

Starting from this initial position, in which demands for commodities 1 and 2 are supplied through imports, I will measure the effects of various factors which would render investment in one or both sectors profitable. In each case, a calculation will be made of the amount of investment that will take place under alternative assumptions as to investors reactions.[16] The social efficiency of these reactions will be measured by the reduction in the total cost of supplying the given demands. Total cost in turn equals capital plus labor used, with labor valued at its opportunity cost of 1.5.

The two assumptions about investors' behavior can be stated as follows:

(i) *Individual reactions*: Investment will take place in sectors which yield profits greater than or equal to the existing marginal productivity of capital (taken as 1.0) at *present prices* and in amounts determined by *present demands* for the commodity.

(ii) *Coordinated reactions*: Investment will take place in sectors and in amounts which together will supply the outside demands at the minimum total cost. (For the linear case I, this assumption can be stated in terms of individual profitability at *future prices*.)

These assumptions represent the extreme range between no foresight and socially optimum decisions on investment. They are not intended as descriptions of the actual behavior of unplanned and planned economies, but as a basis for estimates of the maximum difference in performance.

[14] Except for iron ore, for which there is no demand if steel is not produced.

[15] The solutions for both prices and quantities were made with the Gauss-Seidel method of iteration. The method as applied to input-output systems is explained in Evans (12).

[16] The maintenance of the original pattern of supply also requires investment in exports, but it will keep the original prices unchanged.

The second part of the assumption as to individual reactions will not be applied to sectors in which domestic production is already established, because no investment could take place in a power-using industry, for example, without an expansion of power production. The amount of induced investment required in sectors where production is already established will therefore be assumed to take place even with individual reactions. This assumption is necessary in order that a given set of alternatives be feasible—i.e., satisfy all the restrictions.

The cost of each set of alternatives can be measured in one of two ways. The first is to calculate the production required in each sector and from this result to determine the amount of labor and capital needed throughout the economy. This has been done for the six basic solutions in Table II. In the initial situation (solution 0) the outside demands are supplied from imports, and production takes place only in sectors 7 and 8, exports and "other inputs." The total cost of this production is 2052 units of labor and 4383 units of capital. Using the assumed opportunity cost of 1.5 for labor, the total cost of this alternative is 7461. The total cost of the other alternatives is calculated in the same way.

The use of prices provides a second method of calculating the total cost of each set of alternatives, which is more interesting from an economic point of view. Each price represents the total capital used directly and indirectly to produce a unit of net output. In the initial situation of example B in Table III below, the prices of commodities 1 and 2 are shown as 3.26 and 4.20. Multiplying the outside demands by these prices and adding gives 7460 as the total cost as before (except for rounding). This result corresponds to the "dual" solution of a linear programming system.[17]

Under the assumptions made, any profitable investment will necessarily reduce the total cost of factors required to supply the given final demands. The difference between the amounts required under the two assumptions about investors' reactions provides a measure of the quantitative importance of the interdependence of investment decisions. In considering some types of policy, it is desirable to allocate this difference to individual sectors. When this is done, we will have a partial measure of the type of external economies which Rosenstein-Rodan had in mind: the difference between social and private profitability resulting from the recognition of interdependence.

MEASUREMENT OF THE EFFECTS OF INTERDEPENDENCE

Investment will take place in an industry[18] only if its marginal productivity is greater than or equal to that assumed for the rest of the economy. Assuming that investments which were profitable in the past have

[17] The calculation of the price solution is explained further in the Appendix.
[18] I assume no difference among plants in an industry except for the scale effects discussed under case II below.

TABLE III

Effects of Coordination on Profits and Prices: Case I

Investment Assumptions*	Import Assumption†	Solution N.	Profitability of Investment‡				Prices							Total Cost§
			1	2	3	5	1	2	3	4	5	6	7	
Example A:														
(1) Initial position	a	0					3.40	4.80	4.40	5.04	4.00	4.43	4.00	8200
(2) Individual investment in 2	a	2	−.01	+.58	—	—	3.40	4.22	4.40	5.04	4.00	4.43	4.00	7620
(3) Coordination of 1 and 2	a	4	+.12	+.59	—	—	3.28	4.21	4.40	5.03	4.00	4.42	4.00	7490
Example B:														
(4) Initial position	b	0					3.26	4.20	4.40	5.04	4.00	4.43	4.00	7460
(5) Individual investment in exports	b	0	−.01	−.01	+.70	+1.42	3.26	4.20	4.40	5.04	4.00	4.43	4.00	7460
(6) Coordination of 2, 3, 5	b	3	−.01	+.20	+.70	+1.42	3.26	4.00	3.70	4.68	2.58	4.32	4.00	7260
Example C:														
(7) Coordination of 1, 2, 3, 5	a	5	+.17	+.79	+.70	+1.42	3.23	4.00	3.70	4.68	2.58	4.32	4.00	7230
	b	5	+.03	+.20	+.70	+1.42								

* The necessary expansion in sectors 4 and 6 is assumed in all cases.

† Import assumptions: (a) $m_1 = .85$, $m_2 = 1.2$,
                     (b) $m_1 = .815$, $m_2 = 1.05$.

‡ Profitability per unit of output at input prices indicated, with output price that of the initial position.

§ Total cost equals ($1000 P_1 + 1000 P_2$).

already been made, one of the following conditions must obtain if investment in steel or metalworking is now to become profitable:

(i) *The availability of technology* which is more efficient at existing
prices of inputs and outputs than that already in use;

(ii) *A change in cost* of one of the exogenous inputs, such as a fall in
the price of labor or capital;

(iii) *A rise in the cost* of obtaining foreign exchange (i.e., a change
affecting activity E_7 in Table I;

(iv) *Coordinated planning*, provided unused resources exist in one of
the supplying sectors;

(v) *The expansion of demand.*

These factors may produce investment in one or several sectors, and
the results may or may not be different as between individual investment
decisions and coordinated decisions. In this section I will try to identify
the more important types of external effects—cases in which the results
of the two assumptions are different—and to measure their quantitative
significance in the example I have chosen.

It will be useful to separate the case in which there are internal economies of scale from that with constant costs throughout, since it is often
asserted that external economies are merely the result of internal economies
elsewhere in the economy. I will take up the constant cost assumption first
as case I, since it is analytically simpler although empirically less important.

In order to make the analysis easier to follow, I will use the same set
of interindustry data (eqs. 1–6) throughout. This permits the use of the
basic solutions given for sectors 1–8 of Table II for both cases. Economies
of scale are assumed to affect only the labor and capital coefficients, which
are outside of the interindustry system.

For each case, the same three examples, illustrating some of the initiating factors listed above, will be worked out and the magnitude of the external effects measured.

Case I: External Effects with Constant Costs

The principal effects of interdependence in production can be classified as *effects on users* and *effects on suppliers*.[19] Each type will first be
illustrated separately by assuming only partial coordination among investment decisions, and then their combined effect will be shown by assuming
complete coordination.

Example A: Effects on users. External effects of investment in industry Y on users of commody Y can be illustrated by Scitovsky's example

---

[19] I have abstracted from less direct effects, such as the use of common factors
of production, by assuming an elastic supply of exogenous inputs at constant costs
over the relevant range of demand. All produced inputs are therefore available at
constant cost.

of the effects of an innovation in Y. Assume that it is now profitable to invest in the production of steel, which had previously been imported. In example A of Table III, the import price of steel has been taken as 1.2 to illustrate this possibility. The initial prices, as calculated above, are given in line (1) for all commodities. The import price of metal products has been set just under the cost of production with current prices, however, so that without coordination investment will take place only in steel. The effect on steel cost and the total cost are shown in line (2). If coordination takes place, however, investment in sector 1 will also be profitable because of the lower cost of steel, and a larger investment in sector 2 will be needed to supply the increased demand. (This is the situation envisaged by Scitovsky in the example previously cited.) No change in the source of supply of other inputs is assumed, so the reduction in the total cost of supplying the given demands—from 7620 to 7490—can be attributed entirely to the coordination of investment in steel and the steel-using industries. Others of the initiating factors listed above—a fall in the cost of labor or capital, or a rise in the cost of securing imports—can produce the same effect.

It should be emphasized that, under the assumption of constant costs, the difference between uncoordinated and coordinated investment in this case is only one of time. Once the investment in steel has been made, it will be profitable to invest in metalworking unless the price of steel is kept above its cost. Furthermore, if *both* sectors are unprofitable at the initial prices of imports, coordination will not make them profitable. Both of these conclusions will be changed in succeeding examples.

Example B: Effects on suppliers. When expansion in one sector increases demands for inputs, no external economies are created if the price of the inputs reflects the opportunity costs of the factors used to produce them. When increased demand in one sector leads to a demand for immobile factors which have no alternative uses, or for commodities produced from immobile factors, however, the situation may be different.

In the present example iron ore and coal illustrate this possibility. The market for them is limited by transport costs, particularly in areas where transport facilities are not well developed.[20] If an industry which can use them locally is established, however, they may be much cheaper than would the imported material, as has been assumed here.

Example B in Table III illustrates the effect of investment in the steel industry on the profitability of investment in coal and ore supplies. If it is assumed that there is no market for these commodities outside the region because of high transport costs,[21] additional investment in these sectors will not take place unless steel production (or some other use) is estab-

[20] The case becomes more significant when we make the more realistic assumption of economies of scale in transportation.

[21] An example is provided by the coal and iron ore deposits in Columbia, which cannot be economically transported to the coast.

lished locally. On the other hand, steel production on the basis of imported materials is unprofitable. In this case, there will be no investment in any sector without coordination of all three. With coordination, the cost of supplying the existing demand for steel is reduced from 4200 to 4000.

A similar external effect on suppliers may be produced by a reduction in the cost of a factor which affects profits in all sectors. Assume that the opportunity cost of labor is reduced (e.g., by using its calculated value instead of market cost) from 1.5 units of capital to 1.0. (A reduction in the supply cost of capital or a rise in the cost of foreign exchange would have a similar effect.) Investment in both sectors 1 and 2 will then become profitable to individual investors, but the amount of investment undertaken in sector 2 will be 18 per cent less than if there is coordination, since the demand from sector 1 will not be taken into account initially. The difference in the cost of supplying the given demands is 130 in this case.[22] As in example A, coordination will affect only the timing of investment because it will be profitable to expand investment in sector 2 when the demand for steel from sector 1 becomes apparent.

Example C: Effects on both suppliers and users. Example C in Table III shows the effects of complete coordination of both the suppliers and the users of the steel industry. In this case, all commodities are produced locally and nothing is imported. As compared to partial coordination in example A, prices drop in both sectors 1 and 2, and there is a reduction of 260 in the total cost of supplying the given demands. As compared to partial coordination in example B, only the price of metal products drops and the saving is much smaller.

A comparison of example C with the initial assumption of example B shows the maximum external economies that can be attributed to coordination alone in the present example when there are no economies of scale. In the initial position, no investment is profitable by itself, and demand would continue to be supplied from imports at a cost of 7460. Coordinated investment in all sectors reduces the cost of supplying the same demands to 7230. The saving is attributable to the existence of local resources of coal and iron ore which can be economically exploited with coordination but not otherwise.

Case II: External Effects with Economies of Scale

The introduction of economies of scale not only makes external effects more important in the examples given previously, but it makes possible some types which do not exist in the case of constant costs. These will be taken up after the empirical basis for introducing economies of scale has been discussed.

The nature of economies of scale. Despite the theoretical importance of economies of scale, their quantitative significance has been investigated

---

[22] The calculation is not shown because the mechanism is similar to that in example A.

only in a limited number of industries. The available evidence suggests that the economies of producing a larger volume of output occur mainly in the direct use of capital and labor and in inputs (maintenance, overhead costs of various kinds) related to them. The quantities of materials needed to produce a given commodity seem to vary little with output unless the increase in scale makes possible the use of a different type of process. The value of such materials may fall with increases in the amount purchased, due to internal economies in other sectors, but this results from the working of the model itself.

Most studies of scale effects apply to plants or processes rather than to whole industries. The determination of cost variation for a whole industry must take into account location factors and market structure—e.g., whether the increase will come from one plant or several, from new plants or the expansion of old, etc. In the present example, these problems are important mainly in the metalworking sector because in steel and its suppliers it can be assumed that the increase in output will come from a single source.

Steel is the sector in which economies of scale are of greatest importance in the present case. Fortunately, the Economic Commission for Latin America has made a detailed study (13) of economies of scale in the steel industry based on design data for plants of various sizes; some of the results are summarized in Table IV. Production cost in the smallest plant

TABLE IV

ECONOMIES OF SCALE IN STEEL PRODUCTION*

| | Capacity of Plant† | | | | Decrease from |
Cost	50	250	500	1000	50 to 1000
Cost per ton :‡					
Raw materials	33.84	31.26	31.26	25.68	8.16
Maintenance and misc...	20.59	11.11	10.57	9.83	10.76
Capital charges	122.93	101.20	87.10	85.05	37.88
Labor cost	32.00	15.20	8.57	6.60	25.40
Total cost	209.36	158.77	137.50	127.16	82.20
Total investment per ton	492	405	348	340	152

* Adapted from data in *A Study of the Iron and Steel Industry in Latin America* (13),pp. 112–16.

† Capacity in 1000 tons of finished steel per year.

‡ The costs (in dollars) are taken from engineering calculations for hypothetical integrated plants of different sizes located in the eastern United States. Labor costs are taken here at 50 per cent of U.S. costs and charges for depreciation and profit at 25 per cent of capital invested to reflect Latin American conditions. (These are not the capital charges used in the original study, which are unrealistically low.) Data for iron, steel, and finishing stages have been consolidated.

considered is 65 per cent higher than in the largest, and this does not exhaust the economies which are possible with a smaller range of products.[23]

To use these data in the interindustry analysis, I have based the input coefficients of Table I on a plant of 250,000 tons, which is typical of Latin American steel production. Economies of scale will be assumed only in the use of capital and labor, which account for perhaps 90 per cent of the cost reduction shown in Table IV if the price of inputs is kept constant.[24] For this and the other sectors of the model, capital and labor will be treated as a single input, which is represented by a linear equation[25]

$$f_i = \bar{f}_i + \gamma_i X_i \tag{12}$$

where

f_i is total use cost of capital and labor at the prices assumed,

$\bar{f}_i$ is a constant, and

γ_i is the long-run marginal cost of labor and capital.

A linear function fits the data for steel production costs quite well above 250,000 tons. At the representative size of plant chosen, the ratio of marginal to average cost of labor and capital inputs is about two-thirds. This ratio has been used to determine the input function for sector 2 in Table V, with the constant term fixed so as to equate total cost in cases I and II at the initial demand of 1000.

The input functions for the remaining sectors were established on the same principles but on a hypothetical basis.[26] It would be hard to specify a typical situation for mining, transport, and power production without assuming a specific location.

No economies or diseconomies of scale have been assumed in exports. Total cost has been assumed to be equal for each sector in cases

[23] The plants are designed to produce 80 per cent of the range of steel products typically demanded in Latin American countries. The remainder would not normally be economical and would be imported. See Table VIII.

[24] All of the reduction shown in the cost of raw materials is due to economies of scale in the transport sector.

[25] Capital and labor inputs in chemical process industries (which include metallurgy) have been found to conform quite well to a relation of the following form:

$$f = f_0 \left(\frac{X}{X_0} \right) \psi.$$

Wessel and Chilton (14) give engineering data for chemical plants in which the value of ψ averages about .6 for capital and .2 for labor. ψ is the ratio of marginal to average cost. Equation 12 may be regarded as a linear approximation to this function which holds over a specified range.

[26] The greatest economy of scale is assumed in transportation, the least in mining.

TABLE V
INPUT FUNCTIONS FOR LABOR AND CAPITAL: CASE II

Sector	Input Function for Combined Input*	Total Cost Equal to Case I at†	MC/AC‡
1	$f_1 = 500 + 1.25\,X_1$	$X_1 = 1000$	.71
2	$f_2 = 1000 + 2.00\,X_2$	$X_2 = 1000$	.67
3	$f_3 = .80\,X_3$	$X_3 = 0$	.84
4	$f_4 = 2.5\,X_4$	$X_4 = 0$	.66
5	$f_5 = 1.1\,X_5$	$X_5 = 0$	.85
6	$f_6 = 1.75\,X_6$	$X_6 = 0$	.49
7	$f_7 = 3.7\,X_7$	All values	1.00

* Expressing labor in capital units at the ratio of $1.5 : 1.0$.

† I.e., output at which total cost for labor and capital are the same in both cases I and case II.

‡ Marginal cost in case II divided by average cost in case I.

I and II at the values of exogenous demand for each commodity, which are those that the individual investor takes into account.[27]

The form of the analysis is such that it can readily be adapted to utilize cost studies of the kind usually prepared in connection with investment programs.

A comparison of cases I and II. When economies of scale exist in supplying sectors, external economies will be larger because the increase in demand from the using sector will make possible cheaper production by the supplier. I will now analyze the same examples as before with the assumptions just made as to input functions for capital and labor in order to show the significance of introducing economies of scale.

Table VI has been constructed by applying the alternative input functions of cases I and II to the basic quantity solutions given in Table II.[28] Unlike case I, a coordinated investment will be profitable with the given economies of scale without any innovation, and so I have assumed the import prices of example B throughout. The use of factors in each sector shows that in example A most of the difference between the two cases comes from the larger output in sector 2, but in example B the difference is almost entirely due to the other supplying sectors. The difference is most pronounced in example C, where investment in all sectors is coordinated,

---

[27] This assumption results in a constant term of 500 in sector 1 and of zero in the other sectors. It might have been more realistic to assume a constant term in sectors 3 and 5, where no production exists in the initial position, but the difference in result would be small.

[28] For case I, this calculation serves as a check on the results of the price solution given in Table III. For case II, marginal cost prices can also be used to determine total factor use, but the quantity solution is the more convenient. The price solution for this case is given in the Appendix. With economies of scale, the optimal solution will be a basic solution, as it was in the linear case.

TABLE VI

DIRECT FACTOR USE BY SECTOR AND EXTERNAL ECONOMIES: CASES I AND II

Sectors Coordinated*	Econo-mies of Scale	Solution N.	Direct Factor Use in Sector†							Total Factor Use‡	Difference from Initial Position		External Economies in Sector 2
			1	2	3	4	5	6	7		Case I	Case II	
(1) Initial Position	0	0	0	0	0	0	0	0	7460	7460			
Example A:													
(2) 2	I	2	0	3272	0	80	0	81	4038	7471	+11		
(3) 1, 2	I	4	2260	3992	0	138	0	140	961	7491	+31		
(4) 1, 2	II	4	2260	3772	0	95	0	78	961	7166		—294	.030
Example B:													
(5) 2, 3, 5	I	3	0	3295	100	100	174	337	3260	7266	—194		.020
(6) 2, 3, 5	II	3	0	3287	88	69	151	188	3260	7043		—417	.046
Example C:													
(7) 1, 2, 3, 5	I	5	2260	4019	123	162	217	453	0	7234	—226		.023
	II	5	2260	3790	108	111	189	252	0	6710		—750	.097

* Import assumption b is used for all 3 examples.
† Direct factor use in the sector includes the use of "other inputs."
‡ Figures vary slightly from those given in Tables II and III because of rounding.

because in this case the economies of scale in the supplying sectors (particularly transportation) reach substantial proportions.

The Allocation of External Economies by Sector

The savings in factor use which result from coordination pertain to the whole set of investments, rather than to any one of them, because all are necessary to the result. If all investments in the economy were centrally planned, there would be no need to try to allocate this type of external economies because the determination of the optimum integrated plan would be sufficient. In economies, however, in which not all investment is under government control, the question arises as to how external economies can be taken into account in policies designed to improve the efficiency of individual investment decisions. This problem arises concretely in the less well-developed countries in the attempt to establish investment priorities for the economy as a whole or within certain areas, such as manufacturing. These priorities are intended to guide the allocation of loan funds or foreign exchange, or to be used as a basis for other measures by which the government influences investment.

The rationale for allocating the benefits of coordination to one sector or another must derive from the institutional setting. In the extreme case, it may be assumed that if one investment is made and its output sold at the price of the optimal solution, then investment in supplying industries and using industries will follow if the return on these investments is equal to the marginal productivity of capital elsewhere in the economy. In the present example, investment in the steel industry may have this effect, and, in fact, many governments undertake direct investment in the steel industry partly to stimulate investment in related industries. Let us calculate, therefore, the effect that taking account of external economies has on the profitability of investment in steel.

External economies may be thought of either as an addition to the value produced by a plant or as a reduction in its cost. Since I have assumed given demands in this paper, it is more convenient to take the latter approach.[29] The savings due to the coordination of investment shown in Table VI can be taken therefore as being equivalent to a reduction in the investment required in the steel industry. The profitability of investment is increased thereby, and the difference provides a measure of external economies in sector 2. In example I B the calculation would be as follows:[30]

[29] In an earlier discussion (15), I suggested that external economies be treated as an addition to the value added in production, although I did not indicate how they might be measured. If this approach were adopted, the additional value would be the additional production achievable with the factors saved.

[30] In each case I have used the scale of investment without coordination (1000) as the basis of comparison. Input costs are derived by taking the price of capital equal to its marginal productivity (.25) in exports.

	Market Prices	Shadow Prices
Price of output	1.050	4.20
Cost of inputs	.379	1.517
Profit margin	.671	2.683
Capital per unit of output	2.700	
Capital saved per unit of output (194/1000)	—.194	
Adjusted capital per unit of output	2.506	
Profitability: Original	.248	
Adjusted	.268	
External economy	.020	

The concept is somewhat more complicated when there are economies of scale in steel production because the average productivity of investment in the plant is less than the marginal productivity of additional increments of capacity. This phenomenon will lead to some overbuilding of capacity for the given demand at any moment in time, a factor which I ignore. Here I have calculated the average productivity of investment in the same way for case II as for case I, with the results shown in the last column of Table VI.

The external economies measured in this way add some 8 to 10 per cent to the productivity of investment in the steel industry in case I, and up to 40 per cent with coordination of all sectors in case II. If possible economies in the supply of exogenous inputs of goods and services (which account for about 15 per cent of all costs) were taken into account, the figure would be somewhat higher. The inclusion of external economies of this magnitude might make the difference between an unpromising steel project and one which should be included in a development program.

The Size of the Market

The effect of small markets combined with economies of scale in production is one of the main explanations given for the lack of growth of poor countries.[31] In analyzing external economies, I have so far taken the size of the market as given. In case II, the demand for each commodity was taken to be just below the size which would make investment attractive to an individual entrepreneur. Let us now abandon this assumption and determine the difference that coordination makes in the minimum scale at which investment becomes profitable. I will consider first sectors 1 and 2 separately and then the optimum pattern of investment for the whole complex.

[31] See Nurkse (2).

Investment in individual sectors. The analysis of investment in individual sectors will compare the effect of variation in exogenous demand on the cost of supply under four assumptions:

(i) *Imports;*
(ii) *Uncoordinated investment* in one sector;
(iii) *Coordinated investment* in supplying sectors 3–6;
(iv) *Coordinated investment* in all sectors.

The cost of supplying demands of any size in each sector under these assumptions is given by the equations in Table VII.

TABLE VII

COST OF SUPPLYING IN EACH SECTOR UNDER VARIOUS ASSUMPTIONS*

Assumption	Sector 1	Sector 2
(i) Imports	$S_1 = 3.26Y_1$	$S_2 = 4.2Y_2$
(ii) Uncoordinated investment	$S_1 = 500 + 2.78Y_1$	$S_2 = 1000 + 3.22Y_2$
(iii) Coordination of sectors 3–6	$S_1 = 500 + 2.739Y_1$	$S_2 = 1000 + 2.782Y_2$
(iv) Coordination of all sectors	$S_1 = 500 + 2.429Y_1$ $+ (1000 - 1.418Y_2)$ where $Y_2 < 1040$	$S_2 = 1000 + 2.782Y_2$ $+ (500 - .831Y_1)$ where $Y_1 < 1040$ $Y_1 > 600$

* Source: Appendix.

The differences among the last three equations arise as follows:

(ii) Uncoordinated investment takes account of economies of scale in the given sector but assumes average cost of inputs as given by the initial prices of Table III (line 4);

(iii) Coordination of sectors 3–6 takes the cost of these inputs as determined from the input functions of Table V;

(iv) Complete coordination makes the same assumptions as (iii) and, in addition, determines the net cost of supplying the given sector—i.e., 1 or 2—when the demand in the other is held constant. If uncoordinated investment in sector 1 is unprofitable but investment in sector 2 makes it profitable, the investment in sector 2 is credited with the difference between the cost of supplying commodity 1 from domestic production and from imports. These functions, therefore, are valid only over the range in which uncoordinated investment in the other sector is not profitable.[32]

[32] In sector 2 there is no saving over assumption (iii) and no justification for investment in 1 unless Y_1 is greater than 600—i.e., unless the second term is negative. In sector 1, the last term can be either positive or negative.

A comparison of the several alternatives is given for each sector in Figures 1*a* and *b*.[33] In each case, I have assumed a single value of production in the other sector (the general case is taken up in the next section). In sector 1, imports are profitable up to a demand of 1040 at the assumed

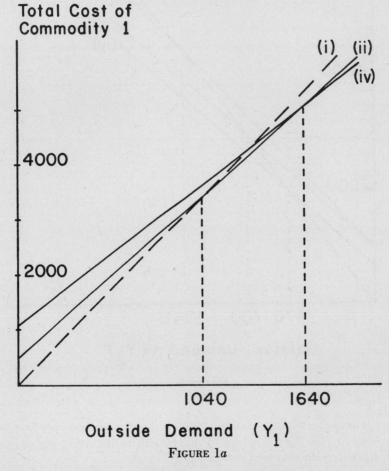

Minimum Scale of Investment
Sector 1. Metal Products
$(Y_2 = 300)$

Total Cost of Commodity 1

Outside Demand (Y_1)

FIGURE 1*a*

value of Y_2, and investment in sector 1 alone gives the lowest cost supply from this point to a demand of 1640. Thereafter, investment in both sectors is profitable with coordination. In sector 2, coordination of the supplying

---

[33] In sector I, curve (iii) is omitted because it is only slightly below curve (ii).

Minimum Scale of Investment
Sector 2. Steel Production
(Y_1 = 1000)

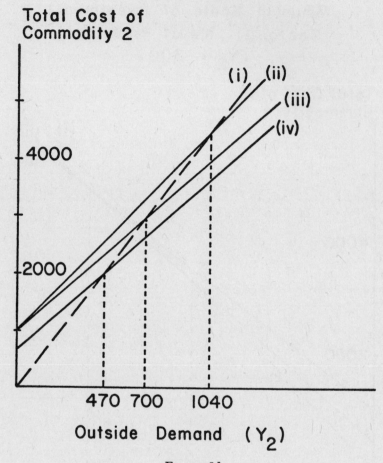

FIGURE 1*b*

sectors lowers the minimum scale at which investment becomes profitable from 1040 to 700. Coordination of investment in the using sector lowers it still further at the assumed demand in sector 1.

The pattern of investment over time. The preceding analysis can be generalized to shed some light on the optimal pattern of investment over time. When investment is completely coordinated, there are four alternative combinations of production and imports that may be most efficient at different combinations of demand:

(A)   Imports of both 1 and 2
(B)   Production of 1, imports of 2
(C)   Imports of 1, production of 2
(D)   Production of both 1 and 2

Effects   of   Demand on Optimal Investment

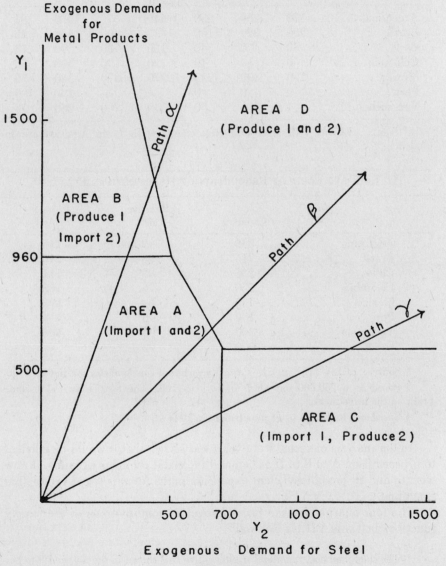

FIGURE 2

TABLE VIII

A. PRODUCTION AND IMPORTS OF CRUDE STEEL*
(1000 metric tons per year)

	Production			Imports			1955 Imports as % of Total
	1946	1950	1955	1946	1950	1955	
Argentina	170	250	250	440	870	1450	85
Brazil	230	820	1160	430	400	400	26
Chile	30	70	340	100	80	90	14
Colombia	0	10	40	120	190	300	88
Mexico	270	390	730	270	370	340	32
Peru	0	0	0	—	—	190	100
Venezuela	—	—	50	340	700	860	93

* Source: ECLA. (All steel-producing countries in Latin America are included.)

B. RELATIVE COSTS OF PRODUCTION OF HYPOTHETICAL PLANTS†

	Capacity	Relative Cost‡	Import Prices§
Argentina	850	92	115
Brazil	716	85	110
Chile	230	82	111
Colombia	250	76	108
Mexico	430	83	108
Peru	150	90	110
Venezuela	300	94	106
U.S.A.	1000	72	—

† Source: ECLA (13), p. 51. Capacity is based on domestic market in 1950.
‡ Based on a 250,000 ton plant in U.S. as 100. The figures do not include profit on the investment.
§ Based on Pittsburgh price plus freight in 1948.

In the analysis of sector 1 above, it was shown that it would be efficient to proceed from A to B to D as demand for metal products expands. I now wish to find all possible efficient expansion paths for this set of production functions.

The four alternatives can be expressed as combinations of the supply functions in Table VII, as follows:[34]

[34] The combined cost function for alternative D is shown in the Appendix to be:
$$S = (500 + 2.429\,Y_1) + (1000 + 2.782\,Y_2).$$

Alternative	Sector 1	Sector 2
A	i	i
B	iii	i
C	i	iii
D	iv	iv

The areas in which each alternative is most efficient can be delineated by solving each pair of equations simultaneously to find the boundary at which the two alternatives have equal cost. The results of this analysis are given in Figure 2.

Figure 2 shows that any one of the three sequences from A to D may be the most efficient, depending on the proportions of demand for the two commodities. The possibilities are illustrated by the three expansion paths shown. Path α represents the ratio $Y_1/Y_2 = 3.0$ and gives the sequence A-B-D as in the example in Figure 1. Path β has the ratio 1.0 and leads directly from A to D, while path γ has the ratio $.5$ and leads to A-C-D.

Although this model is much too simplified to permit a direct application of the results, it indicates at least that industrial development may take different paths. To take only Latin American examples, it may be suggested that, roughly speaking, Peru and Venezuela recently have been in area A, Argentina in area B, Chile in area C, and Brazil and Mexico in area D, as indicated by the data in Table VIII on production and imports. All of the countries mentioned have local sources of iron ore, but the scale at which steel production becomes profitable varies with costs of production and imports.[35]

EVALUATION

The main purpose of this analysis has been to develop a model which could measure some of the principal effects of interdependence on investment decisions. In evaluating the results, it is necessary to see first whether the simplifications made in setting up the model change the nature of the conclusions. I will then try to point out some of the theoretical and practical implications of the results achieved.

The Theoretical Formulation

Effect of the simplifying assumptions. The most important simplifications made in the analysis appear to be the following:

(i) *The omission of income effects.* In taking as given the final demands for the commodities studied, I have calculated the saving in factor use resulting from the coordination of investment rather than the increase in income generated. Factor use is measured in investment units, and so the increase in income achievable with the factors saved can be determined by multiplying the total by the marginal productivity of capital

---

[35] Steel production has now been established with government help in all these countries, but the timing may or may not have been optimal.

(.25 in export prices). In example II C, an increase in output of 188 (9.9 per cent of the outside demands) could be produced with the factors saved.

The argument for including additional income effects as part of external economies has not been stated very clearly. If market prices of labor or other resources exceed their opportunity costs, this fact is a source of difference between private and social benefit, but it is not necessarily a result of the interdependence of productive activities. If opportunity costs rather than market prices are used for labor and other resources, the method used here will include this effect in the calculated return to capital.[36]

The income effects which have not been included are those stemming from economies of scale in sectors outside the model. An increase in total demand will lower the average cost of production in each sector where scale economies are significant and will give rise to a real saving for the economy. These effects can be measured only in a model covering the whole economy in which resources rather than demands would be taken as given.

(ii) *Agglomeration effects.* Agglomeration effects derive from the physical propinquity of different types of production. In part they consist of the Marshallian type of external economies—creation of a pool of skilled labor, common services, etc.—which can result from the expansion of one or several industries in one place. In part they are due to a reduction in the physical quantities of certain inputs required—particularly transport and storage. To take account of these factors adequately would require a regional model, but some of them can be included in the prices at which imports are assumed to be a substitute for domestic (or local) production. For example, it is estimated that a metalworking plant in Latin America which relies on imported steel has to keep a stock equal to six to nine months of consumption to allow for longer delivery times, while a plant using local supplies needs only a three-month supply.[37] The cost of carrying the larger stock should be charged to the import activity. (In the present example, an extra six-month supply of steel increases the capital coefficient by .1 and lowers profits in metalworking by 12 per cent.)

(iii) *Partial vs. general equilibrium.* The model used here is a truncated interindustry system in which the exogenous inputs used in the sectors studied were assumed to be available at constant prices. As the total inputs employed in the omitted sectors represent only about 15 per cent of the

[36] This difference may, of course, prevent individual investors from reaching the socially desirable decisions.

[37] One suggestion of the importance of having a local supply of steel is the spurt in metalworking production which has accompanied the establishment of steel production in each Latin American country. (See ECLA (13), pp. 59–67.) It is hard to evaluate this experience, however, because the countries concerned suffer from balance of payments difficulties and imports are periodically restricted.

total factor requirement, the use of a more complete model is not likely to change the calculation of labor and capital requirements significantly. Since I have assumed a given outside demand, the use of labor is changed only to the extent that production in the sectors analyzed is more or less labor-intensive in the aggregate than production in the export sectors for which it substitutes. It has been assumed here that the industrial complex would use less labor and more capital than the primary production for export which it replaces. In a complete model, the accuracy of the initial assumption as to the relative value of labor and capital could be tested in a complete solution, but it cannot be said a priori whether the external economies calculated with equilibrium prices would be greater or smaller.

(iv) *Substitution.* Substitution in production and consumption is omitted from the present model, although substitution in production could be allowed for by using alternative activities with varying input coefficients. Any substitution effects resulting from the price changes produced by investment coordination would add to the total economies achieved.

(v) *Changes over time.* The preceding analysis has concentrated on one future period and ignored the fact that both demands and the expected efficiency of production with new techniques will change over time. In a more complete model, the discounted sum of values and costs in each alternative would have to be compared in order to determine the optimum timing for investment in each. Economies of scale cause plants to be built in advance of the growth of demand,[38] and hence the more complete analysis would lower the break-even point between domestic production and imports in both the individual and coordinated cases. It would probably be lowered more in the coordinated case, particularly if coordination justifies the use of a lower discount rate.

A second dynamic phenomenon, the fact that the efficiency of new plants which must train their labor force may be expected to increase over a considerable period, is usually allowed for in static analysis by assuming "normal" operating conditions at some time in the future. This simplification would not lead to a difference between the individual and coordinated decisions unless different discount rates are used.

Each of these simplifying assumptions is thus seen to be either neutral or to have the effect of understating the magnitude of the external economies resulting from coordination. Of the factors mentioned, agglomeration effects are probably the most important, as well as the hardest to measure. The other four could be included in the present type of model if it were desirable to do so.

Dynamic and static external economies. The analysis of the effects of investment necessarily assumes that a certain amount of net investment

[38] This phenomenon has been investigated in Chenery (16).

takes place in a growing economy. The cases studied have traced the difference between the response of individual investors to various factors that might make investment profitable—innovation, a change in relative factor prices, unused resources, or the growth of demand—and the optimal response of the whole economy. Since these differences are due mainly to the fact that present prices do not provide accurate guides to the optimal allocation of investment resources, it seems appropriate to call them dynamic external economies. If the further adjustments envisioned by static equilibrium theory take place, some (but not all) of these differences will disappear.

In the examples of case I, the external economies resulting from innovation or from a fall in the price of one of the inputs are purely dynamic phenomena. If there is no further increase in demand, individual investors will eventually arrive at the same result as coordinated investment, since it is assumed that they are not barred by indivisibilities, ignorance, or other market imperfections. This does not mean that the economies of coordination are illusory even in this case, however. If a certain amount of investment is being made each year, the increase in output will be higher with coordination than without it, and the rate of growth will be greater.[39] The adjustment to a condition of static equilibrium may therefore never be made.

In the remaining example of case I, in which coordinated investment is profitable because of unused resources, the elimination of growth does not produce any tendency for individual investors to arrive at the same result as coordination because the reason for the existence of unused resources is the absence of complementary investment in several interrelated sectors. Neither is there any tendency for the difference to be eliminated in the examples of case II, where there are economies of scale.

The difference between the effects of the initial assumptions of growth (increasing factor supplies) and stationary equilibrium (given factor supplies) is shown in Fleming's criticism (7) of the use made of external economies by Rosenstein-Rodan and Nurkse. On static equilibrium assumptions, potential external economies from a given investment are largely offset by rising factor costs. When there is positive net investment and a growing labor force, the question is one of alternative uses of these additional factors, and there is no a priori assumption that a coordinated program which realizes external economies will utilize more of any factor than the alternative investments that would take place without coordination. In fact, it is quite possible that coordination will use less of both capital and labor to obtain the same result as uncoordinated investment.

---

[39] This case is studied in the context of a programming model for the whole economy in Chenery (17), where a difference in growth rates of 10 to 20 per cent is suggested by the difference in marginal productivity of investment.

Although I have been analyzing an essentially dynamic phenomenon, the method used has been that of comparative statics—comparing the results of alternative behavioral assumptions at a given moment in the future. The method is adequate for the assumption of perfect coordination, and also for the case where there is no tendency to depart from the existing pattern of production and prices, since in both cases the expectations of investors are fulfilled. An explicitly dynamic model would be needed to trace out intermediate cases when the expectations of investors are not fulfilled. I am, therefore, not able to estimate the extent to which uncoordinated investment falls short of the ideal, except in the case where it leads to a perpetuation of the existing sources of supply. All of my comparisons (except example I A) were made with this limiting case of an unchanging production pattern.

Importance of External Economies

If my assumptions as to the economies of scale in the principal sectors are at all realistic, it can be concluded from the analysis (p. 101) that the economies of coordination are likely to be substantial in the case studied; furthermore, the external economies may be significantly greater if account is taken of the factors omitted from the analysis. I can only speculate as to the probable importance of external economies in other parts of the economy. Irrigation, for example, is similar to the steel-metalworking case in several respects: the existence of large economies of scale in the supply of inputs (dam building, etc.), the significance of the cost of the commodity produced (water) to agricultural processes using it, and the existence of immobile resources (dam sites, arid land) without alternative uses.

Other overhead facilities—transportation, power—resemble the steel mill in having large economies of scale, although the cost of their product is usually a smaller fraction of the cost of production of users. The most distinguishing feature of overhead facilities, however, is that their services must be supplied locally, and imports do not provide an alternative source. The case for planned investment in such facilities is, therefore, particularly strong, but the variety of uses which they can serve may make it less important to influence the decisions of individual investors in using industries.

Among manufacturing industries, the example studied is perhaps the most important case. Interrelated chemical process industries, such as petroleum refining and petrochemicals, may provide examples in which the economies of coordination are comparable, particularly when the intermediate products are not readily salable.

One may perhaps conclude from this kind of observation that dynamic external economies are sufficiently important to affect the optimal pattern of development throughout the transitional period from a primary-producing economy to one with well-developed overhead facilities and diversified industry. The effect of recognizing external economies is to make it more desirable to undertake interrelated activities together on an adquate scale than to increase production on all fronts simultaneously.

The existence of dynamic external economies has sometimes been used as an argument for the necessity of a large spurt in investment to get a process of cumulative growth under way. In a closed economy with economies of scale this might be true, but when a large proportion of manufactured goods is imported, emphasis can be placed first on one group of investments and then on another. In any case, it is doubtful that democratic governments have much leeway in picking the level of investment, and the more realistic problem is to make the best use of what is available.

Implications for Development Policy

The most important policy question raised by the preceding analysis is the extent to which the government has to intervene in order to secure the benefits of coordination. This is a very large subject, on which I have only a few scattered comments to offer. I will take up three types of mechanism for coordination: (i) integration under private control; (ii) the Lange-Lerner system of centrally administered prices; and (iii) direct control of investment.

Private integration. The main form of private coordination is the integration of several investments under a single ownership or control. It is likely to take place where the external economies are substantial and the sectors involved are not too numerous. The exploitation of natural resources provides a common example; mining, specialized transport, and primary processing are often developed together in order to produce a salable commodity when the domestic processing industry does not already exist.

From the public point of view, the drawback to private coordination is the large amount of capital required for an integrated investment, which is often not available to a single firm in an underdeveloped country, and which, if made, leads to a monopolistic position because of the difficulties of entry. These arguments do not apply so strongly to foreign investment for export, where such integration is very common.

With private integration of investment, some of the benefits of coordination are likely to be lost because the capacity of the auxiliary facilities (machine shops, power, transport, etc.) will usually be designed to satisfy the needs of the integrated firm only rather than to serve other potential users. The investment which might be profitable in other sectors, therefore, may not take place.

Private coordination is likely to occur only when it is institutionally feasible to capture a substantial part of the external economies through integration, price discrimination, or otherwise. In the steel complex, the integration of the sectors supplying the steel mill is quite common in under-developed countries (although limited in the U.S. by the antitrust laws), but the integration of steel production and metalworking is less common because of the diversity of products; it is also less desirable socially because the monopoly problem would be made much worse.

Indirect coordination through administered prices. The discussion of the Lange-Lerner system of administratively controlled prices and decentralized production decisions has been concerned with the ability of such a system to maintain an efficient level of production in each industry.[40] Here the question is whether or not a correct calculation of future equilibrium prices would lead individual investors to the optimal investment decisions.

In my case I, with constant returns to scale, the shadow prices of the optimal solution would lead to the right choice of investments, but not necessarily to the right magnitudes.[41] In order to determine the proper prices, the government would also have to calculate the corresponding quantities, however, and publication of these estimates might furnish adequate guides to the probable demand for various products. This is one of the main functions of a development program. The actual path by which the economy would move from its initial position to a future equilibrium would have to be explored in a dynamic model, but it would appear that, where economies of scale are not too great, prices could serve as the main instrument of coordination, unless the lags in private responses in critical sectors were too long. (The administrative problems raised by this procedure are serious but will not be explored here.)

Direct coordination of investment. Although marginal cost pricing (combined with a subsidy or other method of covering total cost) leads to the optimum scale of use of an existing capital good when there are economies of scale—as in the classical railroad examples—it is not adequate to produce the optimum amount of investment in new facilities. To secure the optimal choice of investments in the examples of case II, the total cost of various alternatives must be compared. As in the short-run analysis, the marginal conditions determine the optimal scale of output, but the total cost calculation determines whether the investment is desirable at all.[42]

The policy implication of this result is that the magnitude of the initial investment as well as the price of output may have to be controlled in order

[40] The argument and the exceptions to it are summarized in Bator (9).

[41] See Dorfman, Samuelson, and Solow (10), pp. 61–63.

[42] The situation is no better at the level of mathematical programming, where no systematic procedure exists for distinguishing a local maximum from the optimum solution other than the comparison of all possibilities. See Arrow (18).

to secure all the external economies.[43] If the optimum plant could be built by successive expansions, there would be less argument for determining the optimum scale in advance, but in the range of output where economies of scale are most important—whether in dam construction, power plants, or steel mills—this is unlikely to be the case.

Given, then, that some control of the magnitude of investment may be needed, it may be possible to limit it to a few key sectors in an industrial complex. In my example, the construction of the optimum size steel mill, power plant, and transport facilities would make profitable to private investors the optimal investment in coal, ore production, and metalworking. Of course, if any of these products is monopolized, the price will be higher and the quantity of output lower than the optimum. It is particularly important to prevent monopoly pricing of inputs to other industries because, unless the effects of decreasing costs are externalized, the investment in other sectors may not take place.

The sectors in which correct initial investments are critical to securing the optimal results are those having the most significant economies of scale and those for which imports do not provide a substitute. These properties are combined in most overhead facilities, and the case for government ownership or control has long been recognized. As between steel and metalworking in the present example, establishment of either one might make the other profitable, but the greater economy of scale[44] and monopoly position of steel argue for its selection.

The preceding discussion should not be taken as an endorsement of indiscriminate building of steel mills or other basic industries through government intervention. What has been shown is that the benefits to the economy of such investments may be understated by their expected profitability to an individual investor, and that coordinated planning may tip the balance in their favor. In the absence of any measure of the quantitative significance of external economies, however, the benefits of such investments may easily be overestimated by the governments of underdeveloped countries. The main purpose of this paper has been to present a framework for objective comparison of the alternatives. Given elastic demand and supply and a somewhat lower capital coefficient in the export sector of the example used here, the rational policy would be to increase exports notwithstanding the existence of unused mineral resources and potential external economies.

[43] The question of the optimal scale of output and the feasibility of various forms of marginal-cost pricing are discussed for the case of irrigation by Margolis (19).

[44] The economy of scale in some sectors of metalworking (e.g., automobile production) may be equally great and justify government action.

APPENDIX

THE CALCULATION OF PRICES AND TOTAL COSTS

Case I: No Economies of Scale

Two types of prices are used in the solutions given in Table III. *Present prices* are those to which the individual investor responds in deciding whether to invest. *Future prices* are those which satisfy the conditions of marginal cost pricing given by equation 11 after a given set of investments has been made. Present prices are also assumed to satisfy equation 11 for the sectors included in the model, although the exogenous inputs may or may not have prices representing their opportunity costs. Future prices are therefore equal to present prices if the source of supply is unchanged, as in example B, line (5).

The determination of the optimum pattern of investment with coordination of all sectors is (in case I) a problem in linear programming. It can be stated as follows: to minimize total cost of production, as measured by the prices of the exogenous inputs, subject to the restrictions in equations 1–8 of Table I. The dual variables (u_j) or shadow prices of this solution are identical with the future prices and may be defined as:[45]

$$\begin{array}{c}(i \neq j)\\ u_j = \sum_i a_{ij} u_i + c_j \qquad (j = 1 \ldots 7)\end{array} \qquad (13)$$

where c_j is the cost of the exogenous inputs (8–10) in each activity.

The solution to equation 13 can be determined in a number of ways, including the iterative procedure suggested above and the use of the inverse of the basis. The second method is given by the following equation:

$$u_j = \sum_i r_{ij} c_i \qquad (14)$$

where r_{ij} is the element in row i and column j of the inverse matrix. For the optimum solution, in which all commodities are domestically produced, the first two columns in the inverse and the calculation of the corresponding shadow prices are shown in Table IX.

As indicated earlier, the total cost of supplying the exogenous demand is given by:

$$S = u_1 Y_1 + u_2 Y_2. \qquad (15)$$

Case II: Economies of Scale

With decreasing average costs, the dual variables can still be defined by equation 13 with c_j taken as marginal cost, since I have assumed con-

[45] See Dorfman, Samuelson, and Solow (10), Chapter 7. The equation is the same as eq. 1 with c_j substituted for the cost of exogenous imports, since $a_{jj} = 1.0$ by assumption.

TABLE IX
Calculation of Dual Variables in Cases I and II

	Columns in Inverse Matrix		Case I			Case II		
Rows			Sector 1	Sector 2		Sector 1	Sector 2	
(i)	r_{i1}	r_{i2}	c_i	$c_i r_{i1}$	$c_i r_{i2}$	c_i	$c_i r_{i1}$	$c_i r_{i2}$
1	1.000	0	2.26	2.260	0	1.76	1.760	0
2	.222	1.007	3.27	.726	3.293	2.27	.504	2.286
3	.018	.080	1.25	.022	.100	1.10	.020	.088
4	.016	.025	3.99	.062	.101	2.74	.043	.069
5	.028	.113	1.54	.043	.174	1.34	.038	.151
6	.029	.083	4.06	.117	.337	2.26	.065	.188
Dual variables (u_j)			—	3.231	4.005	—	2.429	2.782

stant marginal cost over the relevant range of output. The total cost of production must include all constant terms in the input functions (12) of Table V, however. The equation for total cost of supply then becomes:

$$S = \Sigma_i \bar{f}_i + u_1 Y_1 + u_2 Y_2 \qquad (16)$$

where the constant terms $\bar{f}_i$ apply to all sectors supplied from domestic production. The values of u_1 and u_2 for case II are also computed in Table IX. Substituting them in equation 16 gives the total cost with coordination as

$$S = 1500 + 2.429\, Y_1 + 2.782\, Y_2. \qquad (16a)$$

To derive the equations in Table VII above, I assume the outside demands in one sector to be constant and determine the cost of supplying various levels of demand in the other sector. The overhead costs are allocated by holding the cost of supplying the other (fixed) demand constant at the cost of imports, which is subtracted from the total supply cost. The equations in Table VII can therefore be derived from equations 16 as follows:

$$S_1 = S - 4.2\, Y_2, \qquad S_2 = S - 3.26\, Y_1. \qquad (17)$$

The calculation of the dual variables u_j from equation 13 for each assumption is shown in Table X.

Assumptions

(i) *Imports.* The supply functions are merely the cost of imports.

(ii) *Uncoordinated investment.* The values u_i are taken from Table III, line 4; c_j is the marginal direct cost from Table V.

(iii) *Coordination of sectors 3–6.* The u_i are those of the coordinated solution for sectors 3–6 and the same as (ii) for sector 2.

TABLE X

CALCULATION OF DUAL VARIABLES FOR EQUATION 17*

Inputs	Sector 1 Input Cost			Sector 2 Input Cost	
	Case (ii)	(iii)	(iv)	Case (ii)	(iii) + (iv)
2	.92	.92	.61	—	—
3–6	.10	.06	.06	.95	.51
7	.51	.51	.51	.27	.27
c_j	1.25	1.25	1.25	2.00	2.00
u_j	2.78	2.74	2.43	3.22	2.78

* Each entry is the corresponding $(a_{ij}u_i)$ from equation 13.

(iv) *Coordination of all sectors.* The values of u_j for each sector are those computed in Table IX. In this case, where there is domestic production in both sectors 1 and 2, equations 17 become:

$$S_1 = S - 4.2 \ Y_2 = 1500 + 2.429 \ Y_1 - 1.428 \ Y_2,$$
$$S_2 = S - 3.26 \ Y_1 = 1500 + 2.782 \ Y_2 - .831 \ Y_1. \tag{17a}$$

(These equations apply only over the range for which imports are the economical alternative without coordination and in which domestic production in the other sector would be profitable with coordination.)

References

1. P. N. Rosenstein-Rodan, "Problems of Industrialization in Eastern and South-Eastern Europe," *Economic Journal*, June–September, 1943.

2. R. Nurkse, Problems of Capital Formation in Underdeveloped Countries. Blackwell, Oxford, 1953.

3. W. A. Lewis, "Economic Development with Unlimited Supplies of Labor," *Manchester School*, May 1954.

4. H. W. Singer, "Economic Progress in Underdeveloped Countries," *Social Research*, March 1949.

5. G. Myrdal, Economic Theory and Underdeveloped Regions. Duckworth, London, 1957.

6. T. Scitovsky, "Two Concepts of External Economies," *Journal of Political Economy*, April 1954.

7. M. Fleming, "External Economies and the Doctrine of Balanced Growth," *Economic Journal*, June 1955.

8. H. W. Arndt, "External Economies in Economic Growth," *Economic Record*, November 1955.

9. F. Bator, "The Anatomy of Market Failure," *Quarterly Journal of Economics*, August 1958.

10. R. Dorfman, P. A. Samuelson, and R. M. Solow, Linear Programming and Economic Analysis. McGraw-Hill, New York, 1958.

11. H. B. Chenery and T. Watanabe, "International Comparisons of the Structure of Production," *Econometrica*, January 1959.

12. W. D. Evans, "Input-Output Computations," in T. Barna (ed.), The Structural Interdependence of the Economy. Wiley, New York, 1956.

13. United Nations, Economic Commission for Latin America, A Study of the Iron and Steel Industry in Latin America, II. G.3, Vol. 1, 1954.

14. H. E. Wessel, "New Graph Correlates Operating Labor Data for Chemical Processes," and C. H. Chilton, " 'Six-Tenths Factor' Applies to Complete Plant Costs," in Data and Methods of Cost Estimation, a collection of reprints from Chemical Engineering, 1953, 1952.

15. H. B. Chenery, "The Application of Investment Criteria," Quarterly Journal of Economics, February 1953.

16. H. B. Chenery, "Overcapacity and the Acceleration Principle," Econometrica, January 1952.

17. II. B. Chenery, "The Role of Industrialization in Development Programs," American Economic Association Proceedings, May 1955.

18. K. J. Arrow, "Decentralization and Computation in Resource Allocation," to appear in R. W. Pfouts (ed.), Economic Essays in Honor of Harold Hotelling (to be published).

19. J. Margolis, "Welfare Criteria, Pricing and Decentralization of a Public Service," Quarterly Journal of Economics, August 1957.

The Theory of Tax Incidence Applied to the Gains of Labor Unions

GEORGE W. HILTON

Several writers have recently considered the problem of the incidence of the gains of a labor union (1, 2, 3). This is clearly a matter of some interest, both for analytical study of the labor market and for discussion of public policy toward collective bargaining. Since this is a problem analogous to the incidence of a tax, it may be useful to set forth explicitly the elementary theory of tax incidence as applied to the gains of labor unions.[1] This theory also yields incidental implications concerning trade union behavior which are quite useful. Finally, it provides a further demonstration of the similarity of the theory of monopoly to the theory of tax incidence (6).

A wage increase secured by a trade union will affect an employer in the same fashion as an excise tax on his payroll. By raising his marginal cost function, it will induce him to reduce his volume of output. If he is competitive and if the wage increase is unique to him, the consequence of his reduction in output on the price of the product will be negligible. If the resources are unspecialized, the effect of his diminution in demand for them will also be negligible. If the industry is at equilibrium, the earnings of entrepreneurs are devoid of profit and equal to the earnings of persons of equal ability elsewhere, adjusted for the nonpecuniary advantages and disadvantages of the various industries, and of self-employment relative to wage-earning. Thus the wage increase will reduce the entrepreneur's earnings below this level in the unionized industry. Since, being competitive, he is confronted with a perfectly elastic demand function for his product and perfectly elastic supply functions for his productive factors, he will find that his earnings are no longer sufficient to attract him to the industry, and, unless he can establish his plant in some area where he can escape the union, he will leave the industry. From this it follows that a

---

[1] This approach to the problem is suggested by Henry C. Simons (4) and H. Gregg Lewis (5).

union has little to gain in organizing a single employer in an industry where the product is undifferentiated and produced by a large number of firms, and where the resources are unspecialized. An adverse cost differential will simply drive him out of business. In industries of this general description—the clothing trades, job printing, trucking, and the building trades—there has been a tendency for multi-employer collective bargaining.

If the wage increase affects enough of the industry so that the reduction in output is significant in the market for the product and the reduction of demand in the market for the resources, then the wage increase can be shifted forward to the consumers of the product or backward to the suppliers of the resources, depending on the relative elasticities of demand for the product and supply of the resources. In an industry in which the resources were entirely unspecialized, the increase could not, in the long run, be passed on to the suppliers of the resources(7) but would necessarily be shifted forward to the consumers of the product. At the opposite extreme, in a portion of an industry confronted by infinitely elastic demand conditions, but possessing specialized resources, the incidence of the wage increase will be entirely upon the economic rents of the specialized resources. For example, a wage increase affecting all of the coal mines in a single limited area selling in a national market would be borne by the owners of the coal-bearing land. If any of the cooperant resources is earning a monopoly gain, the incidence of the wage increase will fall on it in the same fashion as on an economic rent.

The longer the time period one considers, the less specialized an industry's resources are likely to be, and the greater are the opportunities for making substitution in the production function. Capital items which in the short run are complements to labor of a given sort, and inelastic in supply to the industry, in the long run, when they are scrapped and the proceeds of the depreciation account used for replacing them, will be both more elastic in supply to the industry and capable of serving as substitutes rather than complements for the labor service. In addition, the structure of relative costs, which a successful trade union will alter, is a principal determinant of the direction of technological change (8). The common belief that the relative allocation of factors of production is given by technological complementarity, determined by exogenous technological drift, is essentially a short-run view. If it is accurate at all to say that the elasticity of substitution with respect to the wage rate is zero, it is accurate only for a short time period, but, in any longer period, empirical verification of the effects of a change in wage rates becomes increasingly difficult, if not, at the present state of our analytical devices, impossible. Consequences of changes in wage rates become inextricably merged with consequences of other changes in demand- and supply-conditions. Similarly, the longer the time period one considers, the greater will be the substitutes available for the product of the industry in question, and thus the greater will be the elasticity of demand for it. That is to say, success of a union will stimulate not only changes in technology in its own industry, but substitution of other products in consumption for its own.[2] In the long run, therefore, opportunity for forward-shifting of the increase will decline in much the same fashion as the opportunity for shifting backward to the cooperant resources.

If the employer is a monopolist or a monopsonist, not all of the wage increase will be shifted in this fashion. His monopoly gain is in the nature of an economic rent, since he would be attracted to the industry at some lower rate of remuneration than he is currently receiving. Thus a union may secure part of its gain at the expense of monopoly profits of an employer in the same fashion as it might from the economic rents of the cooperant resources. Similarly, an employer who is a monopsonist with respect to his labor force will, himself, bear part of the gains secured by the union. As several writers have pointed out, under conditions of monopsony, a union by securing its initial—but only its initial—contract, can increase both the volume of employment of its members and their wage rate (9, 10). In this instance, the advance is secured out of the monopsony gain of the employer, and there is an incidental welfare gain to society. Under conditions of monopsony, the employer pays the wage required to attract the number of employees who will equate the marginal factor cost of hiring with the values of their marginal products. Imposing a trade union wage contract under conditions of monopsony, if it raises the volume of employment, also raises the marginal products of the employees newly attracted to the employer. The sacrifice of a smaller marginal product in the industries, or with the employers the workers have left in order to gain a higher marginal product in the formerly monopsonized industry, yields an increase in social output.

Conversely, however, organization of a union in a competitive labor market yields a welfare loss to society. If the union, by increasing wage rates, causes a displacement of laborers to other occupations or other employers, the increase in labor supply will tend to reduce the wages and, thus, the marginal products of laborers in the other occupations.[3] Society in this fashion suffers a welfare loss, since it would have been better off had the transfers not taken place. Alternatively, it would be better off if the transfers were reversed: each time a laborer was taken from an unorgan-

[2] One of the best examples of this principle is found in Chapter XV of Mark Twain's *Life on the Mississippi*, "The Pilot's Monopoly." The steamboat pilots took advantage of a technological complementarity (two pilots to a steamboat) and of the extreme difficulty of learning the occupation to operate a highly successful union. In the process, they increased the costs of steamboat transportation, and, Twain believed, contributed to the decline of the industry relative to the railroad.

[3] Machlup places great emphasis on this form of incidence of gains of a union (3).

ized position at a lower wage and placed in a position at a higher rate in an industry or with an employer being freed from organization, society would give up a smaller marginal product in order to achieve a larger one until equality was reached. Society suffers two further losses from trade union activity: if the union generates an excess supply of labor service at its standard rate, there is a loss involved in the unemployment of resources; strikes, slowdowns, lockouts, and other industrial disputes entail a loss of output.

In summation, if a trade union is successful in raising its members' wages, the gain will be derived from the consumers of the final product in inverse proportion to their elasticity of demand for it, from the suppliers of the cooperant resources in inverse proportion to their elasticity of supply to the industry, and from the entrepreneurs in the industry if they are securing a gain from a monopoly or monopsony position. In addition, except in the situation where the union is dealing with a monopsonist, society as a whole bears part of the incidence of the gain through the welfare loss involved in the less-favorable allocation of resources, and in whatever idleness is created.

This analysis of the welfare loss involved in union activity seems to have a considerable measure of agreement, at least on an implicit level. Most opponents of trade unionism argue by analogy to the theory of monopoly [e.g., Simons (4)], and most academic proponents believe that monopsony is widespread, either because of collusive arrangements or, more frequently, because of imperfect knowledge and mobility [notably the Webbs (11)]. Academic debate on trade unionism demonstrates not so much a divergence in values as a difference in factual interpretation.

The foregoing conceptual scheme is useful for several purposes. First, it helps provide an explanation of the relative strength of unions. A union should be successful in direct proportion to the opportunities for shifting its gains forward or backward. Unions in industries that are characterized by inelastic demand conditions for their final products, or monopoly positions of employers, or inelastic supply conditions of cooperant resources ought to be relatively successful. This is consistent with Alfred Marshall's joint demand analysis. Marshall argued that the elasticity of demand for a factor of production varied directly with the availability of substitutes for the factor in the production function, the elasticity of demand for the final product, the percentage of total cost represented by the expenditure on the factor in question, and the elasticity of supply of the cooperant factors (12). It is a commonplace observation that unions tend to be most successful when confronted with inelastic demands for their members' services. Indeed, if the demand for their members' services is elastic, a wage increase secured by the union will reduce the aggregate expenditure on their wages rather than increase it. Since the elasticity of demand for the services of the members of a union tends to increase over time, it follows that a union ought to be more successful in the short run than in the long. This presumption is consistent with Paul H. Douglas' conclusion that the principal impact of unionization on wages in the period 1890 to 1926 was in the early years of organization, and that, in the mature stages of collective bargaining, organized workers showed no more rapid increases in wages than unorganized (13).

Second, this framework is useful in helping to explain certain characteristic activities of labor unions. For example, cartels among employers, which several unions have endeavored to establish, are an effort to create a monopoly gain against which the incidence of a wage increase may fall. As is well known, the United Mine Workers advocated a compulsory cartel of bituminous coal mines beginning about 1928, secured it under the National Industrial Recovery Act of 1933, and perpetuated it under the Guffey Acts of 1935 and 1937 (14). The United Textile Workers of America with the Ellenbogen Bill of 1935 (15) endeavored to establish a similar cartel in the cotton textile industry, but were unsuccessful. The Amalgamated Clothing Workers established a cartel in the men's clothing industry in 1939 (16). Most unions of journeymen barbers endeavor to maintain cartels of master barbers, often with the help of local governments. Union participation in cartels of contractors is familiar in the building trades. Efforts to put down products rival to those of the union's industry is an effort to reduce the elasticity of demand for the final product in order to facilitate shifting of wage increases to consumers (17). Advocacy of tariff protection for the product of the union's industry serves the same purpose (17). Prohibition of the export of wool, that favorite policy of weavers' organizations in mercantilist times, was an effort to reduce the elasticity of supply of the most important cooperant resource. Efforts to preserve narrow areas of jurisdiction may be an effort to take advantage of inelasticity in supply of a cooperant resource, as well as a means of reducing the percentage of total expenditure on the wages of members of the union. For example, the unwillingness of the Brotherhood of Locomotive Engineers to amalgamate with the Brotherhood of Locomotive Firemen and Enginemen is rational, since in the present arrangement entry into the BLE is restricted mainly by the long years of acquiring seniority in the BLF&E. Entry into the BLF&E is relatively free. Under this circumstance, it should be true that the BLE secures the monopoly gain involved in organization of engine service, and that members of the BLF&E receive approximately competitive earnings. In addition, the arrangement serves to shift the burden of idleness, which is significant in an industry characterized by unstable demand conditions, to the members of the BLF&E (18).

H. Gregg Lewis has demonstrated that, under certain circumstances, a union may find it wise to take its gain in the form of a tax other than an excise on the wage bill. If a union is being troubled by substitution of capital for the services of its members, an ordinary wage increase will add to the employers' incentive to make the substitution. Taking the gain in the form of a tax on output will be neutral with respect to the combination of the factors [(5), p. 284]. Use of the proceeds for maintenance of a welfare fund is entirely consistent, since a union suffering adverse technological change is particularly likely to be troubled with excess supply of its members' services. One method of dealing with this problem consists of supporting some of them in idleness. A welfare fund does this both by supporting members beyond a given age through superannuation benefits and by supporting members who are temporarily unemployed through unemployment compensation payments. Even a union that is not chronically troubled with excess supply is likely to encounter instability in demand for the members' services over time. A welfare fund can also be used for medical benefits in dangerous trades. The principal example of a welfare fund financed in this fashion is furnished by the United Mine Workers, a union particularly characterized by replacement of the members by capital equipment. The practice is quite ancient, however, since a levy by weight of coal was used by the keelmen of the Tyne and Wear to finance their hospital and benevolent fund in the eighteenth century. The situation is quite a close parallel to the United Mine Workers, since the keelmen's manual process of loading sailing vessels with coal was being replaced by mechanical loading from overhead spouts (19). As W. H. Hutt has pointed out, payments from union funds of this sort are similar to arrangements in a cartel in which some of the members' plants are maintained in idleness and supported out of the monopoly gain of the operating members (20). The idle members of the cartel are supported by the operating members as *quid pro quo* for remaining in the cartel and refraining from undercutting the cartel's price list. In the same fashion, a system of superannuation and unemployment benefits is an aid in maintaining the union intact under conditions of excess supply of the members' services.

The common practice of requiring time-and-a-half for overtime of union members serves a similar purpose. It is in the nature of a tax applied by a union to give employers an incentive to distribute employment widely over the membership.[4] This is a particularly simple method of rationing idleness among the members of a union.

Third, the analogy to the incidence of a tax is useful in laying the basis for a judgment whether trade unionism is in total an equalitarian or inequalitarian force in the economy. This is clearly a question of first importance, since the American policy of requiring collective bargaining of employers is largely based on a belief that the consequences are equalitarian. Unfortunately, the evidence available at present is inadequate for a judgment on this matter, since the literature on the effect of trade union-

---

[4] For a discussion of this and other purposes of this practice, see Lewis, "Hours of Work and Hours of Leisure" (21).

ism on the structure of wages and the distribution of income cannot be described as conclusive. Paul H. Douglas initiated the modern enquiry on this point with his observation, previously mentioned (13) that between 1890 and 1926 the impact of unionization was mainly in the early years of organization. Arthur Ross, using the same data, argued that trade unionism had been a decided source of advantage and a significant influence on relative earnings in the same period (22). Other economists who have dealt with this general problem have, in the main, reached conclusions similar to Douglas'. Harold M. Levinson, studying the period 1914–47, found a substantial shift from entrepreneurial income to employee compensation in the decade 1919–29, but found no indication that union activity was responsible for it. For the years 1933 to 1947, Levinson (23) found a shift of income of 4.2 per cent to employee compensation, mainly at the expense of rent and interest, but again he was unable to attribute it unambiguously to trade unionism. Between 1920 and 1933 he found a significant positive correlation between strength of unionism and trend of money wages, but neither between 1914 and 1920 nor between 1933 and 1947. Milton Friedman, writing in 1950, estimated that probably only about 10 per cent of the labor force received wages that had been increased by as much as 15 per cent by union pressure (2). He concluded that the majority of wage increases secured by unions would have occurred in their absence. He based his argument, as Stanley Jevons had done, on the simultaneous rise in income of domestic servants and other unorganized laborers (24). Stephen Sobotka believed that the most successful unions in the building trades had probably increased wages of their members in a range from 10 to 20 per cent (25). Albert Rees concluded that wage increases secured by the United Steelworkers between 1945 and 1948 were probably less than would have been achieved in absence of organization (26). Paul Sultan was unable to find that unions had altered the ratio of wages to all income distributed in heavily organized industries (27). Friedman and Kuznets in their study of incomes in independent professional practice estimated that the American Medical Association had increased the earnings of physicians by only 15 to 20 per cent in spite of exceptionally favorable circumstances for restrictions (28).

From this body of literature, one cannot make a definitive judgment, but the most likely conclusion is that members of the craft unions in the building trades, railroading, printing, entertainment, and certain other occupations have probably achieved increases in wages of less than 20 per cent above what they would have received in absence of their unions. If a union adopts no policies that give evidence of excess supply of labor at the union wage rate—excessive dues and entry fees, apprenticeship requirements, discrimination on the basis of race, sex, or other arbitrary condition, devices for rationing idleness, impediments to technological change, and the like—and if there is no chronic difficulty in securing employment in its industry, there should be a *prima facie* presumption that the wage rates it has achieved are not far from a market-equating level.[5] Since few of the modern industrial unions behave in this fashion, it seems unlikely that they have substantial redistributive effects.[6]

It is useful, however, to consider the problem whether there is any a priori reason to believe that the redistributive effects of the gains of trade unions would be equalitarian. If one is to argue that collective bargaining is, in general, an equalitarian force, one must demonstrate that the opportunities for shifting the incidence of the gains of the union are superior for laborers in low income brackets than in high, and that the incidence falls on persons in higher income brackets than the union members who are receiving the benefits. The first of these propositions is particularly unlikely. Poverty in America is mainly a problem of agriculture. The lowest income groups among employed persons are agricultural laborers, particularly in the South. Among hired agricultural laborers, the elasticity of demand for labor by a single employer is so high, and the difficulty of dealing jointly with any large number of farmers so great that relatively little effort has been made to organize agricultural employees. A very large number of the low-income persons in agriculture are self-

[5] If these devices are efforts to deal with an excess supply of laborers at the union rate, rather than the source of union power (cf. Friedman (2), p. 213; Lewis (5), p. 283; Machlup (3), p. 430), the question arises whether there is a welfare loss in outlawing them. The Taft-Hartley Act prohibits the most lurid of these practices, along with the closed shop. If the sources of union power are of other origin, prohibiting restrictions on entry into the union may simply drive the union to greater use of devices for rationing idleness among its members, which is likely to entail greater welfare losses than the malallocation of resources stemming from the exclusion. The problem is analogous to that of the relative welfare losses from a monopoly and a cartel. A monopoly will produce its output at a higher price and at a lower rate than a cartel, but a cartel that is unable to restrict entry will encounter the problem of "excess capacity" and find it necessary to make arrangements of the sort already mentioned for support of part of the industry in idleness. Thus a successful union that is prohibited from restricting entry may entail greater welfare losses than one that is closed. Cf. Hutt (20); Patinkin (29); Simons (30), pp. 54–56.

[6] Similarly, the evidence under discussion implies that the macro-economic consequences of American collective bargaining are not very great. In particular, the argument that the upward pressure of unions on wages is a significant force for inflation, apart from expansionary monetary and fiscal policies, is inconsistent with Rees' conclusion that the rise in wages in highly-organized industries was impeded by unionization in the inflation of the late 1940's (26). This argument also fails to explain why collective bargaining should have produced inflation at some times (say, 1957), but not at others (say, 1951–55), since the power, goals, and tactics of unions do not change markedly. Neither the movement of union wage rates relative to all others, nor the political effectiveness of unions, nor the change in total union membership indicates that collective bargaining is becoming increasingly significant in America. Indeed, a stronger case can probably be made on these grounds that it is becoming less significant.

employed and, therefore, exempt by definition from benefit by trade union-ism.[7] Domestic servants present virtually the same barriers to organization as agricultural employees. It is widely recognized that, among industrial workers, the most poorly paid positions tend to be those with the least discretion, and thus those for which capital may most easily be substituted. The greater success of the Brotherhood of Locomotive Engineers, in comparison to that of the Brotherhood of Maintenance of Way Employees is in part a reflection of the percentage of total cost of operating a railroad attributed to each, but to a great extent it is a result of the greater ease of substituting capital for the maintenance-of-way laborers. The Diesel-electric locomotive was to some extent a substitute for the services of engineers, since it permitted the railroads to operate longer and faster freight trains at less frequent intervals. It also reduced the skill demanded for actual control of the locomotives, but it did nothing to eliminate the discretion of engineers in train speeds, and it did not change the complementarity of one engineer to one train. Maintenance-of-way employees exercise so little discretion in their work that they are highly susceptible to replacement by machinery. In the course of 27 years, absolute employment in maintenance of way has been reduced by more than half, and the proportion of maintenance-of-way employees to all railroad personnel has fallen from about a fourth to a sixth (31). Short-run success of a union in raising wages under such circumstances is self-defeating, since it increases the pecuniary incentive of the railroads for replacement. A rational union leadership under these conditions could act only with great circumspection. At the opposite extreme, the great success of physicians in organization reflects, in part, the large degree of discretion involved in their profession.

It is much more difficult to discuss the equity of the incidence of the gains of successful union members. If it is true that the benefits of trade unionism have been concentrated among skilled employees in the build-

[7] The federal government's effort to relieve poverty among farmers by a system of price supports is quite parallel to its labor policy. The minimum wage provision of the Fair Labor Standards Act is the equivalent of an agricultural price support, and the maximum hours provisions of marketing quota. School-attendance laws, child-labor laws, the former GI Bill, the requirement that one retire from the labor force in order to draw one's superannuation benefits under the Social Security system, and other policies to reduce the size of the labor force are in the nature of acreage restrictions. Unemployment compensation is in the nature of a surplus purchase. Immigration restrictions are parallel to tariffs on foreign agricultural commodities, and the Wagner and Taft-Hartley Acts are somewhat stronger counterparts of the Capper-Volstead Act, which exempted agricultural marketing cooperatives from the antitrust laws. The consequences on employment and resource allocation of minimum wage legislation and collective bargaining pointed out by Stigler (10) and Simons (4) are simply the analogues of the observed consequences of American agricultural policy. This analogy does not, of course, imply that all features of American labor policy are undesirable.

ing trades, railroading, printing, and other traditional areas of the old-line craft unions, it is unlikely that the incidence of the benefits is equalitarian, since none of these is a craft characterized by poverty relative to the labor force as a whole. Since we have no adequate quantification of monopoly gain in the economy, we have no method of estimating the extent of incidence of union gain at the expense of monopoly profit. Harold Levinson's findings that there was no significant reduction in profits as a share of aggregate income in unionized industries between 1929 and 1952, in spite of a fivefold rise in unionization (32), indicates that the magnitude of this sort of incidence is probably limited. Incidence at the expense of monopsony gain is probably even more limited.

Monopsony is mainly a problem in industries in which there are relatively few employers, and in which the employees earn substantial quasi-rents. Under these conditions, employers have a considerable incentive to collude to eliminate the quasi-rents, and can avoid the difficulty of maintaining a collusion of a large number of members. Professional athletics is the principal example of such an industry, and in most countries its entrepreneurs have established collusive arrangements against their employees, usually elaborately implemented and carefully policed.[8] Since, even with the efficient administration and relative freedom from Sherman Act prosecution that American professional baseball has enjoyed, the collusive arrangement has failed to eliminate the quasi-rents of the employees (although it may have reduced them) or to create exceptional earnings for the employers, it is very improbable that less formal collusions create a significant gain for the employers who participate in them. Incidence of the gains of a union on the economic rents of co-operant resources is probably important in the extractive industries, but limited in manufacturing. One is led to conclude that the principal incidence of unions' gains is on consumers of final products, where there is less presumption that the gains are equalitarian than in the case of incidence either on the entrepreneurial share or on property incomes.

On the other hand, political pressure of members within a union frequently results in a narrowing of skill differentials in organized plants [(7), p. 254]. This, however, is merely a part of the secular reduction in skill differentials observed over the labor market as a whole, and it is difficult to separate the consequences of union pressure from the workings

---

[8] Cf. Rottenberg (33). The difficulty of administering a collusion among any large number of employers is perfectly demonstrated by amateur athletics. A collusion among university athletic departments not to pay football players is unquestionably legal and is not subject to the moral objections directed toward most other collusions. It is so much to the interest of any one institution to break out of the collusion that the arrangement shifts from an effort not to pay football players to an effort not to pay football players very much. The national authorities who administer the collusion are essentially engaged in a delaying action against the march of college football players toward the values of their marginal products.

of market forces (34). On the whole, the net contribution of trade unionism in this respect is probably equalitarian.

Collective bargaining has many facets. It may have no substitute as a safeguard for individual employees against arbitrary and discriminatory treatment, although personnel management sets this up as one of its principal goals. The political actions of trade unions may be desirable. Given the minor effect on distribution of income and allocation of resources that unions are thought to have in America, the most important criterion for judging the movement is probably the desirability from the point of view of anticyclical policy of increasing the inflexibility of the wage structure. Neither logic nor the available evidence offers much support for the defense of trade unionism on equalitarian grounds.

Finally, the application of the theory of tax incidence to the behavior of labor unions serves a heuristic purpose. It helps to demonstrate precisely what is involved in a denial of the marginal productivity theory and replacement of it with a theory, as yet undefined, derived inductively from empirical studies of industrial relations [e.g., Ross (22)]. It involves not only denial of the generally-accepted principles of tax incidence, but also denial that wage formation is an integral part of the general process of price determination and resource allocation. The development of the marginal productivity theory of distribution by Wicksteed, John Bates Clark, Marshall, and their contemporaries was, essentially, recognition that a combination of Jevonian utility theory and the principle of diminishing returns demonstrated an identity of wage determination with price formation of other sorts. Thus, when dealing with the incidence of a tax, one could treat shifting to wage incomes or to prices of nonhuman resources in parallel fashion. It was for purposes of analysis such as this, rather than for description of unique situations, that the theory was designed. Denial of the theory is essentially rejection of the validity of such parallels. It involves rejection of both Wicksteed and Marshall, for it requires demonstration that the laws of distribution are uncoordinate, and that *natura facit saltum.*

References

1. Martin Bronfenbrenner, "The Incidence of Collective Bargaining," *American Economic Review*, XLIV (1954), 293–307.

2. Milton Friedman, "Some Comments on the Significance of Labor Unions for Economic Policy," in D. M. Wright (ed.), The Impact of the Union. Harcourt, Brace, New York, 1951, Chap. X, p. 216.

3. Fritz Machlup, The Political Economy of Monopoly. Johns Hopkins Press, Baltimore, 1952, p. 407.

4. Henry C. Simons, "Some Reflections on Syndicalism," in Economic Policy for a Free Society. University of Chicago Press, Chicago, 1948, p. 143.

5. H. Gregg Lewis, "The Labor Monopoly Problem: A Positive Program," *Journal of Political Economy*, LIX (1951), 282–83.

6. Alfred Marshall, Industry and Trade. Macmillan, London, 1919, p. 410.

7. George J. Stigler, The Theory of Price, 2d ed. Macmillan, New York, 1952, p. 257.

8. Yale Brozen, "Determinants of the Direction of Technological Change," *American Economic Review*, XLIII (1953), pp. 288–303.

9. Joan Robinson, The Economics of Imperfect Competition. Macmillan, London, 1933, pp. 292–304.

10. George J. Stigler, "The Economics of Minimum Wage Legislation," *American Economic Review*, XXXVI (1946), 358–65.

11. Sidney and Beatrice Webb, Industrial Democracy. Longmans, Green, London, 1902; especially Part III, Chap. II, pp. 654–702.

12. Alfred Marshall, Principles of Economics, 8th ed. Macmillan, London, 1920, pp. 385–86.

13. Paul H. Douglas, Real Wages in the United States, 1890–1926. Houghton Mifflin, Boston, 1930, p. 564.

14. Waldo E. Fisher and Charles M. James, Minimum Price Fixing in the Bituminous Coal Industry. Princeton University Press, Princeton, 1955, pp. 26 ff.

15. A Bill to Rehabilitate and Stabilize Labor Conditions in the Textile Industry of the United States. 74th Congress, 1st Session, 1935, H.R. 9072.

16. Robert J. Myers and Joseph W. Bloch, "Men's Clothing," in Harry A. Mills (ed.), How Collective Bargaining Works. Twentieth Century Fund, New York, 1942, Chap. VIII, pp. 436–43.

17. George J. Stigler, The Theory of Price, 1st ed. Macmillan, New York, 1946, pp. 295, 292.

18. George R. Holton and H. Ellsworth Steele, "The Unity Issue Among Railroad Engineers and Firemen," *Industrial and Labor Relations Review*, X (1956), 48–69.

19. T. S. Ashton and Joseph Sykes, The Coal Industry of the Eighteenth Century. Manchester University Press, Manchester, 1929, p. 197.

20. W. H. Hutt, "Participating Idleness in Labour," in The Theory of Idle Resources. Jonathan Cape, London, 1939, Chap. VIII, pp. 114–36.

21. H. Gregg Lewis, "Hours of Work and Hours of Leisure," *Proceedings of the Industrial Relations Research Association*, IX (1956), 196–206.

22. Arthur M. Ross, Trade Union Wage Policy. University of California Press, Berkeley, 1948, Chap. VI.

23. Harold M. Levinson, Unionism, Wage Trends and Income Distribution, 1914–1927. Michigan Business Studies, Vol. X (1951), No. 4.

24. W. Stanley Jevons, "Trade Societies: Their Objects and Policy," in Methods of Social Reform. Macmillan, London, 1883, pp. 116–17.

25. Stephen P. Sobotka, "Union Influence on Wages: The Construction Trades," *Journal of Political Economy*, LXI (1953), 127–43.

26. Albert Rees, "Postwar Wage Determination in the Basic Steel Industry," *American Economic Review*, XLI (1951), 389–404.

27. Paul E. Sultan, "Unionism and Wage-Income Ratios: 1929–51," *Review of Economics and Statistics*, XXXVI (1954), 67–73.

28. Milton Friedman and Simon S. Kuznets, Income from Independent Professional Practice. National Bureau of Economic Research, New York, 1945, p. 137.

29. Don Patinkin, "Multiple Plant Firms Cartels and Imperfect Competition," *Quarterly Journal of Economics*, LXI (1946–47), 173–205.

30. Henry C. Simons, "Economics 201, the Divisional Course in Economics" (mimeo.). University of Chicago Bookstore, Chicago, 1944.

31. William Haber *et al.*, Maintenance of Way Employment on the U.S. Railroads. Brotherhood of Maintenance of Way Employees, Detroit, 1957, p. iii.

32. Harold M. Levinson, "Collective Bargaining and Income Distribution," *American Economic Review*, XLIV (1954), 308–16.

33. Simon Rottenberg, "The Baseball Players' Labor Market," *Journal of Political Economy*, LXIV (1956), 242–58.

34. M. W. Reder, "The Theory of Occupational Wage Differentials," *American Economic Review*, XLV (1955), 833–52, especially pp. 849–50.

The Scope and Limits of Futures Trading[1]

H. S. HOUTHAKKER

The economic analysis of institutions is not highly regarded or widely practiced among contemporary economists. The very word "institution" now carries unfavorable associations with the legalistic approach to economic phenomena that was respectable during the first three decades of this century. There is little reason to regret the triumphant reaction that swept institutionalism from its dominant place. Nevertheless, economics can still learn much from the study of institutions. The analytical problems that arise are often both a challenge to conventional theory and a useful reminder of the relativity of accepted doctrine.

The subject of the present paper is futures trading in commodities. It does not go into technical details, nor does it present empirical evidence. Its aim, rather, is to investigate from a theoretical standpoint why futures markets exist at all and why they exist only for a rather small number of commodities. Because of the intimate connection between futures contracts and inventories much attention is paid to the analysis of the latter, particularly in Sections I and II. The effects of uncertainty are discussed in Section III, while Section IV is devoted to the heterogeneity of the cash market. Section V sketches the development of futures trading, and Section VI relates this to hedging. Section VII brings together the strands of the argument.

I. FOUR TYPES OF STOCKS

The stock of a commodity at a certain time is the difference between the total quantity produced up to that time and the total disappearance up to that time. The change in stocks during the period between two dates is, therefore, equal to the difference between production and consumption during that period. If the quantities produced and consumed[2] during a

[1] This paper results from continuing research on commodity markets initially undertaken with the support of the Cowles Commission (now Foundation) for Research in Economics, under a grant from the Rockefeller Foundation. I am much indebted to Arthur M. Okun for valuable comments.
[2] Although consumption is not the only form of disappearance, destruction being another form, we shall often use "consumption" and "disappearance" syn-

period are equal, stocks do not change, and if production and consumption have been equal at all times, stocks must be zero.

There are few commodities of which stocks are always zero (services and electric power are the most conspicuous examples), and not many more of which stocks do not change over time (e.g., natural gas in a pipeline). Of all other commodities, therefore, production does not always equal consumption. The main reasons that differences between production and consumption occur are the following:

1. The cost of production may not stay the same over time; more particularly, it may vary as a result of natural causes. Thus, it is cheaper to enlist the aid of sun and rain to grow wheat that can be harvested in the summer and stored until it is consumed than to build hothouses from which wheat can be obtained as it is needed. Similarly it is economical to reserve some wheat from an abundant crop for use in subsequent years in which nature may be less benevolent.

2. If production costs per unit depend on the maximum rate of output, and if demand changes over time, storage may help to even out production and thereby reduce costs. Thus, the demand for toys has a peak at Christmas, but the capacity of the toy industry can be kept down, so that unit costs will be lower, if production is spread out over the whole year and the output stored.

3. Large quantities may cost less per unit than small quantities, and it may then be cheaper to obtain large quantities at intervals and store them until they are used up. This factor is particularly important in distribution.

4. Differences between production and consumption may finally emerge against original intentions rather than on any of the efficiency grounds mentioned previously. Production may have been planned to equal estimated consumption, for instance, but, because of favorable weather, production may exceed the plan, or consumption may fall short of the estimate. Storage is then one way of taking care of the surplus.

In each of these four cases a crucial role is played by the carrying costs, which comprise the total outlays necessary for holding stocks. Carrying costs have three components: the cost of storage in the narrow sense (warehouse and insurance charges), the loss (if any) due to spoilage and deterioration, and the interest on the investment which stocks represent.[3] The second component may actually be negative for commodities which improve with age, such as wine; total carrying costs may then also be negative, and stockholding correspondingly stimulated. Disregarding this

onymously. Note also that "production" and "consumption" will throughout be used in a technological sense: by "producers" of wheat, for instance, we mean farmers and not merchants or shippers; the "consumers" of wheat are flour millers and not households.

[3] The cost of hedging (if any) will not be regarded as part of the carrying cost.

case, however, it is evident that in the first three cases mentioned above any advantage in production cost must exceed the carrying cost if storage is to be efficient. In the fourth case the carrying cost will have to be less than the expected increase in value between the time the commodity is put into storage and the time it is taken out.

II. SEASONAL AND CARRY-OVER STOCKS UNDER
PERFECT FORESIGHT

Of the four cases of a difference between production and consumption, the first and the last are the most relevant to the staple commodities with which this paper is concerned, though the third case will also be referred to occasionally. Let us, therefore, consider the first case separately to begin with, under the assumption that the future is predictable with certainty.[4] Evidently the fourth case (unplanned stockholding) is not consistent with the latter assumption, and we must therefore exclude it for the time being. The second and third cases are compatible with perfect foresight, but they will also be disregarded. It should be added that the hypothesis of perfect foresight may lead to absurd results when pushed to extremes, but for the present limited purpose it is harmless enough.

Suppose first that there are no year-to-year changes in the weather, all climatic variations being seasonal in nature, that production and consumption depend only on the price of the commodity considered, and that the entire production becomes available at one instant, whereas consumption is spread out (not necessarily evenly) over the year. If the price (except for seasonal variations) stays the same year after year, annual production and annual consumption will each remain on the same level from year to year, and there will be one price (again apart from seasonal variations) at which annual production and annual consumption are equal. There will then be no carry-over;[5] the only stocks held are those necessary to distribute the annual crop over the crop year. At any time these seasonal stocks must therefore be equal to the total consumption during the remainder of the crop year. This total subsequent disappearance, which itself depends on the prices charged during the rest of the year, may be regarded as the demand for storage at that time.

The gross return from storing the commodity from one day to the next consists of the increase in the spot price between those two days. Depending on the size of that increase, there will be a certain supply of storage: the larger the increase, the larger the stocks people will be prepared to hold, for the costlier the storage facilities that can be used profitably. The actual

---

[4] For a more elaborate discussion of this problem see Samuelson, "Intertemporal Price Equilibrium: A Prologue to the Theory of Speculation" (1), pp. 181–221. I did not see that paper until after the above was written.

[5] By "carry-over" we always mean stocks carried from one crop year into another, and not stocks held within a single crop year.

day-to-day increase in the spot price, therefore, has to be such as to equate the supply and demand for storage, which means that the increase has to be equal to the marginal carrying cost (the carrying cost in the most expensive storage facility necessary to satisfy the demand for storage).

It is not possible to say a priori whether the marginal carrying cost, and hence the rate of increase of the spot price, will rise or fall during the crop year. On the one hand, storage costs in the narrow sense will decline because stocks shrink all the time and can be housed in ever cheaper facilities, but, on the other hand, the spot price goes up all the time, and the interest charge therefore becomes proportionally heavier. If these two effects happen to offset each other, the rate of increase will be constant; the spot price will increase linearly until the end of the crop year, when it falls to the new crop level (cf. Figure 1). In general, however, the two effects will

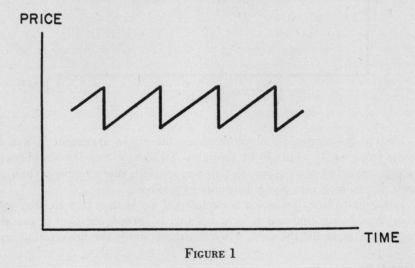

FIGURE 1

not offset each other, and the seasonal pattern of the spot price is then more complicated than in Figure 1. It will still be true that the spot price rises during the storage season and drops suddenly when the new crop is available.

Under the above assumptions, consumption per unit of time will fall during the crop year, resuming again as the new production reaches the market (cf. Figure 2). The reason for this is the rise in price when stocks are held, and this effect may be reinforced by a tendency to postpone consumption when a fall in price is due. The extent of the decline in consumption depends on the magnitude of the price rise and on the elasticity of demand. If the latter elasticity is low and the carrying costs small compared with the price itself, as is the case with many raw materials, consumption will hardly decline at all during the crop year. On the other hand, carrying costs may be so large and the demand elasticity so high (as in the case of some fruits and vegetables) that consumption drops to zero soon after harvest, and no stocks are held for part of the crop year.

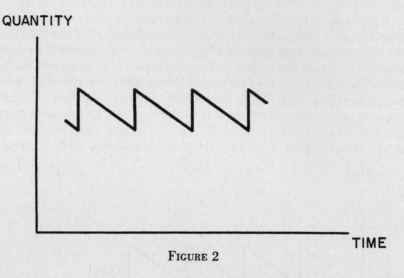

FIGURE 2

Despite the numerous simplifications, the above argument is not as remote from reality as might be thought. To some extent the simplifying assumptions offset each other, so that the whole is more realistic than its parts. Let us look into some desirable extensions.

In the first place, not much is changed if we assume that the harvest, rather than being confined to one instant, is spread out over a certain period, as is normally the case. (See Figure 3, where the broken line rep-

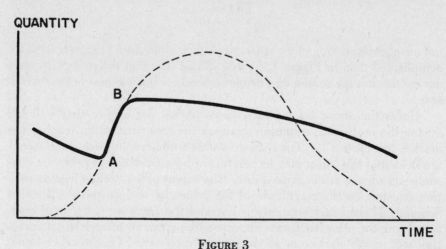

FIGURE 3

resents production and the full line consumption.) The price will continue to rise by the marginal carrying cost as long as consumption stays above production, that is, as long as stocks have to be held. At A, production and consumption are equal and the price can start to fall. It does not fall immediately to the new-crop level, however; for, if it did, demand would increase discontinuously and again exceed production. For a while, therefore, the price falls gradually in such a manner as to keep current consumption equal to the newly forthcoming supplies. The extent of the price fall is limited by the demand for storage, that is, by the consumption at the end of the crop year. If the price fell too far early in the season, not enough would be left for subsequent demand, which in the present model is assumed to be known. At B in Figure 3, stocks again are accumulated and the price starts to rise by the marginal carrying cost.

The new seasonal price pattern is shown in Figure 4. There is evidently

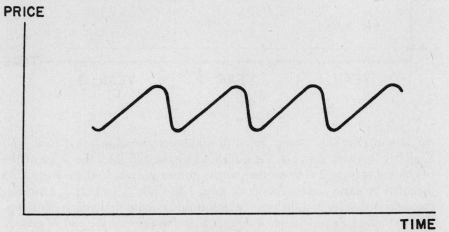

FIGURE 4

a strong incentive to spread out production in the way shown in Figure 4, for those who sell their crop early or late get a higher price. The reason that most producers nevertheless harvest when the price is lowest is the seasonality in production costs mentioned as the first reason for differences between production and consumption, since in this model the price at harvest must always be equal to production cost.

A second modification that needs to be made has more effect on the price pattern. In practice, production and consumption do not depend only on the price of the commodity considered but also on a host of other factors, which for the moment must still be assumed to be known with certainty. For simplicity we confine our discussion to the most important factor, viz., the weather, and we assume (not altogether unrealistically) that the weather is the only determinant of the size of the annual crop, but that consumption still depends only on price. We start from Figure 1, since the complications of Figures 3 and 4 can easily be supplied by the interested reader.

Consider then Figure 5. In year 1 the price pattern is determined by

PRICE

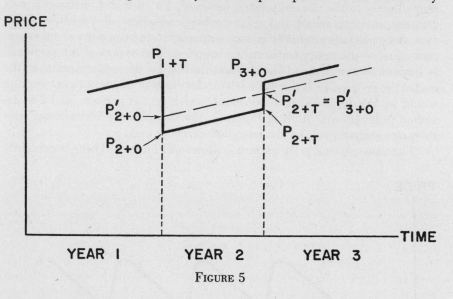

FIGURE 5

the size of that year's crop, so as to make consumption equal to it, and similarly in years 2 and 3. As indicated by the full line, the price at the beginning of year 2 is lower than at the end of year 1, so there will be no incentive to carry over stocks from year 1 to year 2. In year 3, however, the crop is smaller and the price which would equate that year's consumption to that year's production is higher than the price at the end of year 2. This means, in effect, that the demand for storage at the beginning of year 2 consists not only of consumption during year 2, but also of the excess of consumption over production in year 3. Prices in year 2 will therefore be raised to the level of the broken line in order to free some of the 2-crop for 3-demand, and the price in year 3 will, accordingly, be lower than if there were no carry-over. If the crop in year 4 is again so much smaller that the price at the beginning of that year (before carry-over) is higher than the price (including carry-over) at the end of year 3, there would be a further demand for storage in year 2, and the broken line would again be moved up.

The carry-over consequently serves to distribute large crops over years with smaller crops in much the same way as seasonal stocks distribute the production from low-cost months to months in which production (if any) is costlier. The extent to which this is possible depends again on the carrying cost, the deterrent effect of which is cumulative. Let p_{1+0} be the price at the beginning of year 1 if the 1-crop is equal to the 1-demand (not including any carry-over), and p_{1+T} the corresponding price at the end of year 1; similarly for p_{2+0} and p_{2+T}, etc. We have seen that there will be a carry-over from year 2 to year 3 if p_{3+0} would be higher than p_{2+T}. If there is a carry-over, p_{2+0} will rise, say, to p'_{2+0}, and so will p_{2+T} to p'_{2+T}; p_{3+0} will fall to p'_{3+0}, which equals p'_{2+T}. Now if year 4 is also to get a share of the 2-crop, the pre-carry-over price p_{4+0} has to be higher than p_{3+T}, which exceeds $p'_{2+T} = p'_{3+0}$ by the carrying cost during year 3, while p'_{2+T} itself is again higher than p_{2+T}. The obstacles in the way of year 4's getting part of the 2-crop are thus more formidable than in the case of year 3.

The carry-over works in only one direction: it distributes large crops over subsequent years, but does nothing to supplement small crops that were not preceded by larger ones. Nevertheless, as has already been mentioned in connection with Figure 2, some relief in small-crop years may come from postponement of consumption when the price is about to decline because the next crop is known to be large. The existence of such a tendency to postponement, which amounts to substitution of later for present consumption, is probable but not necessary. It is also conceivable that the known increase in subsequent supplies may encourage the starting of new consumption processes while current supplies are still short; in that case, present and subsequent consumption are each other's complement because both are complementary with a third commodity. Whenever the tendency to postpone consumption prevails, *negative storage* may be said to take place.

III. SOCIAL AND INDIVIDUAL UNCERTAINTY

It is now time to abandon the most drastic of the simplifying assumptions made in Section II, namely that of perfect foresight. In doing so we will also make room for the fourth type of stockholding from Section I.

Suppose first that noneconomic conditions such as the weather are completely foreseeable by everybody, and that every individual knows with certainty what he himself will do under any combination of economic conditions (prices, etc.) that may arise in the future, but that he is not certain about the decisions of other persons under those conditions and has no interest in predicting their decisions. Thus A knows how much wheat he himself will want to buy a year from now if the price is $1.00 per bushel, or $1.10, or any other price, but he does not know how much other people will want to buy or sell, and therefore he does not know either what the actual price will be. Similarly B knows what the weather will be in the coming year, and how much he himself will consequently harvest, but he does not know what price he will obtain. Such a state of affairs is characterized by *social uncertainty*; it is uncertainty due exclusively to the fact that many individuals take part in production and consumption.

Social uncertainty can be eliminated by *forward trading* which consists in buying and selling with delivery at a later date; it should not be confused with futures trading, about which we shall speak in section V. In the above example there would be a market for wheat deliverable one year from now. In this forward market B could offer his crop for whatever it will fetch, and A could cover his needs to the extent that prices warrant. Those who want to hold stocks of wheat for one year could sell them forward in this market, and the difference between the forward price and the current spot price would tell them whether such stockholding is profitable given their carrying cost. The forward price resulting from these various transactions would be equal to the spot price that would prevail in the absence of social uncertainty, and unintentional stocks (the fourth case of Section I) will not emerge. This conclusion only holds, however, when every individual participates in forward trading to the full extent of his foreseeable position. This amounts to assuming that everyone accepts the forward price as a perfect prediction of the spot price. There is no need to consider whether or not the latter assumption is already implied in the assumption of social uncertainty; in any case the two assumptions go naturally together.

The consequences of *individual uncertainty* are more interesting. Individual uncertainty is present when not all individuals know exactly what they will do under different economic conditions at later times, for instance because they do not know what noneconomic conditions will exist or because they dislike the effort of looking ahead. Individuals may, of course, still have more or less precise ideas as to their later decisions and they may still be willing to anticipate these decisions by buying or selling in the forward market. When they thus anticipate their decision, however, they may find, when the time comes, that a different decision would have been better. Thus the producer B, just mentioned, may have sold forward part or whole of a later crop, but when this crop is harvested he may find that he would have obtained a higher price if he had sold spot at harvest time. The buyer of his crop will have a corresponding advantage.

The possibility of subsequent rejoicing or regret will no doubt affect the extent to and the price at which traders are willing to buy or sell in the forward market. Nevertheless there will be at any time, for every forward price quoted, a definite quantity (possibly zero) which each trader offers or demands. This quantity will in general not be the same as in the absence of individual uncertainty and it will of course depend on many factors besides the forward price. At any time the buying and selling preferences of all traders can be added to form total demand and supply, which the forward price will bring into equilibrium.

In this respect the forward market under individual uncertainty is not different from the forward market under perfect foresight or under social uncertainty. This similarity does not mean, however, that individual uncertainty can be removed by forward trading in the same way that social uncertainty can be. By forward trading an individual can make the outcome of his activities independent of the course of prices between the present and the date when these activities are completed. As far as he is concerned any difference, favorable or otherwise, between the actual spot price at delivery time and the forward price at which he traded then enters into the category of bygones that are bygones, except to the extent that he may be led to reconsider his forecasting procedures; but for the economy as a whole the matter is not so simple.

Consider the case where a crop turns out to be so small that the spot price at harvest time is much above the previously quoted forward price. Consumers who have bought forward at the low price will have made their plans accordingly, and though some of them may now resell their purchases, others will proceed as if nothing had happened. The new crop will therefore be used partly for purposes which would not have been profitable under the actual spot price. Moreover, the relatively low forward price will have discouraged the holding of a carry-over which would have helped to offset the small crop. Both of these effects, the higher level of demand and the lower level of supply, will act to the detriment of those who have sold forward, and who might have produced or stored more if they had known the actual spot price at harvest time. The result of forward trading therefore has been not that the risks of a small crop have been eliminated, but merely that they have been shifted from forward buyers to forward sellers. Conversely, the risks of a large crop have been shifted from forward sellers to forward buyers.

If the forward market were used only by producers and consumers it would already serve an important function. No matter how much the forward price differs from the ultimate spot price, and how much production and consumption may consequently be distorted from the levels that ultimately turn out to be appropriate, the plans of consumers and producers would at least be coordinated, since total forward supply and total forward demand have been brought into equality by the forward price. It is true that complete coordination can be achieved only if all producers and consumers participate in forward trading, and we shall see below that there are obstacles to such complete participation, but this need not concern us at the moment. Under conditions of individual uncertainty, even complete participation of producers and consumers would be no guarantee that the forward price would agree with the ultimate spot price. There are other traders, however, who might profit from a discrepancy between these two prices without themselves engaging in production and consumption, and who are therefore prepared to enter the forward market. We are referring to speculators.

In a very wide, and therefore unilluminating, sense all decisions that extend over time are speculative, since they imply some degree of confidence that later events will coincide with the expectations behind the decision. A more precise definition of speculation can be given, but this would lead us too far; for the moment, the every-day notion should be borne in mind.

Anybody, whether inside or outside the trade, who feels sufficiently confident that the ultimate spot price will turn out to be above the currently quoted forward price can expect a profit if he buys forward, takes delivery when it is due, and resells the merchandise thus acquired in the spot market. Conversely, if he thinks the ultimate spot price will be below the current forward price he may sell forward and meet his commitment at delivery time by buying in the spot market. Again, it is not necessary to know the exact shape (if any) of the speculators' "expectations" as to the ultimate spot price. All that matters is how much, for each level of the currently quoted forward price and any other relevant factors, they will want to buy or sell. The actual forward price will be determined by the total demand and supply for forward delivery, irrespective of whether it comes from producers and consumers or from outsiders.

Speculation is not confined to the forward market. If a trader thinks the spot price will rise by more than his carrying cost he may buy spot rather than forward and hold the merchandise as long as he sees fit. In the spot market, however, it is only possible to be "long," that is to be in a position to profit from a rise in price, whereas in the forward market one can also be "short," namely by selling forward without possessing the merchandise sold. In the spot market, morever, being "long" entails the actual holding of merchandise, but in the forward market longs need only buy contracts for later delivery.

IV. THE HETEROGENEITY OF THE CASH MARKET

We have so far spoken of "the" spot market and "the" forward market. This usage requires qualification, and not merely because there are different commodities such as wheat, corn, etc., each with its own spot and forward market. Even for what is commonly regarded as "one" commodity, the spot and forward market are far from homogeneous. We shall see that this has had a far-reaching effect on the organization of trade.

One important source of heterogeneity is geographical dispersion. The price of wheat in Oregon is not wholly independent of the price of wheat in New York, for if the two prices moved too far apart wheat could be profitably shipped from one state to the other, or suitably located buyers would switch from one source to the other. But these equilibrating tendencies are certainly not strong enough to ensure a very close correlation between the two prices. Supply and demand conditions in the two states may, in fact, be so different that they might be thought to constitute two different markets.

The difficulties of such a view become apparent, however, when we consider that there are several other states between Oregon and New York, each of which we should then regard as a different market. Different though conditions at the extremes may be, in Illinois and Indiana they can hardly fail to be so alike that one would rather regard these states as forming a single market. But if Illinois and Indiana are one market, would not Illinois and Iowa also be one market, and Iowa and Nebraska? In the absence of any economically meaningful boundaries would not the four states together then form one market? Clearly we could continue this process of joining neighboring states until Oregon and New York are united again. The spot market thus appears as an aggregate of interrelated and not sharply delimited sub-markets.

Much the same holds for the physical, rather than the geographical, heterogeneity of any commodity. Wheat, for instance, is produced in an almost infinite number of varieties and qualities, which for commercial purposes have to some extent been standardized into grades. These grades are more or less adequate substitutes for each other, and their prices therefore tend to move together, but not exactly so. Supply and demand conditions for No. 1 White and No. 4 Hard Winter may be quite different, but the large number of intermediate grades again makes it impossible to draw any meaningful market boundaries.

The spot market, therefore, lacks homogeneity in two respects: location and quality. In the forward market, delivery time is a further source of heterogeneity. Traders may want to contract for delivery at any time from tomorrow until a few years from now, and neighboring deliveries are close substitutes for each other. Indeed, the spot market is nothing but one end of the forward market, and for many purposes it is best to regard them as one, the *cash market*.

The complicated nature of the cash market, with its many segments all mutually dependent, is not merely a challenge to the economist, who finds his usual tools of analysis too crude to do full justice to it. Its consequences for the traders in the commodity concerned are more serious. Heterogeneity of a market results in a high level of transaction costs, which in turn causes an increase in risk. Transaction costs are the sacrifices necessary to conclude a transaction. The simplest example is a broker's commission, which is paid for the service of bringing a buyer and seller together. In a market for a homogeneous commodity with a multitude of buyers and sellers hardly any trouble would be involved in making such an encounter possible, but the more specialized the requirements of each trader are, the harder it is to find another trader whose requirements match those of the first trader. To take an example from another area, a person who wants to sell his house may incur much trouble and loss of time until he finds someone who is willing to buy this particular house at a price that is agreeable to both. Until the prospective seller has found a counterpart he runs the risk that the value of his house may change. The situation in the cash market for a commodity is quite similar.

The task of matching producers and consumers is performed by middlemen, who may be either brokers, merchants, or scalpers. Brokers do not trade for their own account, and their charges therefore represent transaction costs in pure form. Merchants do buy and sell for their own account, and, since they usually perform also such services as grading, storing, and shipping, their income cannot be identified with transactions costs. An important part of their function, however, consists in providing a ready demand for producers and a ready supply for consumers, and to this extent their income consists of transaction costs. Certain traders, known as scalpers, make their living exclusively from short-term price fluctuations, particularly in the futures markets. If, for instance, a large selling order forces down the price, they buy in the hope that buying orders from outside will soon come in to offset the initial price fall, which the scalpers' purchases thus help to keep within bounds. Scalpers' activities do not always have this beneficial effect; indeed they may sometimes aggravate rather than mitigate price fluctuations, but, to the extent that they contribute to a smooth determination of prices, their income is also part of transaction costs.

Transaction costs are not always incurred by those who trade in the commodity concerned. If a group of middlemen operates a commodity exchange its cost will be part of the expenses of the members and therefore included in their charges or other receipts, but if the exchange is operated by a city, for instance, all or part of its cost may be borne by the taxpayers. The latter case will also arise if a government agency provides free marketing information (such as crop forecasts).

We have already remarked in passing that high transaction costs lead to an increase in risk. The reason is that these costs may be so high as to prevent traders from undertaking transactions which reduce their risks. Thus a producer may want to eliminate the risk of price changes on his growing crop by selling forward, but the net return from doing so, after the cost of finding a buyer is allowed for, may be so small that he may decide to bear the risk after all. This in turn makes the cash market less active than it would otherwise be, and thus makes it more difficult to find trading partners, so that the effects of transaction costs and individual uncertainty reinforce each other.

The intervention of middlemen helps to facilitate the use of the cash market by producers, consumers, and speculators, but it does not solve the basic problem of heterogeneity. Indeed, this problem can never vanish completely, for there will always be geographical, physical, and temporal differences between transactions.

To see along what lines an improvement may nevertheless be obtained, it is instructive to consider the introduction of money into a barter economy. In such an economy the producer of wheat would have to find individuals who are willing to exchange his wheat for the clothing, housing, etc., which he needs and which they can supply themselves. His efforts to find such trading partners would no doubt be considerable, or alternatively he would have to take large risks in waiting until they present themselves. The introduction of money makes it possible for him to avoid a large part of these transaction costs and risks. He can now sell his wheat for an intermediate commodity, money, with which he can then buy the goods he wants, for these goods will be offered for money by *their* producers. It is consequently no longer necessary for a producer to seek trading partners who produce things he needs; any trading partner who has money is now suitable. This reduction in transaction costs and risks is the fundamental reason for the use of money. It explains why money exists even though it has no usefulness of its own and is merely a general claim on other commodities.

The cash market for a commodity presents all the difficulties of a barter economy in miniature. The introduction of an intermediate good that can serve as a claim on other objects of trading would be equally valuable, even if that good had little or no usefulness itself. To a large extent this need is satisfied by the futures contract.

V. THE FUTURES MARKET

As was true of money, the evolution of the futures contract was largely unplanned, and guided mainly by the slow but sure process of piecemeal adjustment to the needs of trade. Even today different stages of development may be found side by side in different commodity markets. It is not within our scope to trace the history of futures markets;[6] a few words must suffice.

The origins and antecedents of futures trading are partly lost in the mists of Dutch, Scotch, and Midwestern antiquity; judging from the history of many of our commercial institutions, there were probably precursors in Northern Italy, but I have found no references to this effect. It is therefore hard to say when futures contracts similar to the present type were first used. In the cases of Amsterdam and Chicago it seems clear that such devices were initially introduced because of uncertainty as to the nature and availability of shipments that were still "to arrive"; this factor is even today of some importance in a few commodity markets.

In the pre-railroad days in Chicago, for instance, merchants who had bought wheat in outlying territories could not be sure when their purchases would turn up, and what the quality would be. Until arrival they therefore ran a price risk, which in those days of poor communications must have been especially serious. The "to arrive" contracts solved these problems. It was essentially a forward contract in which the time of delivery was not precisely specified and in which the price was fixed on the assumption that the shipment was of some particular grade, adjustments being made when

[6] Cf. Smith (2), Haccou (3), and Working (4) also for further references.

the grade proved to be different. Merchants who expected to receive wheat were thus enabled to sell it before it arrived.

Gradually the "to arrive" contracts became standardized so as to make them of interest to a greater number of traders and thereby reduce the cost of finding a trading partner. Since the delivery period was somewhat indefinite anyway, it came to be standardized to one month. Some months soon turned out to be more active than others; thus there was particular interest in May because Lake Michigan became navigable during that month.

As regards grades, some standardization also developed. The mere evolution of accepted grades was itself a major advance in commercial technique. Certain grades became particularly important because of their predominance in the territory that supplied Chicago; these grades were therefore generally adopted as fixed points for the determination of grade adjustments. The size of the contract also became standardized in round lots of 5,000 bushels.

Although "to arrive" contracts were originally developed for the use of merchants who contemplated actual purchases and sales, they soon attracted the attention of speculators who were not interested in the commodity itself but only in its price. The standardized nature of the contracts made them superior to ordinary spot and forward transactions as a means of speculation. The intervention of speculators, in turn, increased the volume of trading and further lowered transaction costs, at least in those months (such as May) which were especially interesting to traders, and the larger volume in its turn made for greater publicity, which attracted outsiders.

Because delivery conditions on "to arrive" contracts were so flexible, the identity of the buyers ceased to be important to the sellers, and conversely. The contracts accordingly became less and less personal, and the development of the Clearing House, a general intermediary between buyers and sellers, finally depersonalized them completely. Those who had bought contracts need no longer take delivery if they were not interested in actual merchandise, and they need not even approach the seller to annul the contract; all they had to do was to sell the contract to someone else.

At this stage the original connection with "to arrive" dealings had become very faint indeed: the "to arrive" contract had evolved into the futures contract. This economic evolution had its counterpart in the realm of law. As the contracts became more remote from ordinary transactions in the cash markets, it became more dubious whether they were not mere gambling deals and legally unenforceable as such. The large-scale utilization by speculators made this question all the more acute. The courts established the rule that futures contracts were binding only when actual delivery was contemplated. A clause to this effect appears to this day on brokers' statements.

Since traders can avoid delivery by buying or selling the contract before delivery is due, the presumption of intent to make or take delivery is largely a legal fiction. It nevertheless has a vitally important bearing on the relation between the futures price at delivery time and the spot prices at that time. Apart from certain technical complications the futures price upon the expiration of the contract has to be equal to the spot price of at least one deliverable grade. This ultimate equality influences the decisions of at least some buyers and sellers of the contract throughout the life of the future (i.e., the time during which it is traded). Although buyers, for instance, can avoid delivery by selling before expiry, and usually do so, they may "stand on delivery," and so may some sellers.

The possibility of delivery makes futures contracts analogous to banknotes under a convertible currency. If there is only one deliverable grade, this fulfills the place of gold under the gold standard; when there are several deliverable grades, the situation is analogous to a multiple standard such as existed in many countries before the silver standard and, afterwards, the gold standard were established. The peculiarities of a multiple standard first led to the formulation of Gresham's law; and, in fact, the substitution between deliverable grades is nothing but an instance of Gresham's law.[7]

Although the possibility of delivery helped to maintain a relation between spot prices and futures prices it also led to abuses. Short sellers got into difficulties when they were unable to buy in their contracts before expiration or to obtain actual merchandise with which to meet their obligations. When deliverable stocks were small, large traders could exploit the plight of the shorts by operating "corners" or "squeezes," which are attempts to monopolize the long side.[8] The exchanges themselves, who regulated and administered futures trading, were not always diligent in preventing such excesses, for the beneficiaries from corners and squeezes were often their own members, and the victims were usually outsiders. Laws were revived or enacted which made manipulation of the futures market a criminal offense, but until the establishment of government agencies with adequate powers of supervision and investigation, it was often hard to prove manipulation.

The danger of corners and squeezes kept many potential traders from using the futures markets for speculation and hedging. The most effective weapon against this danger is extension of deliverability. The larger the variety of grades that can be tendered on futures contracts, the smaller the possibility that the deliverable stocks will be controlled by a corner. Deliverability of a grade, however, is not enough to make delivery feasible,

[7] This analogy was suggested by Professor Holbrook Working.

[8] In a "corner" such an attempt extends beyond the futures market into the spot market; a "squeeze" is confined to the futures market but may occasionally also be attempted from the short side.

for the premiums and discounts for nonstandard grades may be such as to restrict effective deliverability to one grade, in accordance with Gresham's Law. Moreover, deliverability depends not only on the grade but also on the location of the stocks involved.

Thus before 1930 the New York cotton contract called for delivery in New York. In the nineteenth century, when cotton was grown in the southeast, manufactured in New England, and exported through Atlantic ports, New York was a natural location for delivery, since stocks had to be held there in any case. As cotton growing moved westward and cotton manufacturing southward, however, New York came to lie outside the normal channels of the cotton trade, and ordinarily stocks would be held in the south. Manipulation of New York futures became easier and made their use by the trade increasingly inadvisable. After much official pressure the contract was finally changed so as to make delivery in southern ports acceptable and in practice obligatory. This restored the usefulness of the New York contract, which also allows for effective deliverability of a wide range of grades and staples of cotton. It is no doubt due largely to the flexible provisions of the contract that futures trading occupies such a vital place in the marketing of cotton.[9]

Effective deliverability of a broad range of grades and locations is desirable not only because it makes manipulation more difficult; it also widens the range of spot prices with which the futures price is correlated through the delivery mechanism, and this is particularly important for hedgers. On the other hand, it makes futures contracts increasingly unsuited to the acquisition or disposition of actual merchandise, and makes them more and more akin to money.

VI. FUTURES CONTRACTS AND HEDGING

Illuminating though the comparison of futures contracts with money is, it should not be pushed too far. The careful reader will already have been put on his guard by the fact that in the preceding discussion different types of money were used as objects of comparison at different points. As we shall now see, futures are in fact more akin to bonds than to ordinary currency.

The principal differences between futures and currency are (1) futures contracts are dated, rather than payable on demand as currency technically is, and (2) their use is confined to one "commodity" (albeit a heterogeneous one) rather than to all commodities. The latter factor explains why, for example, "wheat money" (that is, contracts exchangeable at sight into any kind of wheat) cannot survive when "general money" (coins, bills, checks, etc.) is also in existence: the general money, being of wider usefulness, would make the special money redundant, and the additional trans-

---

[9] Cf. Garside (5) for an excellent discussion.

action costs due to having more than one variety of money would make its use undesirable.

This redundancy, however, does not pertain to dated bonds.[10] There *is* scope for "wheat bonds," "cotton bonds," etc., in addition to "money bonds," if the latter term may, for a moment, denote the bonds payable in ordinary currency on a specified date, with which we are all familiar. These "commodity bonds," in fact, are nothing but the futures contracts discussed in Section V, and they are useful because they facilitate the holding of inventories, just as "money bonds" facilitate other capital transactions. To see why this is so it is necessary to go briefly into the subject of hedging; a final answer to the problem will be given in Section VII.

A trader is said to be a hedger if his commitments in the cash market (that is, his spot and forward commitments) are exactly offset by commitments of opposite sign in the futures market. To take the simplest case, if a merchant has 1000 bales of various kinds of cotton on hand, and if he is at the same time short 1000 bales of cotton futures, his cotton inventory is said to be hedged. More particularly he is a "short hedger," the adjective indicating the sign of his futures position. He would also be a short hedger if he had bought 1000 bales of specified quality and location forward (that is, for delivery at a later date) and had again sold 1000 bales in futures contracts. "Long hedging" arises, for instance, in the case of a miller who

[10] In his paper "Le Rôle des Valeurs Boursières dans la Répartition la Meilleure des Risques" (6), Kenneth J. Arrow has shown that under certain conditions (including social and individual uncertainty) the existence of only one type of security, payable in money, will suffice for the coordinated adaptation of every individual's commitments to the risks he deems to be present. Forward trading, as described in Section III above, would consequently be unnecessary, and so would "commodity bonds" in the sense defined in the text. While granting the logical validity of this remarkable result, I am nevertheless inclined to question its empirical relevance, even under the assumptions made by Arrow. The securities he describes are rather like very complicated sweepstake tickets, whose payoff depends on which of many alternative "states of nature" is realized. The notion of a "state of nature" unfortunately raises more difficulties than it solves. Consider, for instance, the case of a farmer who wants to arrange his commitments in accordance with his subjective probabilities concerning the price and size of his growing crop. There is an almost infinite variety of states of nature which he would have to take into account, and whose effect on the price and size of his crop he would have to know. Arrow would then want the farmer to buy or sell a ticket, or combination of tickets, whose price and payoff would yield a maximum of expected utility given his subjective probabilities. Clearly it would be much simpler if the farmer just sold his crop forward; this would, among other advantages, dispense him from the construction of theories about the way in which crop sizes and prices are determined, a task with which even specialists have not made much progress. It is, incidentally, also somewhat misleading to say, as Arrow does, that by means of the securities he describes the number of markets can be reduced. Since the securities themselves would be highly heterogeneous (because of their reference to different states of nature) they can hardly be regarded as constituting a single market.

has undertaken to deliver the flour equivalent of 100,000 bushels of wheat without actually having the wheat in stock (or without having bought it forward) and who at the same time has a long position of 100,000 bushels of wheat futures; it is closely related to "negative storage" (cf. Section II above).

Apart from the long and short hedgers, only one other group of participants in futures trading has to be considered here; *viz.*, the long and short futures-speculators, defined to be those traders whose futures commitments are not offset by cash commitments (if any). A third group of participants, consisting of the "futures-spreaders" who are short in some futures contracts and long to an equal amount in other contracts, has net futures commitments equal to zero, and can be disregarded for the present purpose.

Since in a futures market the total short and the total long position must be equal, any excess of short over long hedging must be matched by an equal excess of long futures speculation over short futures speculation. This equality holds for every securities market, though it is sometimes disguised by institutional conditions; thus corporations, who constitute virtually the entire short side in the market for shares—the *so-called* "shorts" account for only a minute fraction of the total number of shares outstanding—rarely trade in their own issues. The equality also holds for forward markets in commodities or foreign exchange. It does not hold, however, for the spot market, in which it is impossible to be short.

Now it can be shown[11] that most of the time futures position of short hedgers exceeds the futures position of long hedgers. The demonstration falls outside the plan of the present article; ultimately it is based on the just-mentioned asymmetry of the spot market. Though an excess of long hedging over short hedging is by no means impossible, I shall simplify the argument by assuming, from now on, that the normal relation between short and long hedging prevails. In fact it will be convenient to consider only two groups of traders: the short hedgers (excluding those whose positions are offset by long hedgers) and the long futures-speculators (excluding those whose positions are offset by short futures-speculators). The market thus defined is evidently a highly idealized one, whose long side consists only of speculators and whose short side only of hedgers. It is not difficult to bring in the groups of traders who have been "netted out," but I shall not attempt to do so here.

After these preliminaries we can return to our current concern, the theory of hedging. Why does a trader hedge? The customary answer is:

---

[11] This is one of the elements of Keynes' theory of "normal backwardation" upon which much of the following argument is based. A full discussion and reformulation of this theory will be given elsewhere. Some relevant empirical material may be found in Houthakker, "Can Speculators Forecast Prices?" (7), pp. 143–51.

to reduce the risk of having a position in the cash market. If carefully interpreted, this answer is not incorrect, but stated without qualification it is highly misleading. Its defect is the suggestion that the cash position is primary, and the offsetting futures position no more than an afterthought. In an important paper (8) Professor Holbrook Working has emphasized, on the contrary, that traders will normally consider cash and futures transactions in coordination and that the decision to engage in the one kind cannot be independent of the decision to engage in the other. According to Working, the decision to hedge is normally made in anticipation of a favorable change in the spot-futures price-spread, just as a decision to buy spot (without hedging) is motivated by an expected favorable change in the spot price. That this must be so is clear from the fact that the profit or loss on a hedging transaction equals the change over time in the "basis" (as the spread between spot and futures prices is often known) multiplied by the size of the commitment.

By a similar line of reasoning, it is possible to analyze the choice among three alternatives: hedging, long cash speculation (that is, the holding of an unhedged long position in the cash market), and long futures speculation. After the elimination of long hedging and short futures speculation, these are the principal alternatives to be considered. Clearly, the choice among them depends on the total profit obtainable, given the resources with which the trader operates.

These resources are mainly of two kinds: the trader's skill in different types of transaction, and his financial position. The skill consists basically in a knowledge of the special factors, economic, technical, institutional, and personal, that are relevant to the formation of prices. In the cash market the heterogeneity already discussed in Section IV provides ample scope for the exercise of merchandising skill. At the same time this skill is not likely to be found among occasional traders: those who have acquired it, usually after a long apprenticeship or similar experience, will normally find it worth their while to specialize in this line of business. Another important aspect of this merchandising skill will be mentioned in a moment (p. 154).

The type of skill appropriate to the futures market is rather different. Indeed, according to the theory of normal backwardation, no more skill is necessary to make a long-run profit than a determination to stick to the long side. This simple policy enables futures speculators, at least over a sufficiently long period of time, to receive the risk premium which, as we shall see, the short hedgers are willing to pay. There is some evidence that the bulk of speculators' profits is, in fact, derived from this source.[12] Apart from this "general skill," consisting only in being long, there is scope for

[12] Cf. Houthakker (7).

"special skill" which requires an ability to forecast[13] price movements other than the persistent upward tendency of futures prices predicted by the theory of normal backwardation. Such skill appears to be much rarer, and its possessors are likely to be skillful in the cash market as well, because of the overlap in the factors determining prices in the cash and futures markets.

All of these skills can be measured in various ways. The most convenient one for the present summary account is as an annual percentage return on the average value of the physical units (bales, bushels) held in a given line of business by a given trader. Thus, a merchant may be able to make 25 per cent per year on the average value of his stock (which may, of course, turn over several times per year). According to some unpublished calculations relating to corn and cotton futures, the risk premium accruing to long futures-speculators with "general skill" before deducting commissions and other expenses, is of the order of 8 per cent per year on the value of their holdings; Keynes himself, on the basis of unspecified data, had put it at 10 per cent (9, 10).

By measuring skill in this fashion, an implicit assumption is made, namely that the percentage return is independent of the number of physical units to which it applies. Accordingly, there would be no diminishing returns to the exercise of skill. As far as general skill in futures speculation is concerned, this is probably realistic. In the case of commercial skill, the assumption is more debatable and a full analysis would require a subtler argument.

Leaving aside this point, we next observe that, for a trader with limited capital, skill is not the ultimate determinant of profit. The decisive criterion is average return per dollar of owned capital, which can be computed by multiplying skill, as measured above, by the value of holdings which one dollar of investment will support. An example may make this clearer. If the margin required for futures-speculation is 10 per cent of the value of the contract (a not unrealistic figure), plus another 10 per cent which the prudent trader would hold as a cash reserve, then the return per dollar of owned capital is 40 per cent per year if the futures price increases by 8 per cent per year on the average.

In the case of merchandising in the cash market, capital requirements depend on whether inventories are hedged or not. If a well-organized futures market exists, bankers are willing to finance a considerably greater part of the value of hedged than of unhedged inventories. For example, they may advance 90 per cent of the value if hedged, as against 70 per cent if not hedged. Consequently, the merchant has to provide three times as

---

[13] Or, perhaps, ability to bring about price movements through manipulation. As a result of government supervision and regulation the possibilities of manipulation have fortunately been much reduced.

much of his own capital if he does not hedge. It is probably typical of the commercial sector that equity capital (as distinct from loans secured by collateral) is hard to obtain; one item of evidence is that commercial enterprises (apart from department stores) are virtually unrepresented on the New York Stock Exchange. Hence, for the merchant with limited capital, hedging permits a larger scale of operation and, consequently, a better utilization of merchandising skill.

Now it must be granted that the assumptions made (constant percentage return to the value of inventories combined with limited capital) tend to overstate the advantage of hedging. If the return to skill increases less than proportionately to the value of inventories, or if capital is not rigidly rationed but available at an increasing rate of interest, then the advantage of hedging will be smaller than suggested above, but the conclusion will be weakened merely quantitatively and not qualitatively. Leaving these refinements to another occasion, it may be asserted with confidence that hedging is not, or at least not directly, a means of avoiding risk, in accordance with the *adagium* "nothing ventured, nothing gained." Hedging may reduce the risk *per unit* of inventory, but in general it will not reduce the *total* risk.

We must next briefly consider in what way hedging reduces the risk per unit of inventory, where risk will be taken to be identical with variance of return.[14] Hedging, it will be remembered, involves taking commitments of equal size but opposite sign in the cash market and in the futures market. The mere fact that these commitments have opposite signs does not imply a reduction in risk; thus a trader who is long one million pounds of spot coffee and short one million pounds of lead futures is not likely to have reduced his risk per pound of coffee and, for practical purposes, is not hedging. In this example it is evidently debatable whether his long and short commitments are of the same size, since coffee and lead are commonly thought of as different commodities. The issue is not one of semantics, however. As we have seen earlier in this paper, it is often hard to define what constitutes *one* commodity, and rather than philosophize on that elusive question we should recognize from the start that there is an almost infinite variety of objects of trading, distinguished by quality, location, and time, which cannot without arbitrariness be grouped into meaningful, single commodities. A merchant, for instance, who has an inventory of one million bushels of Soft White wheat in a Seattle elevator, and is short one million bushels of Kansas City wheat futures, cannot be said to be hedging *merely* because the word "wheat" occurs in the description of both sides of his balance sheet.

It can be shown that the factor deciding whether or not variance per

[14] This identification, though reinforced by precedent, really begs a great many questions which cannot be discussed in the present context.

unit is reduced is the correlation between the prices of the items on the two sides of a trader's position. More particularly, short selling to offset a long position completely will reduce the variance per unit of the long position if the regression coefficient of the spot price on the futures price is positive and exceeds one-half. The trader just mentioned who was long coffee and short lead futures probably was not hedging because the regression coefficient of the spot price of any kind of coffee on the futures price of lead is no doubt small, especially in the short run. Whether the Seattle wheat merchant of the second example was reducing his unit variance is a matter for empirical investigation, and not one of terminology.

Reduction in the unit variance, it should be added, is only a necessary and not a sufficient condition for the profitability of hedging. Other relevant factors are the availability of credit on hedged and unhedged inventories (though the willingness of bankers to advance different percentages is itself a reflection of the unit variance) and the cost of the hedging operation itself. The latter consists of two parts: the transaction costs of futures trading and—probably more important—the risk premium paid to speculators, which, as we saw earlier, is necessary to keep them in business in the long run. It is conceivable that during certain periods, such as the 1920's or the years just after World War II, mere love of gambling will provide sufficient incentive to speculation, but in the long run something more tangible is needed. The risk premium is paid by short hedgers because it is manifested in a tendency for the price of a futures contract to rise from the inception of trading to maturity, thus causing losses to those who are short. A high risk premium will therefore discourage hedging.

VII. THE FEASIBILITY OF FUTURES TRADING

It is now time to collect the trains of thought pursued in the last three or four sections, and to return to the question raised in the introduction: when is futures trading feasible? We have seen that futures contracts serve the needs of speculators who are not interested in the *minutiae* of the cash market, and who want to confine themselves to the forecasting of price trends that are common to all or most of the varieties of a "commodity." We have also seen that futures contracts are useful to merchants, who can make a better return on their capital if they sell futures as a hedge, and are thus enabled to concentrate on the *minutiae*. In fact the speculators thus help finance the merchants' inventories, even though they do not give direct loans to the merchants or to anybody else: by buying futures contracts from the hedgers they enable the latter to obtain credit on more favorable terms. For this service, according to the theory of normal backwardation, the speculators earn a risk-premium in the long run.

Viewed in this light, futures trading would seem to be one of those marvels that ought to be invented if they did not already exist. Yet the number of futures markets is surprisingly small: in the whole world there are probably not more than 60 or 70 (not counting those that are dormant), and not more than 40 or 50 commodities are traded on them, some commodities being traded on two or more markets. Some of those markets, particularly in grains and cotton, are of central importance in their respective industries, but many others appear to have only a tenuous existence of no more than marginal interest for the marketing process. Nor is the nature of the commodity a very informative guide as to the existence of futures trading: it exists in coffee and cocoa, but not in tea; in copper and other nonferrous metals, but not in pig-iron; in many grains including rye, but not (in the United States) in barley, which is a far more important crop than rye; in cane sugar, but not in beet sugar or salt; in eggs, but not (in recent years) in butter.

It would carry us too far to consider for each of those commodities why there is futures trading, or why there is not. Instead, we may sum up the discussion by looking at the criteria determining the feasibility of futures trading. These criteria are two in number: (a) The correlation between the spot prices of a large number of varieties on the one hand, and the futures prices on the other hand, should be large enough to make hedging worth while despite the risk premium accruing to speculators. (b) The volume of trading in futures contracts should be large enough to make transaction costs distinctly smaller than in the cash market.

The crux of the matter is that these two criteria are opposed to each other. Thus a high correlation between the various spot prices and the futures price could be achieved by defining the contract in a very narrow manner, so that only one or two grades, at one or two locations, are deliverable (for instance only No. 2 Soft White Wheat in Seattle). If that were done the volume of trading would be so small that transaction costs would be the same as, if not higher than, in the cash market. To engage in this kind of futures trading as much commercial skill would be necessary as is required of cash merchants; outside speculators would therefore hardly be attracted. In fact the hypothetical futures contract just described would be almost indistinguishable from a forward contract.[15] Other disadvantages of narrowly defined futures contracts have been discussed in Section V.

When futures contracts have a large range of deliverable grades, on the other hand, there is a danger that they may not be useful to large numbers of potential hedgers because the futures price is no longer sufficiently cor-

[15] Actually the example is not entirely hypothetical. There are facilities for wheat futures trading in Seattle, but they are rarely used. A few years ago the Chicago Board of Trade introduced a special contract for North Pacific Coast wheat in addition to its regular, broadly-based wheat contract; trading was negligible, however, and the experiment was soon abandoned.

related with the particular spot prices in which they are interested.[16] The
extent of this danger depends on two factors: the technical nature of the
futures contract—more particularly, the price adjustments which they provide in the case of delivery of nonstandard grades—and the existence of
a well-developed grading system. The more perfect the grading system,
the better the correlation between spot and futures prices is likely to be
because of the resulting reduction in transaction costs in the cash market.
The highest perfection appears to have been reached in cotton, where
transactions are often made on description only, without actual sampling
of the lots involved. In the case of tea, on the contrary, there apparently
is no generally accepted grading system at all, so that futures trading is
impossible.

Even if a contract suitable for both hedgers and speculators could be
devised, it is by no means certain that interest in futures trading is large
enough to keep transaction costs low. The mainspring of futures trading,
according to the view presented here, is the need to finance inventories in
the face of fluctuating prices. A prerequisite for sustained trading, therefore, is the existence of considerable inventories. This is the reason agricultural commodities are so prominent: the seasonality of production
means that after harvest enormous stocks have to be held, whereas in manufacturing, inventories are relatively much smaller. In manufacturing, including wholesaling, inventories appear to be rarely equivalent to more
than one or two months' consumption; in agriculture they sometimes exceed one year's consumption.[17] Furthermore, the variance of prices differs
greatly between commodities. The price of copper appears to be more
variable than the price of steel; moreover the latter price is more closely
controlled by the firms that hold much of the stocks, thus reducing the need
for hedging. In recent years the Government has done much to stabilize
the prices of agricultural commodities and has also undertaken to hold
large inventories, but the hedging needs of private merchants are still very
large.

Such are the limitations which have prevented futures trading from
spreading beyond a rather small number of commodities. Occasionally,
active markets survive for some time in the absence of large-scale hedging,
just as Monte Carlo and Las Vegas survive by catering to the gambling
instinct. In general, however, futures trading can be understood only as
a response to the trading problems of a heterogeneous cash market with
social and individual uncertainty, where specialization is necessary to keep
the cost of making transactions and of holding inventories to a minimum.

---

[16] This is also the reason—to return to a question raised at the beginning of
Section VI—why "money bonds" cannot do the job of "wheat bonds," "cotton
bonds," etc.

[17] This point was emphasized by Keynes (9).

References

1. Paul A. Samuelson, "Intertemporal Price Equilibrium: A Prologue to the Theory of Speculation," *Weltwirtschaftliches Archiv*, December 1957.

2. J. G. Smith, Organized Produce Markets. Longmans, Green, London, 1922.

3. J. F. Haccoru, De, Termijnhandel in Goederen. Stenfert Kroese, Leiden, 1947.

4. Holbrook Working, "Futures Trading and Hedging," *American Economic Review*, June 1953.

5. A. H. Garside, Cotton Goes to Market. Stokes, New York, 1935.

6. Kenneth J. Arrow, "Le Rôle des Valeurs Boursières dans la Répartition la Meilleure des Risques," in International Colloquium on Econometrics, 1952. Paris, C.N.R.S.

7. H. S. Houthakker, "Can Speculators Forecast Prices?" *Review of Economics and Statistics*, May 1957.

8. Holbrook Working, "Hedging Reconsidered," *Journal of Farm Economics*, November 1953.

9. J. M. Keynes, "Some Aspects of Commodity Markets," *Manchester Guardian Commercial: Reconstruction in Europe*, March 29, 1923.

10. J. M. Keynes, Treatise on Money. London, 1930. Vol. II, pp. 143–44.

The Handling of Norms in Policy Analysis

CHARLES E. LINDBLOM

How do economists handle norms or values in their analyses of policy?[1] This is not to ask where they find their ideas of the Good and the Beautiful—in God, in nature, or by postulate. It is simply to ask how, regardless of their underlying ethic and regardless of what they say they do, economists do, in fact, handle the kind of values pertinent to economic policy.

One specific question to be asked is how the analyst achieves a weighting or aggregation of his values. However complete, a list of values does not permit an analyst to choose among policies if these policies differ in their value-mix. How, then, does he weight, say, freedom as against economic stability?

A second question is how, aside from solving the weighting problem, the analyst makes his values operational so that he can rate alternative policies in the light of his values. How can he formulate both his value position and policies so that he and other observers can determine which of several policies best satisfies the value criteria he is employing.

It is postulated—in the hope that agreement on the postulate is widespread—that value judgments are not empirical propositions subject to the same tests of truth and falseness as are applied to empirical propositions. But a third question to be examined is how economists can achieve some degree of *agreement* on values and on ratings or ranking of policies in the light of the agreed values. Agreement—though not complete agree-

---

[1] This paper explores their actual handling of values in order to make explicit and somewhat more systematic some of our professional methods. It does not prescribe; instead it seeks to uncover elements of method in what appear to be makeshift devices for handling norms in economic analysis. It builds in part upon an earlier paper which explored some commonly employed methods of analyzing public policy issues [cf. Lindblom (1), pp. 298–312] and, like that paper and other similar papers by other authors, attempts to bring to nonquantitative analysis at least a touch of the methodological scrutiny which when applied to quantitative methods has made them explicit, systematic, and communicable, hence capable of commutative refinement. It also carries some implications for decision theory. For helpful criticism, my thanks to David Braybrooke and Henry Bruton.

ment—on values and on ratings is widely thought to be desirable; the pursuit of agreement explains many ill-fated attempts to construct "scientific" norms, as well as the cultivation of the new welfare economics.

Economists do not, of course, wholly agree on values and ratings. On the other hand, if we consider not what economists say about values but how they actually handle them, it seems clear that enough agreement exists to warrant some explanation. Explicit agreement is not the only sign of agreement. If we observe the frequency with which discussion of norms or values is tacitly omitted in policy analyses, we find some impressive evidence of widespread implicit agreement, for discussants will not often agree tacitly to suppress the discussion of norms unless they implicitly agree on them.

The agreement we do achieve is easily underestimated because it emerges largely as a by-product of our own individual attempts to simplify our value problems and is often no more deliberately sought than it is explicitly recorded once achieved.[2]

It is postulated in this paper that economists cannot escape valuation problems merely by observing the values held by the society in which they live and employing these values in analysis. The discovery of agreed values in the community is difficult even when one looks for them. Only in part do large numbers of people agree on values; hence, as one discovers community values, one finds he has discovered conflicting values. This being so, each analyst finds himself burdened with the responsibility of deciding which of the conflicting values or which of various value-mixes he will postulate. He cannot escape the exercise of choice among values, no matter how close he wishes to remain to reporting nothing more than what he observes about him. Only if there were an objective "general welfare" or "public interest"—and few scholars will these days claim that one exists— could an analyst escape the responsibility for choosing among norms or values.

Moreover, many economists do not wish simply to report observed values. As their pursuit of utility theory discloses, they believe that economists may have some special insights into valuation problems such that

[2] One way to achieve agreement on values and ratings, as well as to make headway with the weighting problem, would be to convert as many value questions as possible into empirical questions. This can be accomplished by re-examining one's values to determine which "values" are actually valued only as means to the achievement of other values and which values are, on the contrary, not reducible to means. Once this has been done, the appropriateness of each "value" in the first category becomes an empirical question like any other empirical question in policy analysis.

Granted that this can be done profitably and that many empirical questions masquerade as value questions in a limbo of unsolved questions only because such a scrutiny has not been undertaken, it nevertheless remains true—and we postulate without arguing it—that some nonempirical value questions will inevitably remain; and it is these with which this paper is concerned.

economists as economists, without becoming philosophers, can suggest values or norms or public policy that are something different—in ways we need not go into here—from mere descriptions of the norms that can be observed to be in use in the community.

DIFFICULTIES

How then do economists weight values and how do they achieve some agreement?

Some Fundamental Difficulties

One common picture of the sophisticated economist (or social scientist of any kind) represents him as sharply separating value and empirical materials. He postulates the values required for his intended analysis and then proceeds to resolve choices in the light of them. That this procedure is considered to be a kind of ideal is indicated by occasional criticism of policy analysis in which values remain implicit or are introduced from time to time *ad hoc*.

A closely related way to handle values, it is sometimes suggested, is through a social welfare function in which possible social situations are, by postulate, mapped directly into corresponding levels of social welfare.

Now neither of these two pictures, models, or methods—it is not necessary to decide just exactly what they are—necessarily produces agreement on values or on ratings. The careful postulation of values in advance of analysis does not necessarily move analysts toward agreement. As for the social welfare function, although it is itself a ranking of possible approximations to an ideal and, if written to reflect transitive preferences, would permit an inference as to its author's postulated values, it is nothing more than a precise and complex statement about values and ratings. Hence it offers nothing beyond its own precision as a basis for agreement. That is to say, if you and I as economists each write a social welfare function, we are not necessarily brought to agreement upon norms or ratings.

No doubt the study of characteristics of various hypothetical social welfare functions, not limited to those that approximately express current value judgments, can greatly clarify values or preferences, as illustrated by Kenneth Arrow's *Social Choice and Individual Values* (2); and clarification might possibly encourage agreement. But there is no present basis for agreement in the ability to write social welfare functions, and paradoxically it has even been persuasively argued by the political scientists that clarity of perception of preferences is inimical to widespread agreement.[3]

Quite aside from whether these two methods lead to agreement is the question of whether they are in any case the methods actually used by economists to clarify and weight their values. It is quite possible that they

---

[3] Herring (3), *passim*, but especially p. 102 and Chap. 18.

are, in fact, nothing more than blueprints, appropriate in value analysis only for imaginary men of mental capacities far beyond our own. For it is one thing to say that economists can conceive of systematic postulation and of social welfare functions, but quite another matter to work out values so completely and precisely that they can be systematically postulated or reflected in a welfare function.

Consider the nature of the task of prior postulation of all important values and their rankings as a preface to analysis of a policy problem. Except for deliberately simplified analytic questions, no man can perform the task. Hence, I shall argue that the social scientist who goes through the motions of formal postulation of values as a preface to resolving choices is ordinarily performing a ritual that has little to do with the way that values actually enter into his thinking and influence his conclusions.

In the first place, only in the vaguest way can an individual analyst know or articulate his chosen values except in actual choice situations. We often do not know what we value except by trying some choices and, in addition, the choices we make often actually change our preferences. Just as one infers consumer valuations of commodities from consumer choices, similarly, economists' policy values have to be inferred from actual choices by economists among policies or conditions. We economists do not so much first evaluate, then choose, as instead choose, then inspect our choice pattern for clues to our values.

Second, we economists do not know in advance of analysis what values are relevant to the analysis. In a society in which highway improvement can have such remote consequences as changes in sexual behavior and in family functions, we end up omitting important values; or we postulate that all values are relevant, in which case we founder in a morass; or we undertake analysis before postulating the relevant values. Again, therefore, in our actual thinking analysis and valuation are closely intertwined.

Third, just as we economists do not know our values except through choice situations, we do not know our weights on values except through actual choice situations. In fact, therefore, we do not postulate a system of weights but achieve directly a weighting by choosing directly among alternative policies offering different value-mixes. We do not so much choose alternative policies that satisfy our weighted values as instead discover our value weightings by reacting to alternative policies. Hence, again, valuation and empirical analysis are intertwined.

Fourth, because all relevant valuations are marginal valuations with valuations at the margin varying with varying value-mixes, we could at best only postulate values by postulating schedules of marginal valuations. Our inability to do this is a major difficulty in its own right as well as being the root of the first and third difficulties above. True, we can imagine or conceive of postulating such schedules; but, because we do not know our own marginal preferences well enough, as well as for other reasons, we cannot and do not do so in fact; and if we were to try to communicate to ourselves or anyone else just what our schedules were, the best we could do would be to reveal some points on our schedules by pointing to the choice we make among some specified policies. Again, our choices express our values more than do our prior articulated evaluations.

Our difficulties with postulated values are matched by difficulties in specifying a welfare function in which all relevant policies or conditions are mapped into their corresponding values. It would, of course, be intellectually exhausting to try to imagine all the choice situations we might face—or even the variety of choices that might be faced by policy in the United States—and then try to rate each alternative policy by mapping it into its corresponding value of social welfare as the dependent variable.

One way we economists avoid mental exhaustion on this score is to rely—sometimes deliberately, sometimes not—on the guidance of historical sequences of policy choices. These simplify our valuation problems in the same way that writing a social welfare function complicates them. First, rating only those new policy alternatives that seem to us to be closely related to past sequences of policy moves in the area in question, we greatly reduce the number of alternatives we must map, even if we map both reversals and extensions of past trends. Thus, rather than postulate a welfare function, we postulate a very few select points on it and choose a maximum among these few. Second, because we examine a sequence of actual historical choices in a particular area, we are not wholly without guidance in determining which few alternatives to consider.

Shortcomings of Utility Theory

To the foregoing summary of well-known valuation problems, the reply can now be made that many of the difficulties would either disappear or would be greatly reduced if we could find a general scheme for relating one to another the kinds of values with which economists must deal. In the language of functions, our difficulties would be reduced if, instead of having to construct the social welfare function by independently specifying the value of the dependent variable for each value of the independent variable respectively, we could simply write a formula for the function.

The objection is sound, but its force is lost because we have found no satisfactory scheme or formula. We have tried, however. We have tried to reduce various values to a common denominator of want satisfaction— that is, we have identified "good" with more utility and "bad" with less. Not only is this generally an attempt at simplification, specifically it points the way to a solution both to the weighting problem and to the problem of obtaining agreement—but, as is well known, we can at best derive criteria of only limited use from this approach; and a recapitulation of some of our recognized difficulties with it will show why.

Through utility theory we economists can under some conditions define an "economic welfare" in terms of want satisfactions. Now "economic welfare" sounds like a value or norm. But, as is generally recognized, economic welfare so defined can be a value or norm only for those who so postulate. That is to say, it is not to be taken for granted that wants ought to be satisfied, that it is a "good" thing to satisfy wants. Hence, it is generally acknowledged that economic welfare defined by a level of want satisfaction as a norm is not a road, as has been occasionally argued, to a value-free or "scientific" criterion. If economic welfare or want satisfaction can be made into a serviceable norm, it is only because economists postulate such a value and can agree on ratings of the degree to which various policies and conditions satisfy the norm.

We economists do not always wish to make such a postulate, and certainly we do not agree generally on it. One reason is that we sometimes fear that people do not "really" want what they want. A second and more fundamental reason for our not agreeing that wants ought to be satisfied is this: To believe that people ought to have what they want—that it is "good" if they do—is to practice a kind of ethical or philosophical laissez-faire with reference to the individual; and most economists are willing to practice it only with respect to a limited number of individual wants, primarily wants for marketable goods and services (and not all of these). For the vast number of other wants—the desire to maim, kill, rule, patronize, own, protect, influence, worship, defer to, and be moral, we do not practice laissez-faire. Nor do we believe or agree—to take examples from economic life—that it is good if a seller who wishes to corner a market, adulterate his product, or suppress a patent succeeds in doing so. We have made up our minds—and with a high degree of agreement—that some wants should not be gratified, that it is immoral or unethical to pursue their satisfaction.

What is the distinction that we economists are, in fact, drawing? It is that, while we will sometimes employ want satisfaction as a criterion in a context in which it is assumed that none of the wants are morally reprehensible, we do not necessarily believe in, and certainly do not agree on, using want satisfaction as a criterion for determining what is moral and immoral.[4]

<hr />

[4] This points up, of course, the fact that the use of want satisfaction as a criterion in the very limited context in which economists employ it is quite a different thing from the use of utilitarianism as an ethical system.

As for the utilitarian ethic itself, it presumably offers a way to arrive at moral judgments by asking whether the gratification of the desire, say, to kill or otherwise injure does or does not achieve a net increase or decrease in satisfaction, taking all individuals into account. Hence, it is of course possible to take a position that all moral values should ultimately be anchored in want satisfaction. But while this is possible, it is not by any means the agreed ethic of the economics profession. Hence, again, the professional use of want satisfaction as a base for value judgments at best is almost wholly limited, as has been said, to value judgments in which individual preferences and acts are assumed to be morally acceptable.

Possibly most of the value judgments that economists are called upon to make are applicable to situations in which economists are less asked to judge what is moral than to judge what is in some other sense "better" or "best," as, for example, in policy on wages, agricultural prices, or income distribution (although any of these questions can be turned into moral questions). But even for these nonmoral problems, want satisfaction is often not a satisfactory basis for choice.

We reject want satisfaction as a norm even for nonmoral questions for many reasons. To begin with the most familiar, when there are interpersonal conflicts of interest or preference, many economists do not believe it possible to make valid interpersonal comparisons of utility. And still further, where A can gain only if B loses, economists do not agree on the ratio in which A's and B's wants should be satisfied, do not agree on how in our norms to weight the conflicting preferences. Even if we could make objective interpersonal comparisons of utility, this further difficulty would not be overcome, for knowing what levels of want satisfaction various individuals achieve relative to each other is not the same as deciding upon or agreeing upon norms for relative achievement of want satisfaction. Knowing that A is better off than B tells me nothing about whether he should be.

These two difficulties with want satisfaction as a norm (where there are conflicts of preferences, wants, or interests) can be joined and restated in either of two ways. On the one hand, it can be said that where conflicts exist we economists do not know or agree on what we mean by economic welfare, because many of us do not know or agree on a method of weighting utilities. Not agreeing on what we mean by it, we cannot employ it as a norm. On the other hand, it can be said more directly that we cannot agree on want satisfaction as a criterion because, since many of us do not know or agree on a method of weighting, we cannot say, as between two situations, whether wants are "more" or "better" satisfied in the one situation or the other. Although the first formulation seems to pose a definitional difficulty only, the two formulations are actually identical; and they pose a kind of index-number problem.[5]

Want satisfaction or economic welfare might have little appeal as a norm were it not that for some wants we believe it to be true or approximately true that their gratification for any one individual is without loss to any other. We believe or assume this to be generally the case for goods

---

[5] For what it is worth, it can be noted that the objection to the economic welfare criterion that we do not want some kinds of wants to be satisfied can be construed as a special case of the objection that we cannot agree on weights in cases of conflicting preferences. If I declare that by my norms A's desire to misrepresent his products to his customers should not be gratified, I am in effect weighting the utility A receives from satisfying that want at zero or less.

and services, given the distribution of income. Given the distribution of income, we assume than an individual's preferences for goods and services can be gratified without loss to other individuals because these preferences are satisfied through an exchange process in which it is possible for everyone to gain or at least for many to gain without imposing loss on others. Under these circumstances, and only under these, can we agree on a definition of economic welfare; and only under these circumstances do we agree on economic welfare as a norm, referring to the norm as a Paretian optimum.

We know that it is not strictly true that in exchange relationships in a price system no one loses. We know, for example, that exchange will alter prices and hence adversely affect income shares for some traders and that some transactions have neighborhood effects. Why on the whole we agree to ignore these losses and treat most exchange relationships as though A's gains were never or only rarely at B's expense we shall want to say more about later. For the moment the point is that, in this limited area of policy, agreement is widespread on want satisfaction or economic welfare as a norm. Beyond this area, agreement founders on the twin rocks of interpersonal comparisons and interpersonal weights.[6]

For conflict situations, economists who are willing to attempt interpersonal comparisons have, of course, tried to find acceptable weights. The most common prescription offered as a solution to the problem of weighting is that the sum of want satisfaction shall be maximized for the group or society, this to be achieved by seeking equal marginal satisfaction for all individuals. But why maximize the sum of utilities? It is not obvious that we should, for economists are torn between the principle of equalizing want satisfaction at the margin and equalizing the individual levels of want satisfaction among individuals.

Where, for example, our interests in want satisfaction sometimes incline us to distribution of income in favor of those individuals whose marginal satisfactions from its use would be the greatest, the same interest also inclines us at times to distribution in favor of those at the lowest levels of gratification, regardless of marginal satisfactions. Imagine, for example, two individuals of equal incomes petitioning for a special income share. Given his psyche, A requires slightly more income than B to be as happy as B. B will get more pleasure out of the income share to be awarded than will A. Even if we agree on want satisfaction as a criterion, we do

[6] Because of the limited area in which the Paretian optimum is agreed upon as a norm, its significance has been, as Boulding has pointed out, not so much to provide economists with norms as to "set forth explicitly the distinction between those changes in social variables which can take place through 'trading'—i.e., through a mutual benefit of all parties—and those changes which involve 'conflict,' or the benefit of one party at the expense of another" (4), p. 18.

not agree on how to decide this case; and, quite aside from agreement, many of us are uncertain individually as to how we would decide such a case.

As has often been pointed out, maximizing utility requires that income be diverted to the most efficient pleasure machines, but we are often disposed to identify "good" with a more equalitarian pattern of distribution. Much of the appeal of maximizing utility may be attributed to its supposed equalitarian implications; but, without special assumptions denying important individual differences in capacity for enjoyment, maximizing utility may well, we know, be inequalitarian in its applications.[7]

From another perspective, note that the maximizing principle as a policy prescription wholly subordinates our interest in distribution of utility to our interest in its total amount. As a rule for distribution, it paradoxically implies that distribution is important only as it affects the total. For those who give distribution a more prominent place in ethics, the principle has to be rejected.

It is clear from an inspection of the literature of economics that for all these and other reasons the maximizing principle is not agreed upon as a criterion for conflict of interest questions.[8]

There are still further objections to the want satisfaction criterion, whether it is in the form of the maximizing principle or not. The distinctiveness of want satisfaction as a norm where it can be applied to an individual not in conflict with other individuals is in its inhibition of the observer or judge. It prescribes as "good" whatever the individual prefers; it represents, as we have said, a kind of philosophical laissez-faire. If this distinctiveness has been its source of appeal for the narrow range of value questions that it is indeed widely agreed upon, when the same norm is extended to distributional and other conflict of interest questions, the appeal is lost, for the principle is no longer the expression of philosophical laissez-faire. In its extended application, the norm requires the observer or judge to commit himself on relative individual worth.

A quite different source of difficulty with want satisfaction, in any form, as a criterion has been rarely expressed. Economists, unlike psychiatrists, are more concerned with public policy than with personal adjustment; but the want satisfaction criterion is less helpful to public policy than to personal adjustment, and we find economists failing to agree upon its use because, often without articulating their dissatisfaction on this score, they find it irrelevant.

Of course, when an economist analyzes individual market behavior, he may find the want satisfaction criterion extremely useful; but, when he analyzes public policy, he often finds himself concerned, as any reading

[7] As it was, for example, to Edgeworth in (5), p. 64.

[8] See, for example, Lerner (6); Friedman (7), pp. 405–16; and Simons (8), pp. 5–15.

of economics will show, more with the impact of policy on opportunities
for the individual than with its impact on resultant states of mind. This is
understandable on the hypothesis that he assumes a division of labor between government and the individual, in which the former tries to shape
opportunities and the latter to exploit them. Not only—to elaborate the
hypothesis—does public policy often not aim directly at want satisfaction,
it aims instead at creating conditions in which appropriate want satisfying
activity will be called forth from the individual.

Thus to the economist the test of a good policy is often not the level
of want satisfaction directly achieved. And in some cases, he will judge
a policy undesirable even if it raises the level of want satisfaction if it does
so by some process that reduces the demands upon the individual to exert
himself within the framework of conditions arranged through public policy.
In short, all other objections to want satisfaction as a criterion aside, it
does not command agreement because economists often want policy to
produce opportunities for the individual rather than the results of these
opportunities and do not want the results on any easier terms than through
individual response to opportunities.

Finally, economists cannot agree on want satisfaction as a criterion
because they often wish to distinguish among different specific kinds of
wants and are little interested in the net balance of gratification and deprivation for the individual. In their analyses of policy, economists achieve
a higher degree of agreement on the desirability of each individual's achieving some minimum level of education, physical well-being, or money income, for example, than on the desirability of his achieving some minimum
level of satisfaction in general. In short, we economists come closer to
agreement on specific criteria than on a criterion that aggregates for the
individual as does want satisfaction. We deal in specifics not merely because aggregation is difficult, but because we value the pattern of specifics;
and, to relate this point to the immediately preceding, we value specifics
because we are often interested in a pattern of specific opportunities for
the individual rather than in a result aggregated as his balance of satisfaction or deprivation.

The economist's concern with specific opportunities for the individual
rather than with results aggregated in terms of an individual's level of
satisfaction can be seen in the history of his interest in public policies on
income redistribution. While he has experimented with general theoretical
arguments for more equality that are rooted in utility theory, the main
stream of economic thinking has been directed at specifics and at opportunities. The impact of inequality on educational opportunity, on health
and physical development, on the home environment of children, on occupational and social mobility, and on political influence—these inquiries
have reflected the actual standards brought to bear by economists. The
general impact of inequality on the psyche, on relative general levels of

want gratification, has been subordinated. And, it is worth noting, one does not find the bulk of economic writing on questions of income distribution in explicit papers and books on that subject but finds it instead scattered throughout the literature of taxation and other applied fields. For, on the whole, economists are called upon to take a value position with respect to income distribution only as specific questions arise.

In summary, utility analysis as a basis for norms is recognized to be (*a*) limited to evaluations of alternatives none of which are morally reprehensible, and (*b*) not wholly satisfactory even for these.

SOME SOLUTIONS

Common Methods

If I now summarize a number of the points so far made, reversing their order of appearance, they can describe not our difficulties as economists with values, but how we in fact meet the difficulties. The following interconnected procedures for handling values are apparently common:

1. In our evaluations, we economists are often rather heavily concerned with specific individual gains or losses rather than with an aggregated level of satisfaction for the individual.

2. We are often concerned not with resultant psychic states, but instead with opportunities afforded by policies or conditions for individuals to achieve desired psychic states; and we do not evaluate the opportunities by reference to want satisfaction eventually achieved by individuals, but by reference to the degree to which the opportunities make possible and encourage individual exertion toward the achievement of want satisfaction, whether the exertion is forthcoming or not.

3. It is also true—and follows from our frequent concern with specifics rather than an aggregate for the individual—that we often, in fact, arbitrarily limit the number of values we take account of. We will, of course, often disregard what we consider to be noneconomic values. More than that, even within the economic area we will ignore important values. We will often neglect, for example, income distribution consequences of measures designed to improve resource allocation, even if we feel somewhat uneasy and sometimes rebuke each other for doing so. Or, as noted above, we will disregard losses to third parties in considering the advantages of free exchange.

4. With a show of respect for the ritual of postulating values as a preface to analysis, we, in fact, often disregard our own and others' postulations as being too vague and incomplete to be relevant to the actual choices we must make.

5. Instead of choosing among values in the light of which alternative policies can be rated, we often choose among alternative policies directly. That is to say, instead of choosing among a group of abstract values, we

compare and choose among combinations of them in which their proportions differ.

6. Hence we choose not among values but among value-mixes.

7. Rather than consider all possible combinations of values embodied in all possible policies, we often restrict our valuations to those that are immediately relevant for the kinds of policy choices open in our society.

8. Now because, in our society, change proceeds almost always through incremental steps, it turns out that we often *evaluate only a restricted set of alternatives which are only incrementally different from each other.* And because a democratic society can survive only where fundamental values and procedures are not rejected except by fringe groups, we can count, so long as democracy survives in the United States, on incremental change and the relatively modest demands it makes upon us for evaluations.[9]

9. Hence, our values are not total or average values but are instead values at the margin.

10. We often count heavily on a continuing *sequence* of incremental adjustments in policy both to clarify and to simplify our own marginal valuations. As we have seen, such a sequence of policies differing only incrementally affords us opportunity to consider fine gradations in valuations, and the character of the sequence limits the number of new alternatives we consider relevant.

11. Finally, we sometimes place a value on certain social processes that resolve conflicts rather than place values on possible outcomes of the conflict. The obvious example is the widespread approval given to the process called majority rule, an approval that excuses us from having to evaluate all the policies decided upon by that process. Now, not on all issues put to majority rule do we abstain from judgment. We may, for example, believe some majority policies to be foolish or immoral. But for a large category of policies we are indifferent to outcomes provided only that the outcomes are chosen by majority rule. Similarly, to other government policies not put to majority vote, we are indifferent so long as they are worked out by legitimate and customary negotiations among government officials. There are probably more of these conflict-resolving processes to which we give our implicit approval than we stop to count.

The device of evaluating conflict situations by process rather than by solution produced is in one important sense comparable to evaluating non-conflict situations according to levels of want satisfaction achieved. For, just as accepting want satisfaction in the no-conflict situation is to practice a kind of ethical laissez-faire, so does the acceptance of a conflict-resolving process, whatever its results, represent a kind of ethical laissez-faire in conflict situations.

---

[9] For a fuller exposition of the meaning and significance of incremental change see Lindblom (1).

How Weighting Is Accomplished

Despite the emphasis in the above enumeration on the limitation of valuation to specifics and to small numbers of values, the need for weighting values is by no means eliminated. In fact, the practice of ignoring some values suggests a serious failure in weighting. How then is weighting achieved by these methods? How does the analyst using these methods compare the value of more higher education with the value of better highways?

The first answer is, of course, that these procedures in several ways enormously reduce the amount of aggregating or weighting that needs to be done by any individual analyst. This can be seen by considering details of the methods in this light. For example, whatever one may think of arbitrarily limiting the number of values considered, it is undeniable that for any given analyst such a limitation in itself greatly reduces *his* task of aggregating. For another example, his need for aggregation is further limited because he attempts no wide-ranging evaluation but limits himself to actual policy choices. And these choices are in turn restricted because, in a society like ours, policy choices are made largely among only incrementally different alternatives to present policies. He further reduces his task of weighting by attempting in effect only marginal evaluations of the values embodied in incremental policies. Finally, as is obvious, he achieves a great limitation of the need for aggregation when he accepts any results of certain conflict-resolving processes as desirable, thus enjoying the advantages of a kind of philosophical laissez-faire.

In all these respects the enumerated methods succeed in minimizing the problem of aggregation because they make the most rather than the least out of constraints on alternatives to be considered. We are often tempted to talk about values without constraints—that is, we abstract from all "practical" considerations. We are tempted to debate a question such as ideal distribution of income after expressly ruling out the constraints upon our alternatives imposed by incentive considerations, politics, or the stickiness of social change. But the enumerated methods take the opposite tack: the more constraints that can be piled on a choice the less remains to be settled as a condition of making the choice. Making the most of constraints leaves less weighting to be done, just as it simplifies analysis in other ways.

The second answer to the question of how weighting takes place is that these methods offer some specific aids to the individual's attempts to accomplish the limited amount of weighting he cannot escape. Consider again specific characteristics of the enumerated methods. To begin with, only a small part of the aggregating he must do must be done in any one decision situation. That is, given these procedures, at any one decision-making situation, the only values that must be weighted against each other are those with respect to which the alternative policies or value-mixes differ. The analyst's weighting problem is thus factored into many smaller problems. Moreover, the weighting is achieved automatically with the choice taken; he does not first work out a weighting and then bring this weighting to the choice to be made. Furthermore, because he deals with specifics and often with specific opportunities rather than states of mind or other intangibles, he deals for the most part with observables. A hypothesis is that he finds it easier to evaluate observables and tangibles than intangibles. Moreover, because he deals with a succession of incrementally different policies, he acquires familiarity with the kind of choice he faces, so that relative weights pose meaningful rather than remote and hypothetical questions to him.

Weighting and Fragmentation

The third answer to the question of how aggregation takes place is no less important than the first two, but it is less immediately convincing and requires substantial explanation, taking the form of an hypothesis. And whether this third answer is better thought of as identifying a method of aggregation or as identifying a substitute for aggregation is open to debate.

The most troubling—and at the same time the most unavoidable—of the methods enumerated is the arbitrary omission of some important values from consideration in any one decision. Troubling as it is, there is no escaping it, for we cannot pretend to be either patient or intelligent enough to achieve a grasp and weighting of all the nontrivial values—or even all the nontrivial economic values—that might in nontrivial ways be affected by a policy we choose. Policies produce ramifications that sometimes run in an astonishing variety of directions, as is easily seen by taking almost any example of policy. An agricultural price support program presumably has many important economic consequences that emerge through its impact on rural-urban population shifts, many others that emerge through its impact on group conflicts and partisan politics, still others that emerge through its impact on international economic relations, and so forth. What was intended by most of the advocates of a policy may turn out to have much less significance than indirect and remote incidental consequences.

If we as individual analysts cannot take into account, let alone weigh, all the important values or even the important economic values that may sooner or later be affected by the policies we appraise, what *do* we do? The hypothesis is that we take account of the variety of values that runs beyond our intellectual grasp by depending, with only half-conscious appreciation of it, upon a process that I shall call fragmentation of analysis and fragmentation of policy-making. Fragmentation of analysis and policy-making refers to situations in which there exists a very large number of different analysts and policy-making individuals or groups, each approaching its own problems of analysis or policy-making from a distinctive limited point of view.

Where analysis and policy-making are fragmented, any one analyst or group of policy-makers makes the assumption—usually tacit—that consequential values ignored in their analyses or formulations of policy are central concerns of some other analyst or policy group. To the extent that this assumption is true, there is achieved in the society, though not by any one individual in it, a kind of weighting or aggregating of values. No doubt fragmentation produces such a result in at least some circumstances, for the market or price system is a system of fragmentation. The hypothesis transposes the market idea and fits it to the group process of politics.

For example, everyone knows that highway construction in the United States today promises great unknown consequences for the character of urban, suburban, and country living, therefore somewhat more indirect consequences for family organization, patterns of recreation, and attitudes toward arts and letters as one alternative form of recreation. Yet in the analysis of when, under what conditions, and where to build highways, more "practical" considerations of national defense and relief of congestion will so dominate as to give short shrift to some of the consequences mentioned and wholly ignore others. But if, as problems of family organization appear, some analysts somewhere will work on them and some policy-makers somewhere will formulate policy to deal with them, then it cannot be said that the values were ignored or given no weight.

It is customary to think of an analytical process as going on in one mind or within the minds of a small group. But the analysis of policy problems can also be seen as a social process; and the whole story of how analysis is undertaken is not told until the relations among individual analysts are looked into, even if they do not formally or explicitly cooperate with one another.

Just how does the weighting take place in fragmentation? Not, I have suggested, in any one analyst's mind, nor in the minds of members of a research team, nor in the mind of any policy-maker or policy-making group. The weighting does not take place until actual policy decisions are made. At that time, the conflicting views of individuals and groups, each of whom have been concerned with a limited set of values, are brought to bear on policy formulation. Policies are set as a resultant of such conflict, not because some one policy-making individual or group achieves an integration but because the pulling and hauling of various views accomplishes finally some kind of a decision, probably different from what any one advocate of the final solution intended and probably different from what any one advocate could comfortably defend by reference to his own limited values. The weighting or aggregation is a political process, not an intellectual process.

As limiting cases, at least two different aggregation processes can be recognized in fragmentation. One is bargaining: the various limited evaluations are represented by various groups who must come to terms before a policy in some given area can be formulated. The second is without a common name, but it is the process in which each of various groups has a substantial degree of autonomy or discretion over some area of policy-making conceded to it. In this case, aggregation is accomplished by each group's reinforcing or countering each other's policies, either passively or actively.[10]

Fragmentation goes very far in the United States. It has been estimated that we have over 100,000 governmental units in the United States. Taking the one largest of these, the federal government, it is itself not a monolithic, decision-making organization but is composed of almost countless formal and informal decision-making units, each looking upon public policy from its own point of view, each therefore protecting or advancing a somewhat different assortment of values from that of any other.

Fragmentation of policy and analysis goes far to explain why we sometimes neglect distributional consequences of policies aimed primarily at, say, improved resource allocation while simultaneously proving the theoretical impossibility of abstracting from the one while dealing with the other. The long-standing debate, for example, on the appropriateness of marginal-cost pricing in a firm-industry of decreasing cost is explainable on the hypothesis that we are torn between theoretical conviction of the inseparability of allocation and distribution, on one hand, and strong inclination to treat pricing solely as an allocation problem on the other. To pursue this example, we do not believe that distributional consequences of marginal-cost pricing will necessarily come to be recognized as a separate and identifiable problem in public policy. But we act often as though we were assuming that, if the consequences of various policies, including resource allocation policies, turn out to be inconsistent with our preferences on income distribution, then sooner or later both analysts and policy-makers will attack the emerging problems of income distribution.

Or consider the controversy over the principle of compensation of losers by gainers in moving from one policy to another. If in a "second" situation compensation is possible but is not actually paid, is the "second" situation in any sense better than the "first"? That it is better is understandable on the assumption that it makes sense to call the "second" situation better in a society in which through fragmentation an equitable distribution is maintained even if no specific redistribution takes place in connection with the move to the "second." For in such a society, it is quite possible that what we could call "good" results would follow from a general policy of pur-

---

[10] What happens, one may ask, if the analyst's recommendations reach the ear of not a single policy-making group? Clearly fragmentation does not then achieve a weighting of the *analysts'* values. To analysts this is no doubt regrettable; on the other hand, if commonly the principal purpose of aggregation is to make policy recommendations, the analysts' inability to influence policy relieves them of the necessity for aggregation.

suing resource allocation policies for the sake of resource allocation and quite separate distribution policies for the sake of distribution.

The weighting of values achieved through fragmention is very rough. But that the process can be observed in the United States is clear; and, conversely, that it achieves a poorer weighting than would be achieved if individual analysts tried to take all important values into account, is not at all clear.[11]

How Agreement Is Facilitated

Finally, let us consider how the enumerated methods produce agreement. It is not necessary to discuss agreement on values and on ratings separately, because the methods, as already explained, join the two. In appraising the amount of agreement achieved, it should be remembered that the methods leave valuations in large part tacit, agreement implicit and epiphenomenal, hence somewhat disguise the agreement achived. Moreover, agreement reached through these methods is quite consistent with much explicit and elaborately articulated ideological disagreement, which is, however, largely irrelevant to the actual choices being made. It seems to be a characteristic of discussion of policy that words about values make the most of disagreement while the actual handling of values in analysis quietly achieves some important degree of agreement.

To begin with, in pragmatic methods such as those enumerated, much agreement emerges simply because the practitioners share a common culture which not only disposes them to some important degree of consensus on moral values but does the same for valuations in which moral values are minimal or absent.

Unique to these methods, however, is the extent to which agreement is engendered by making the most of limitations or constraints on policy choices. As already seen, constraints minimize the weighting problem. For the same reason, they encourage agreement; that is, the more constraints, the fewer points remaining on which to disagree.

Furthermore, a heritage of successive incremental policy moves which have been the foci of past evaluations give all analysts a commonly shared background of experience in evaluation. Our hypothesis is that this facilitates agreement.

Another hypothesis is that because empirical and value analysis are closely intertwined and because empirical propositions are, by definition, the kinds of propositions on which it is possible for analysts through appropriate observations and experiments to agree, agreement on fact pulls analysts toward agreement on values.

Still another hypothesis is that these methods often make it possible for analysts logically to agree on evaluations of alternative policies regard-

[11] For a discussion of the relation of fragmentation to empirical analysis see Lindblom (1).

less of what they consider to be their disagreements on ultimate values, for ultimate values become irrelevant except as they are weighed and employed in actual policy evaluations, where quite different sets of ultimate values are logically consistent with the same policy. The contrasting situation, at the other extreme, is that in which two analysts believe that they must agree on values and weights in the abstract before they can permit themselves to ask whether they agree on the application of these values and weights to a policy choice.

Another hypothesis is that in the practice of these methods we often find ourselves agreeing on what we are against, even if we cannot agree on what we are for. Hence, we agree that a commonly experienced situation is intolerable; we agree in large part on a "next step" designed to remove us from the intolerable position; and we disagree only in the degree to which we ask ourselves questions about more distant goals of policy which are increasingly removed from the kind of policy choices that can be and are being made for the present. At the extreme, analysts can agree that disagreements on abstract values are often simply disagreements on utopias, from which policy choices are far removed.

And, at the risk of laboring the obvious, to the extent that analysts evaluate conflict-resolving processes rather than concern themselves with evaluation of results of these processes, agreement on a few processes is equivalent to agreement on countless policy alternatives.

Of all these aids to agreement, two are probably most noteworthy: taking advantage of constraints on alternative evaluations, and tying valuation closely to empirical analysis.

Agreement and Fragmentation

If the arbitrary exclusion of some important values from any given analysis is commonplace and if we are dependent upon fragmentation to achieve an integration, the need for agreement is significantly altered. Agreement is still desirable among analysts working on the same policy problem with the same limited set of values; but among analysts working on different problems or on the same problem with different limited sets of values, as is the case where analysis is fragmented, agreement is unnecessary. It is unnecessary because none of these analysts need discuss his differences with any other analyst or come to terms with him. Generating agreement at the political policy-making level is sufficient, and this can be achieved through fragmentation of policy-making.

Agreement on values among analysts is necessary only to the degree that agreement on policy is sought by an intellectual resolution of policy disagreement. To the extent that policy disagreement is resolved not in any individual's or group's mind but in a political process in which a line of policy emerges as the resultant of many forces, analysts gain little by agreeing on values.

Is this merely to say the obvious—that if analysts cannot agree in the face of decisions, some kind of agreement will emerge in the political process? No, the point goes beyond that. Where analysis and policy-making are fragmented, political processes may achieve a consideration of a wider variety of values than can possibly be grasped and weighed by any one analyst or policy-maker. It is this accomplishment at the political level that makes agreement among analysts less necessary. If political processes merely settled disputes without responding to a multiplicity of interests or values, as would be the case without fragmentation, then not only agreement among analysts, but agreement on a comprehensive set of values would still be much to be prized.

To be concrete, consider again as an example public policy on income distribution. Income distribution is a resultant of public policies on taxation, social security, public education, national parks, highways, housing, agricultural prices, collective bargaining, and veterans, and still other subjects. Each of these policy areas is approached by analysts and by policy-makers each of whom works with his own limited set of values. Income distribution will thus reflect both a multiplicity of analyses and a multiplicity of policy-making groups. That economists in these different areas do not agree with each other on values creates no problem of communication among them because they are not called upon to communicate with each other. Nor does their failure to agree discredit them in the eyes of those who use their analytical services, for each policy-making group realizes that it is approaching a problem from a limited set of values and is not distressed to find that the experts to whom it turns are doing the same.

Imagine for contrast a monolithic government in which, in the absence of fragmentation, income distribution is not a resultant of a multiplicity of conflicting and reinforcing decisions but an object of explicit central policy. In this case, central policy-makers would attempt an intellectual resolution of all important values; hence it would be important that each analyst be comprehensive in his consideration of values. If now the analysts did not agree among themselves on values, their disagreements would undermine the confidence with which policy-makers could employ them.

Finally on fragmentation, it can be noted that, to the extent that fragmentation in policy-making comes to be understood as a conflict-resolving process, it, like majority rule, can become one of the explicitly agreed processes that make agreement on some classes of specific policies unnecessary. Even where it is not widely recognized as such a process, it has the effect of excusing analysts, we have said, from reaching much agreement that would otherwise be quite desirable; but analysts do not always realize this to be so.

CONCLUSION

In trying to clarify methods and point up possible useful functions performed by apparently haphazard procedures, there is always a real danger of exaggerating the scope or precision of the methods. All the methods discussed are imperfect; some of them are actually crude; and the thesis on the relation of these methods to what I have called fragmentation has to be labeled, with emphasis, an hypothesis.

In addition, some pressing business is left unfinished. Insofar as evaluations reached by these methods are often tacit, and insofar as these methods suppress debate about valuations, these methods may themselves pose serious obstacles to their own improvement. If on one score the analysis of these methods makes the practice of them more self-conscious, hence by ordinary expectations more skilled, it may also be that self-consciousness in these particular methods is inimical on another score to their skilled use. These possibilities have not been explored.

Nor at the moment is anything more said about the critical question of under what circumstances fragmentation achieves a weighting of all important values and under what circumstances it does not. Yet, presumably, such an amorphous process as fragmentation is sometimes workable, sometimes not, in much the same sense that the decentralized decision-making of the market place is sometimes workable, sometimes not.

Of several immediate inferences to be drawn from all the foregoing, one on standards of rationality for government deserves comment, although it digresses. To the extent that fragmentation achieves an aggregating of values, it does so by processes involving widespread conflict among various decision-making centers. The conflict often takes the form of conflicting or inconsistent government policies. It is therefore not appropriate to postulate as a norm that public policy be consistent or to take inconsistency in public policy as symptomatic of irrationality. Although conflict among decision-making centers is sometimes excessive and sometimes does not achieve the aggregation of values that in other circumstances it might, the wastefulness of conflicting government programs in some circumstances should not blind us to the function that conflict is performing in others. What is often called irrationality in government is sometimes to be desired.

References

1. Charles E. Lindblom, "Policy Analysis," *American Economic Review*, XLVIII (June 1958).

2. K. J. Arrow, Social Choice and Individual Values. Wiley, New York, 1951.

3. Pendleton Herring, The Politics of Democracy. Rinehart, New York, 1940.

4. K. E. Boulding, in Bernard F. Haley (ed.), A Survey of Contemporary Economics, Vol. II. Irwin, Homewood, Illinois, 1952.

5. F. Y. Edgeworth, Mathematical Psychics. Kegan Paul, London, 1881.

6. A. P. Lerner, Economics of Control. Macmillan, New York, 1944.

7. Milton Friedman, "Lerner on the Economics of Control," *Journal of Political Economy*, LV (October 1947).

8. Henry C. Simons, Personal Income Taxation. University of Chicago Press, Chicago, 1938.

Alternative Theories of Labor's Share[1]

MELVIN W. REDER

The present state of distribution theory is most unsatisfactory. This statement would probably always command a large measure of assent, irrespective of time or place; but today, in view of some recent contributions, it has perhaps more than ordinary pertinency. This is not because of the poor quality of the recent work, but because of its excessive compartmentalization. The authors who adopt an aggregative approach often write as though relative factor quantities had nothing to do with relative shares. On the other hand, the writers on the Cobb-Douglas function and related matters hardly consider the possibility that wage rigidities, unemployment, and the like might furnish alternative hypotheses to explain their findings. The students who stress profit margins, labor union pressure, and various institutional forces constitute a third stream of thought. And, finally, we have the data gatherers; these hewers and drawers pay little attention to what the theorists are cooking, except for an occasional—and usually correct—remark to the effect that the proposed bill of fare cannot be prepared from the ingredients at hand.

The purpose of this paper is twofold: (1) to compare the more important theories of labor's share with one another and (2) to study the capacity of two of them to explain empirically the behavior of labor's share in the United States.

I

Let us first examine the various theories. These may be placed in three classes: marginal productivity, or, more accurately, supply and demand theories; "mark-up" theories; and "widow's cruse" theories.

[1] This paper benefited greatly from discussions of its author with K. J. Arrow, R. M. Solow, and Lorie Tarshis. Dr. J. C. Harsanyi made a number of valuable comments on an earlier draft, and Tibor Scitovsky's editing substantially improved both style and contents. The ground rules of this volume prevented me from showing the manuscript to Bernard Haley; however, his continuing interest in this subject and his many sagacious remarks upon it have sustained my own interest and greatly influenced my ideas. Mrs. Mary Girschick performed the computations for Table A and the extensive experimentation that preceded them.

Marginal Productivity Theories

With reference to an individual firm, this theory needs no further exposition; it is a staple item in general works on economic theory. In these works, the demand of a firm for a specific factor service is determined (under pure competition) by the firm's production function, the prices of the outputs it produces and of the various factor services it uses or might use. (The monopoly and/or monopsony cases present inessential complications but no serious difficulties so long as the relevant demand and/or supply functions are known.) To get the aggregate demand curve for any one factor service, given the prices of other factors and products, is simply a matter of summing the demands of the various firms at the relevant prices of the factor in question. By an analogous though usually neglected operation, the aggregate supply function of labor (and of certain other factor services) is derived from the preference functions of the economy's households. The equilibrium of the system determines the quantities and prices of the various factors used and products turned out, given the production functions of the firms and preference functions of the households.

The relative share of any factor in net output is the ratio of its total reward (price per service unit times the number of service units used) to the net product of the system. On this theory, changes in the relative share of a factor can be explained only by shifts in production functions and/or by changes in the preference functions of the households that furnish factor services and buy products. Therefore, in order to use this theory to explain the actual behavior of a factor's share, it is necessary to relate the behavior of that share to shifts in the above functions. In a more old-fashioned terminology, this theory seeks to explain the variations in factor shares (and related phenomena) as the result of changes in tastes, techniques, and resources—and nothing else. That is, factor quantities and factor prices are supposed, in this theory, to vary in an interrelated fashion with changes in tastes, techniques, and resources.

Obviously this theory requires an hypothesis as to how these parameters (i.e., tastes, techniques, and resources) of the economic system change, and how their changes affect factor shares. Thus far, only one such hypothesis has been seriously offered: this is the hypothesis related to the construction of "aggregate production functions," particularly the Cobb-Douglas function. The details of this hypothesis will be discussed below (pp. 193–200) when we consider its empirical validity. For the present, it will suffice to mention one of its features: it implies that such market imperfections as would be reflected in a difference between the value of the marginal product of a factor and its rate of remuneration are either (1) nonexistent or (2) uncorrelated with the quantities of any output or input.

The second of these possibilities should be noted carefully; use of the marginal productivity theory via an aggregate production function does not imply an acceptance of the idea that departures from competitive conditions are negligible. It implies only that these departures are uncorrelated with the variables in terms of which the theory operates (i.e., quantities of factors and products). I do not find this possibility absurd *a priori*; it is merely one of those approximations, such as "constancy" of tastes, which is certainly untrue in detail but which *may* be justified heuristically. Whether it *is* justified can be determined only after considering the empirical results that it helps us to obtain. However, this implication of the marginal productivity theory is inconsistent with the idea that market imperfections, monopoly power, policies governing profit-margins, etc., play a role in distribution theory.[2] Some, perhaps most, economists find this unacceptable and have, therefore, looked hopefully toward some sort of "mark-up" theory.

"Mark-up" Theories

I define as "mark-up" theories those which make the distribution of the receipts of a firm, industry, group of industries, or an entire economy depend solely upon the relative prices of factor services and products, but regard these prices as being independent of relative quantities. That is, the ratio of price to average cost is "explained" as the outcome of oligopolistic agreements (explicit or implicit), conventional profit margins, and the like, and not by the presence and amount of excess capacity (of capital goods). Similarly, the wage rate is supposed to reflect union and employer bargaining power rather than the amount and sign of the excess demand for labor.

Now the mark-up theorists do not assert that excess demand in a market has no influence upon price in that market; they would probably concede that a great deal of unemployment would tend (*cet. par.*) to reduce wage rates and that "excess capacity" would (*cet. par.*) tend to reduce profit margins. However, they would insist that other forces are also important in determining such variables as wage rates and profit margins, and that these forces should not be treated as mere "disturbances." This is not, *prima facie*, an unreasonable position; my only objection is that no theory has ever been offered that relates, *in a testable way*, either factor prices or profit margins to such forces as bargaining power, oligopoly agreements, etc. Indeed, these forces have not been defined in such a way that

---

[2] It is easy, in principle, to develop a distribution theory (of the supply and demand type) which makes the demand and supply functions of the factors to individual firms depend upon the relevant degrees of monopoly and monopsony power. At the purely formal level this has been done, in good part, by Mrs. Robinson (1, 2). However, this analysis is of virtually no assistance in empirical work because of the fact that we have no way of measuring, or even indicating the direction of movement of the weighted average elasticities of the various product demand and factor supply curves in any given time period.

we could ever know when they had increased or decreased, except by looking at their alleged effects. Needless to say, this makes it impossible to refute or confirm any statements about the effect of these forces on the variables (e.g., wage rates or profit margins) whose behavior they are supposed to explain.[3]

These remarks can be made more concrete if we consider the outstanding example of an explicit mark-up theory: Kalecki's theory of income distribution.[4] In essence, this theory divides the "value added" by each firm into two parts, prime costs and the remainder; and it is focused on the expression, *product price minus average prime cost*. For any one firm, average prime cost consists exclusively of wages and raw material costs, but, for a closed economy, raw material costs will "wash-out" and we may, after aggregating, identify prime costs with wage payments.[5] Therefore, summing the above expression over all firms, we obtain the nonwage share of national income and, by subtracting this from the total, the wage share.

Of itself, this asserts nothing about the behavior of the relative shares. But Kalecki adds the assumption that the marginal cost curves of firms are, "on the average,"[6] horizontal up to capacity output. If this is granted, we may, for our purposes, substitute marginal for average prime cost in the above ratio. This makes the nonwage share (in each firm) depend exclusively upon Lerner's measure of the "degree of monopoly power"; i.e., *price minus marginal cost*. As can readily be seen, the truth of this statement is guaranteed as soon as average prime cost is assumed equal to marginal cost. Hence, the only empirically refutable statement that Kalecki makes is that marginal cost curves (in some aggregative sense) are horizontal up to capacity output.

Now, it is very unlikely that this statement is consistent with the facts.[7] However, as the issue is not relevant to our main argument, let us accept it. What follows? One and only one thing: given the stock of plant and equipment, the relative shares of labor and other factors depend upon neither the scale of output nor the relative quantities of the factors used. That is, this theory denies that the marginal productivity theory helps to explain labor's share, but does not tell us what does explain it. Adver-

[3] See below (pp. 184–85) our comment on the alleged effect of union power on wage rates.

[4] Cf. M. Kalecki (3), especially pp. 201–8; also (4), Chap. I.

[5] Kalecki, whose principal point of reference is Great Britain, usually treats the ratio of average wage cost to average raw material cost as a parameter, whose level may affect relative shares. However, our simplification changes nothing of importance.

[6] The construction of this average is a much more difficult matter than Kalecki's discussion [in (3), pp. 201–4] would suggest; it involves several implicit assumptions about noncorrelation of relevant variables.

[7] I have argued this point elsewhere: M. W. Reder (5).

tising, oligopoly agreements, union pressure, anything and everything that could conceivably affect the "degree of monopoly power" might—for all that Kalecki's theory implies—do so.[8]

Indeed, it is apparent on careful examination that if there should be a *long-run* change[9] in the labor-capital ratio, this might also affect the relative shares. That is, if capital charges per unit of output should rise relative to average prime costs, Kalecki's theory does not deny that this might lower the wage share—or do the reverse. All that it says is that any influence must alter the "average degree of monopoly power"; whether it *will* do so is not discussed.

The mark-up theory of distribution has a strong appeal to those who wish to emphasize the role of unions in determining labor's share, since it makes it possible to portray the distribution of income as a struggle between unions and employers. Such a portrayal may be a useful and harmless expository device so long as it is not taken for a theory of distribution. The temptation to do this, however, seems difficult to resist.

Consider the argument of Phelps-Brown and Hart who make unions an important factor in the determination of the level of wage rates and leave the distribution of income to be determined by the interaction of the levels of wage rates and product prices.[10] Whether the level of product prices reflects mark-up policy, the forces of supply and demand, both, or some other factors, is not specified. These writers do not claim that unions have an appreciable influence on long-term movements in labor's share, but feel that in certain types of situations, union pressure has exerted a detectable upward pressure on the wage share. Specifically, they argue that where unions are aggressive and product markets "hard" (i.e., prod-

[8] We are discussing Kalecki's theory as though it sought to explain the remuneration of all labor. Actually, it refers only to manual labor, so that shifts between manual and other kinds of labor also affect the relative shares.

[9] In a rather neglected article, "A Theory of Long-Run Distribution of the Product of Industry" (6), Kalecki has offered a "long-run" theory of distribution which is quite different from the more famous (short-run) theory we are discussing in the text. It makes the wage share depend crucially upon the degree of utilization of equipment, as well as upon mark-up policy and the ratio of average wage cost to average material cost. In this article, as in his latest statement [(4), pp. 28–31], Kalecki retreats from his earlier denial that factor proportions and level of output can affect relative shares, and thereby ceases to offer a theory of distribution.

[10] E. H. Phelps-Brown and P. E. Hart (7). The main argument of this justly famous article is not affected by this particular criticism.

Phelps-Brown and Hart are not alone in arguing in this fashion. It is a common type of argument which stems from a (commendable) desire to treat relative bargaining power as an explanatory variable though there is no way to determine its direction of movement. Because of this, bargaining power is identified with a residual; i.e., what cannot be explained otherwise is attributed to bargaining power. This is not, per se, objectionable—though it is always risky. To minimize the risk, it is necessary to analyze the impact of as many as possible of the other pertinent variables.

uct prices do not rise appreciably), labor's share tends to rise. As a description of what has happened this is acceptable; but it explains nothing.

For, as Phelps-Brown himself points out, in some (though not all) cases, hard markets lead to downward pressure on wage rates despite determined union resistance. How are we to know whether unions were more "aggressive" when wage rates rose despite hard product markets, than when (under similar circumstances) wages fell? It is possible that unions were actually "more aggressive" in the cases where wages fell, but employer resistance was still more obstinate. Unless we have some independent measures of union aggressiveness and employer resistance,[10a]—and these have not yet been furnished—using "union aggressiveness" as an explanatory factor of wage behavior is simply to affirm the consequent.

Someone may yet discover that a genuine influence is exerted by unionism upon labor's share; but so far the available evidence is entirely compatible with the view that unionism has had but a negligible effect upon labor's share.[11] In section III, we shall suggest a hypothesis that is consistent with such a lack of influence; but, in any event, we shall henceforth ignore unionism as a determinant of labor's share.

The "Widow's Cruse" Theory

We now turn to a quite different, though related, kind of theory. Based on the analogy of the widow's cruse, it has been expounded in various forms by a number of writers, notably K. E. Boulding[12] and (more recently) Nicholas Kaldor.[13] As Kaldor's version is directly concerned with labor's share, we shall base our exposition on his paper, although many of our comments are applicable to the literature as a whole.

The widow's cruse theory starts with the proposition that, for the system to be in equilibrium, *ex ante* saving and *ex ante* investment must be equal. From this it follows that if the economy is divided into sectors, each with a different marginal (and average) propensity to save, the equilibrium of the system requires that the distribution of income among these sectors be such as to generate the amount of *ex ante* saving that will equal the *ex ante* amount of investment undertaken. In the aggregate, however, the level of income, as well as its distribution, is determined by the condition that (*ex ante*) saving equals investment. This leaves us, in effect,

[10a] In correspondence, Professor Phelps-Brown has indicated that he has further evidence of a qualitative nature that indicates, independently of the results, that unions became more aggressive in certain of the periods to which he refers.

[11] The available evidence is well summarized by Kerr (8), especially p. 279 ff. The reader interested in the relevant literature will find ample guidance in Kerr's footnotes.

[12] Boulding (9), Chap. XIV, and (10), Chap. VI. Also see Bronfenbrenner (11). The present article was completed before the appearance of Weintraub's *An Approach to the Theory of Income Distribution* (12).

[13] N. Kaldor (13), especially pp. 94–95.

with one equation to determine two unknowns: the level of income and its distribution into classes.[14]

Kaldor gets out of this difficulty by considering separately the two cases of full employment and underemployment. In the former case, the level of real income is determined exogenously by the (given) stock of capital and state of productive technique—accepting for the moment the debatable assumption that the full employment of the labor force coincides with the full-capacity utilization of the stock of capital. In this case, with the level of income exogenously determined, the savings-investment equation determines relative shares.

In the underemployment case, it is assumed that the marginal physical product of labor is constant at less than capacity outputs,[15] so that marginal cost depends on the wage rate but not on the level of output.[16] The price level is also independent of output, being some multiple of marginal cost; and this multiple is assumed to be an unique function of the mark-up ratio. Thus, the relative shares are independent of national income, being determined uniquely by the ratio of product price to wage cost per unit of output. Given this ratio, exogenously-determined fluctuations in investment will affect the level of (real) national income but not its distribution so long as there is unutilized capital equipment.

In short, for this case of underemployment Kaldor, in effect, adopts Kalecki's "theory" of income distribution but (properly) does not seriously consider it a theory. Instead, he focusses his attention on the full-employment case,[17] where both factors are fully used and the elasticity of

[14] In general, the number of unknowns is equal to n, where n is the number of income classes. This is because one variable, the level of income, plus the income received by dwellers in $n-1$ income classes determines income received by dwellers in the nth class. Where, as in our case, $n = 2$, we are "short" one equation.

[15] "Capacity output" refers only to the technical capacity of the capital stock. It is assumed that the labor supply is sufficient to utilize the capital stock to its "capacity." There may be more than enough labor to accomplish this (i.e., there may be unemployment), but this is irrelevant, as unemployment is not permitted to affect the wage rate.

[16] I.e., the marginal cost curve has a reverse "L" shape.

[17] Kaldor further restricts the applicability of his model to cases where two minimum profit conditions and one minimum real wage condition are satisfied. The last condition states that the profit share must not be so large that the full employment wage level lies below a subsistence minimum. One minimum profit condition states that the rate of return on invested capital must not be less than the minimum necessary to induce capitalists to risk it, and the other states that there is a minimum rate of return on sales, reflecting market imperfections. (These restrictions are alternative to one another, only the higher of the two being applicable.) The theory that Kaldor advances is restricted in its application to the range of relative factor shares where these restrictions simultaneously apply. Kaldor further restricts the applicability of the theory to situations where the capital-output ratio is independent of the relative distributive shares of labor and capital. This restriction precludes application of the marginal productivity theory, except in the special case where the aggregate production function is of the Cobb-Douglas variety (pp. 200–205).

supply of output is zero. In this case, the level of real income is fixed, and any increase of investment implies an increase in the ratio of investment to national income and, therefore, also an increase in the ratio of saving to income. Assuming fixed propensities to save of both wage earners and others, such an increase leads (if the system is stable) to a shift of income from the sector with the lower to that with the higher propensity to save.

To see what this means, assume (with Kaldor) the wage rate to be constant and wage earners to have a lower propensity to save than do others. Then, an increase in investment must (assuming stability) lead to a rise in product prices which implies a reduction in the wage share (because the quantities of both labor and capital are fixed) sufficient to increase the saving ratio by the same amount as the increase in the investment ratio. If the wage rate rises, for whatever reason, the price level must rise even more in order to achieve the same result.[18]

To put the theory into algebra, consider the following identities (borrowed from Kaldor):

$$Y \equiv W + P \equiv C + I \tag{1}$$

where Y is national income; W wage income; and P other income, identified (for simplicity) with profits; C is consumption expenditure and I investment. From the usual savings-investment identity, we obtain

$$I \equiv S = s_w W + s_p P \tag{2}$$

where S is aggregate saving, s_w is the marginal (and average) propensity to save from wage income and s_p the analogous fraction for profits. Dividing (2) by Y and using (1), we obtain:

$$I/Y \equiv (s_p - s_w) P/Y + s_w \tag{3}$$

where $s_w < s_p$ and $s_w(W/Y) + s_p(P/Y) < I$.[19] As can be seen from (3), an increase in I/Y, the investment ratio, must be offset by an increase in P/Y, the profit share, if $s_p > s_w$.

The only characteristic of these identities worthy of comment is the special form of the consumption functions implied by (2). To treat the savings ratios, s_w and s_p, as constants independent of the level of income is to accept, by implication, a particular and controversial view of the relation of saving to income. This point is elaborated in the next section.

Since Kaldor's theory can be stated in a series of identities, the reader

[18] Alternatively, we could assume the price level to be constant and discuss the behavior of the wage rate. What is at issue is whether the ratio of the wage level to the price level is determinate (given I/Y, the ratio of investment to income) and stable with respect to displacements in I/Y. Kaldor's discussion in the aforementioned article (13) is very incomplete. In a later article [(14), especially pp. 604–14], he offers a somewhat better discussion of stability conditions.

[19] Stability requires $s_w < s_p$, provided that $d(P/Y)/d(I/Y) > 0$. This assumption is plausible; but it is not based on empirical investigation.

might well ask what state of affairs could conceivably refute it; or, less politely, isn't this "theory" a disguised tautology? *The answer is that the empirical content of the theory lies in the implicit assumption*[20] *that the saving coefficients,* s_p, *and* s_w, *are parameters which do not vary over time.* If s_p and s_w are constant over time, then it immediately follows from (3) that changes in the investment ratio must be matched by corresponding changes in the nonwage share.

Obviously, we might construct on these lines a "theory of income distribution" between any *two*[21] sectors of the economy; e.g., rich and poor, peanut-sellers and nonpeanut sellers, etc. Whether any one of these theories is of empirical interest depends entirely upon whether the difference between their respective marginal propensities to save is sufficiently large, relative to variations in investment and the sizes of the various disturbances affecting the parameters of the relevant consumption functions, to account for the observed movements in the division of the national product between the two sectors. Whether the division between wage and nonwage incomes can be usefully explained by Kaldor's model is, therefore, a matter for statistical investigation. To this subject we turn in the next section.

II

To understand the empirical significance of any theory, it is necessary to specify precisely how it is tested. For the purpose of testing we express Kaldor's theory in equations (4) and (4a). Equation (4) defines d, the difference between the actual and estimated values of I/Y. [The sole purpose of writing (4) and (4a) is to contrast them, presently, with (5).]

$$d = I/Y - \text{est.}\, I/Y \qquad (4)$$
$$\text{est.}\, I/Y = s_g + .14\, P/Y + .04\, W/Y \qquad (4a)$$

The expression (4a) is the empirical counterpart of (3), with numerical values assigned to s_w and s_p and the new term s_g added: s_g is the ratio of "Government Surplus on Income and Product Transactions to National Income"; we must insert this term in (4a) in order that, on Department of Commerce definitions, savings equal investment. As soon as we insert

[20] From Kaldor's discussion in "A Model of Economic Growth" (14), it seems clear that he regards s_w and s_p as roughly constant for long periods of time. It is, of course, possible that Kaldor's theory might be empirically meaningful even though s_p and s_w change frequently. In this case, the test of the theory would lie in the observed pattern of covariation of s_p/s_w and I/Y. However, we do not have observations on s_p and s_w at different moments of time, and therefore if the theory is to be tested on time series, s_w and s_p must be assumed to be constant. Of course, it is also possible that the theory might be useful in explaining international or interregional variations in relative shares, irrespective of temporal fluctuations in s_p and s_w, when suitable data become available.

[21] Of course, it is also possible to have three (or more) sectors. But then we need an additional equation for each additional sector (see footnote 14).

numerical values for s_g, P/Y, and W/Y, (4a) provides us, in each year, with an estimate of I/Y on the hypothesis that $s_w = .04$ and $s_p = .14$.

Looked at in this way, the test of Kaldor's theory is its performance as a predictor of movements in the investment ratio, I/Y.[22] What observations are relevant to the test? Clearly, not all observations, for the theory is supposed to apply only to situations of full employment. Hence, the depression years 1930–39 are irrelevant and, for the moment, we shall ignore them. Nothing that Kaldor says would exclude the war years (1915–19 and 1942–45) from the purview of his theory; however, it is generally believed that the savings ratios during these periods were considerably above their normal peacetime levels (i.e., during these periods s_w and s_p temporarily increased), and so we shall also abstract, temporarily, from these years.[23]

What of the remaining years? Are they "full-employment" years in the sense required by Kaldor's theory? Probably not, in a literal sense, for it is very unlikely that an "aggregate" marginal cost curve would have the required reverse L shape. Nonetheless, 1909–14, 1923–29, and 1946–56 were periods of reasonably full employment during which variations in I/Y might have been expected to affect S/Y primarily by redistributing income—or by altering savings ratios—and only to a limited degree by shifting the level of current output and employment. Let us assume, therefore, that the aforementioned periods were sufficiently good approximations to full employment (in the United States) to use for testing Kaldor's theory.

The test to be made is how well the annual levels of I/Y can be predicted, with the aid of equation (4a), from the annual levels of W/Y and P/Y. The success of the theory in meeting this test is indicated by the resulting size of d in equation (4). Kaldor's theory implies that d will be as small in each full-employment period as in the base period 1948–50, whose data were used for calculating the values of s_p and s_w on the assumption that d is approximately zero. (Actually, d is not zero but $+.002$ for the base period with the values of s_p and s_w used.) The annual values of d, and of the variables from which it is computed, are presented in Appendix Table A; a summary of which is presented in Table I below.

As column 4a of Table I shows, the average size of d was $+.002$ in the base years of 1948–50. For the logic of the argument, the values assigned

[22] Since Kaldor's theory is concerned with labor's share, W/Y, and not with I/Y, the reader may wonder why we have not tested the theory by its ability to predict W/Y. It would, of course, have been possible to do so; however, such a test would have been logically equivalent to the one used and would have involved extra calculations.

[23] The selection of the particular years included in the "war periods" was made, frankly, *ex post facto*. That is, we looked at the data to see which years had unusually high saving ratios and defined the "war periods" accordingly. The depression decade was defined arbitrarily as 1930–39.

to s_w and s_p should be considered to be arbitrary; however, they were chosen from among the possible pairs that would make d roughly zero in the base period, with an eye to realism.[24] For the period 1946–56, the average value of d was $-.004$; for 1923–29 it was $+.005$; for 1921–29 it was $-.001$; and for 1909–14 it was $+.020$. I interpret the values of d for either 1921–29 or 1923–29 and for 1946–56 as "small"; i.e., as being not inconsistent with the acceptance of Kaldor's theory. One reason for this interpretation is that the average values of d in each of these periods lies within one standard deviation of the annual values of d when these values are measured from zero. Another reason is that in 1949–56, the average value of d was only about $1/200$ of I/Y and in 1923–29, about $1/20$ of I/Y.

TABLE I

AVERAGE VALUES OF d COMPUTED FROM EQUATIONS; (4a) AND (5)
FOR SELECTED PERIODS*

	(4a)	(5)
Base Period 1948–50	$+.002$	$-.003$
Full Employment Periods		
1946–56	$-.0004$	$-.007$
1923–29	$+.005$	$+.004$
1921–29	$-.001$	$+.003$
1909–14	$+.020$	$+.021$
Other Periods		
1915–19	$+.097$	$+.100$
1930–39	$-.084$	$-.085$
1942–45	$+.122$	$+.118$

* Data from Appendix Table A.

The data for 1909–14 are not so easily reconciled with Kaldor's theory. They suggest that s_w or s_p (or both) might have been higher before World War I than thereafter.[25] However, the quality of the pre-1919 data is such as to inhibit inference. It may be that the greater size of d in 1909–14, as compared with the other "full-employment" periods, is merely a statistical artifact.

[24] The coefficients chosen are roughly consistent with the available estimates of s_w and various parts of s_p made from budgetary data for the period 1948–50. The published estimates to which we refer are in Table 5 of Friedman (15), p. 71. Also see Brady (16), Table H-9, p. 157.

[25] The standard deviation of the annual observations in 1909–14 was .021. Hence the difference between the entries in Table I for 1909–14 and 1946–56 is about two standard deviations of the latter period and one of the former. This would be insufficient to reject the hypothesis that the coefficients for the two periods were the same if one chose to believe it.

But to assert that a set of data are or are not reasonably consistent with a particular hypothesis requires that we also test their consistency with some alternative hypothesis. One obvious alternative to (4a) is that $s_w = s_p$; i.e., the saving ratio is the same for both groups of income receivers. This hypothesis is expressed by (5) which is an analogue of (4a), the only difference being that in (5) we assume that $s_w = s_p = .08$.

$$\text{est. } I/Y = s_g + .08 \tag{5}$$

The results of applying (5) to the data of Appendix Table A are summarized in column (5) of Table I. Comparing columns (4a) and (5) of Table I shows that the hypothesis that $s_w = s_p$ does just about as well as Kaldor's theory; i.e., the differences between the entries for the base period (1948–50) and the given periods are about the same (and small) in both columns.[26] This judgment is confirmed by the fact that the difference between the entries in any row of Table I is substantially less than the standard deviation of annual values of d on either hypothesis.

In other words, it is difficult to choose between Kaldor's theory and our "dummy" alternative expressed by (5).[27] However, while this does not preclude the possibility that variations in the relative shares of national income "explain" variations in the savings ratio, it does mean that variations in the distribution of wage income among workers; of nonwage income among its recipients (especially the ratio of corporate to noncorporate profits); and of exogenous shifts in the savings functions of households, governments, and firms have so combined as to have had just about the same effect upon the savings ratio as shifts in relative shares. If we could state that the coefficients in (4a) were more realistic than those in (5)—and I think they are—this would be a point in favor of Kaldor's hypothesis. However, the method of selecting these coefficients precludes any such argument.

[26] Since both entries for the base period are very close to zero, the reader may, for convenience, treat the absolute size of the various entries as indicating the extent of their disagreement with the hypothesis under consideration.

[27] The reader might also wonder whether the coefficients we have chosen for equations (4a) and (5) might not be improved upon. While it might be possible to choose "better" sets of coefficients for these equations, it is not likely that they would greatly improve the performance of either of the hypotheses considered. Examination of Table I shows that the performance of both (4a) and (5), especially the former, was extremely good for the periods 1946–56 and 1921–29 (or 1923–29). Any attempt to improve performance during 1909–14, would almost certainly worsen performance in the other periods—if s_w and s_p are assumed constant. Put in a slightly different way, the "trouble" with Kaldor's theory is not that (4a) does so badly, but that the alternative, (5), does so well.

One reason (4a) and (5) show such similar results is the limited, though genuine, variation in the relative shares in years of peacetime full employment. This means that though Kaldor's theory might be (empirically) valid, it is not in itself a very important factor in explaining the observed behavior of relative shares.

So far, we have considered the relative performance of equations (4a) and (5) in years of peacetime full employment. Now let us consider briefly the other periods. During the years of World Wars I and II, and their aftermaths, d (on both Kaldor's theory and our alternative) is large and positive. This is readily explained on the hypothesis that a household's expenditure tends to lag its income; therefore, in periods (such as major wars) when income is rising rapidly, aggregate saving ratios tend to be higher than usual. This would cause estimates of savings based on customary saving ratios to be lower than actual savings (and investment). Conversely, during the 1930's actual saving ratios were below customary ones, and our estimates of S/Y were correspondingly in excess of the observed levels of I/Y.[28] As d exhibits the same general pattern during the World Wars and the 1930's, irrespective of which hypothesis we accept, and because Kaldor's theory does not refer to such periods, I shall not attempt to discriminate between the hypothesis on the basis of evidence from these periods.

III

Let us now consider the empirical evidence bearing upon the marginal productivity theory. To test this theory it is necessary that we specify a functional relation among factor prices and quantities so that we can deduce a theoretical pattern of price-quantity covariations with which to compare the actual covariations. In practice, we do this by assuming (1) that the production function either remains unchanged or varies in some particular way, so that the demands for factor services can be deduced once the parameters are estimated and factor and product prices are given. It is further assumed (2) that the supply functions of the factors shift over time, and that the observed price-quantity points (assumed to represent, save for random disturbances, equilibrium positions) are traced out by the intersections of the shifting factor supply curves with the factor demand curves deduced from the fitted production function.

The price-quantity points thus generated are supposed to be positions of "general equilibrium." That is, they are positions where (apart from random disturbances) every firm and every market is in equilibrium, and where each factor is so allocated that the value of its marginal physical product is equal in all uses. There is no point in arguing whether these

[28] This view is similar to that expounded as part of the "permanent income hypothesis" by Milton Friedman in "A Theory of the Consumption Function" (15). However, the lag hypothesis mentioned in the text may be rationalized on several different hypotheses.

It might also be mentioned that the savings functions given in equation (2) are of a specific kind which imply that savings are a constant fraction of income (i.e., are independent of the level of income). This form of savings function was specified, without discussion, by Kaldor. However, it is an essential part of Friedman's permanent income hypothesis that savings functions should be of this form.

assumptions are "sufficiently realistic." The only way to find out is to accept them and see what follows.

To discuss the relative size of two factor shares, those of "labor" and "capital," involves considerable violence to the facts. There are many different kinds of labor and capital, and there is good reason to believe that the quantities of the various grades of labor, at least, have not varied proportionally over time.[29] Consequently, to treat sums of (equally-weighted) hours of labor at different moments of time as though they were homogeneous magnitudes is a tour de force, whose only justification (if any) is pragmatic. The problem of valuing the services of capital goods produced at different dates and possessing varying "technical" capacities creates similar difficulties. However, if the argument is not to be grounded at the start, we must brush these difficulties aside and proceed as if they did not exist.

To derive the demand curves for the two factors, labor and capital, the usual procedure is to fit an "aggregate"[30] production function to annual data of quantities of labor and capital used and output produced. In principle, a variety of functional forms could be fitted to the available data. However, for several reasons that will become apparent, we prefer to concentrate upon the Cobb-Douglas function given by:

$$P = aL^k K^j, \tag{6}$$

where P is product, L is labor, and a, K, and j are estimated parameters.

Estimating the parameters of aggregate production functions (in particular the Cobb-Douglas) from their fits to time series is subject to well-known statistical difficulties.[31] However, these difficulties are largely overcome in a recent paper by R. M. Solow.[32] Solow advances the hypothesis (1) that technical progress is neutral and stochastically independent both of relative factor quantities and the level of output, and (2) that there is constant returns to scale. That is, it is hypothesized that the relative marginal physical productivities of two factors are determined uniquely by the ratio of their quantities. Put in a slightly different way, this states that the aggregate production function is, at any moment of time, identical with what it was at any previous moment, save for a vertical displacement.

Solow shows that where a production function of two factors is homo-

---

[29] That is, the number of unskilled workers has declined relative to the total. This implies that there has been a secular improvement in the quality of the aggregate labor input unit; the consequences of this for the estimated parameters of the Cobb-Douglas function are discussed by Zvi Griliches (17), especially pp. 14–16.

[30] I.e., a function involving the operations of more than one firm.

[31] These have been pointed out by a long list of authors; and most recently by Professor E. H. Phelps-Brown (18).

[32] R. M. Solow, "Technical Change and the Aggregate Production Function" (19).

geneous of degree one, the percentage change in output, at any moment of time, will equal the "rate of technical progress"[33] plus the share of capital times the percentage change in the ratio of capital to labor. If technical progress is neutral, then the aggregate production function takes the multiplicative form,

$$P = A(t)aL^kK^{1-k} \qquad (6a)$$

where $A(t)$ is a variable which reflects technical progress and all economic forces correlated therewith.

The legitimacy of (6a) depends crucially upon the hypothesis of neutrality in technical progress. The evidence in favor of this hypothesis is as follows: if technical progress were neutral and independent of the level of output, then the (percentage) changes in output would be uncorrelated with the percentage changes in the ratio of capital to labor. Solow constructed a scatter diagram of these two variables and, finding no relation whatever between them, concluded that the evidence supported the hypothesis of neutrality. Though at least one other possibility remains,[34] the hypothesis of neutrality has thus far been substantiated and (6a) may therefore be accepted, tentatively, as an aggregate (private nonfarm) production function, for the United States in the period 1909–53.

The principal advantages of (6a) over (6) are as follows; (6a) is fitted to the time series

$$(P/L)/A(t) \text{ and } (K/L)^{1-k},[35]$$

neither of which contains a trend; i.e., we are correlating variables largely free of auto-correlation.[36] Consequently, the statistical instability which

[33] Defined as the percentage increase in product, per time period, with given factor inputs.

[34] I.e., that the production function is not homogeneous of degree one and is "biased" in such a way as to offset the underlying pattern of association of technical progress with changes in factor ratios.

There is some independent evidence for the hypothesis that the production function is homogeneous of the first degree. Professor Solow has told me that he has, since publication, fitted a Cobb-Douglas function where the exponents of L and K were determined independently; i.e., $j + k$ was not forced to equal one. It turned out that the fitted function was $P/A = aL^{.6181}K^{.3381}$. (The agreement of the implied capital share, .3381, with the actual capital share is obvious.) The sum of the exponents, .9562, is within one standard error of unity, as the standard error of the sum of the exponents is .048.

[35] That is, Solow divides (6a) through by L and then by $A(t)$, so that after taking logs we have log $[P/L/A(t)] = \log a + 1-k \ [\log \ (K/L)]$.

[36] The series used by Solow are P/L, $A(t)$, and K/L. $A(t)$ is the factor reflecting technical progress. The K/L series does exhibit an upward trend from 1909 to 1923, but none thereafter.

has plagued previous attempts to fit Cobb-Douglas functions is largely avoided.[37]

A further though related advantage is that while the ordinary Cobb-Douglas function makes no allowance whatever for technical progress, (6a) does. Ignoring technical progress is contrary to common sense and may have been responsible for some of the difficulties in obtaining sensible esti-mates of the coefficients of the fitted functions.[38] A further "practical" improvement of Solow's work over most previous efforts is that he uses labor employed, rather than the size of the labor force, as a measure of L and also corrects K (conceptually) for idle capacity.

There is one important difference between Solow's own discussion of his results and ours. We have focussed our attention on the Cobb-Douglas function, while Solow fitted five different functions. Among these five, the Cobb-Douglas gave as good a fit as any, but there is no purely statistical reason for preferring it to three of the others.[39] However, the Cobb-Douglas function (when it is homogeneous of the first degree) is the only function which has the property of implying that the factors receive the same rela-tive shares *whatever* their (non-negative) quantities.[40] Put differently, the Cobb-Douglas is the only function which has a unit elasticity of substitu-tion at all points (assuming first-degree homogeneity).

[37] Unfortunately, the standard errors of the coefficients of (6a) are not avail-able. However, Professor Solow has told me in conversation that he recalls the coefficients as being many times greater than their standard errors, indicating a high degree of statistical stability. In the calculation mentioned in footnote 34, Solow found that the standard error of the labor exponent is .0662, and of the capital exponent, .0405; i.e., the labor exponent is more than nine times its standard error and the capital coefficient more than eight times its standard error.

[38] For example, negative exponents for capital have been obtained for Ameri-can manufacturing for the 1920's.

[39] I.e., the correlation coefficient between observed and estimated values of $P/A(t)$ was for all functions better than .99 for all functions.

[40] This can be shown as follows: let the total income of capital be equal to rK and the wage-bill be wL where r is the rate of return per unit of capital service and w is the wage rate. The value of output, P, is identically equal to $rK + wL$; $P \equiv rK + wL$. Now the marginal productivity theory implies, assuming (6) to be the production function, $w = \partial P/\partial L = k(P/L)$ and $r = \partial P/\partial K = j(P/K)$; alterna-tively $L(\partial P/\partial L) = kP = wL$ and $K(\partial P/\partial K) = jP = rK$. Substituting,
$$P \equiv (j+k)P;$$
therefore $k + j = 1$. The share of labor is kP/P, and of capital jP/P; hence the ratio of the shares is k/j or $k/(1-k)$ where j and k are constants and independent of relative factor quantities and output.

To obtain this result it is necessary that $L(\partial P/\partial L) = kP$ and $K(\partial P/\partial K) = jP$, j and k being constants whose sum equals unity. Otherwise $L(\partial P/\partial L)$ and $K(\partial P/\partial K)$ could not be constant fractions of product, independent of the levels of P, L and K. But kP/L and jP/L are the derivatives of the Cobb-Douglas func-tion; therefore, only the Cobb-Douglas function is consistent with (1) constant relative shares, (2) variations in L/K, and (3) the production function being ho-mogeneous of the first degree.

This means that if labor's share is constant over time, and if factor markets are cleared by the forces of supply and demand, we must either accept the Cobb-Douglas function as the proper relation among the aggregates of output, labor, and capital or argue that the constant shares result from secularly constant ratios of factor quantities and factor prices. This second possibility is not to be dismissed lightly; however, from Solow's data it appears that for the period 1909–53 employed capital per man-hour varied from a low of $2.06 to a maximum of $3.33 (a variation of 47 per cent about the mid-point of the range). It is pointless to argue abstractly as to whether this is little or much variation; it was sufficient variation to fit a statistical regression of $P/A(t)$ on K/L with "satisfactory" results, but it was not sufficient variation to prevent several different functions (all homogeneous of the first degree) from giving very good fits to the data. In short, in the United States during 1909–53, the fit of the Cobb-Douglas function is to a range of observations not sufficiently "wide" to enable us to choose (on statistical grounds) from among several functions, all homogeneous of the first degree. Our choice of the Cobb-Douglas function must rest upon its analytical properties; e.g., the fact that it implies constant shares.

We must next consider two separate, but related questions: is labor's share (and therefore that of its complement) constant over time; and if so, is the size of the share equal to that implied by the coefficients of the fitted Cobb-Douglas function (or nearly so)?

(1) Before discussing the constancy of labor's share, it is necessary to specify what we include in that share. In Section II we defined labor's share as the share of Employee Compensation in National Income. For our present purpose, this definition is unacceptable; what we need is a concept that includes the value of the services of the self-employed as well as of the wage earners. Also, it is desirable to avoid the complications stemming from the growing economic role of government; clearly the employee share of government product is fictitiously high (judged by the standard of private accounting rules) because of the absence of profits and of charges for the services of government-owned capital. Hence, we restrict our discussion to the private sector of the economy. Finally, because Solow's data exclude Agriculture (they refer to the private nonfarm sector) we are also compelled—if we wish to make use of his results—to confine our argument to the (private) nonfarm sector.[41]

The difference between the definition used in this section of the paper

[41] Another reason is that there is considerable evidence that the marginal productivity of labor is lower in agriculture than in industry, so that shifts out of the former and into the latter would be inconsistent with the hypothesis on which an aggregate production function is based. On the difference between the marginal productivity of labor in agriculture and industry, see M. W. Reder [(20), especially pp. 78–79].

and that used in Section II is very important. The share of Employee Compensation (the concept used in Section II) is *not* secularly constant; on the contrary it has risen appreciably since 1910.[42] However, the share of wage earners plus the imputed earnings of the self-employed (what is sometimes called labor's functional share) in Private non-Farm Product behaves quite differently. It is quite possible that, despite the upward trend in the share of Employee Compensation, labor's functional share has stayed constant in the United States since 1910 or thereabouts. First let us consider the period 1929–52; the salient facts for which are presented in Table II. It is clear that, for the economy as a whole, the share of Employee Compensation rose during this period. However, if we look at the various sub-sectors of the "ordinary business sector," there is no evidence of an upward trend in the employee share in any one of them. This suggests, and Table III confirms, that the economy-wide increase in the share of employees results principally from an increase in their relative numbers in industries with more than average employee shares.

One very important example of such a shift is the relative decline of Agriculture as a labor user with its very low employee share.[43] (The reason for the low employee share in Agriculture is the large fraction of labor furnished by farm operators and their families, most of which is not reported as wages.) Another instance of such a shift is the rise in importance of government which has an unusually high employee share. The relative growth of government employment is primarily responsible for the marked rise in the employee share in "all other sectors" (shown in Table II).

Because of these and similar facts, Denison concludes that, during prosperous peacetime years,[44] there is "substantial stability" in the employee share of income in the ordinary business sector, when account is taken of structural changes in that sector.[45] Excluding government confines our analysis (approximately) to the ordinary business sector, and excluding agriculture eliminates most of the structural change in the ordinary business sector from which Denison abstracts. The remaining major source of structural change is the shift from wage earning to self-employment; but as this does not affect labor's *functional* share, we may interpret Denison's conclusion as tantamount to saying that labor's functional share of private nonfarm output was constant during the prosperous peacetime years of 1929–52.

[42] See D. Gale Johnson (21); also E. F. Denison (22, 23). Johnson's article contains references to the earlier literature.

[43] There is evidence of a positive trend in labor's functional share within agriculture, but this is not so marked as to upset the argument of the text.

[44] I.e., these statements do not apply to the depression years of the 1930's or to the war years, 1942–45.

[45] E. F. Denison (23), especially pp. 258–59.

TABLE II

COMPENSATION OF EMPLOYEES AS A PERCENTAGE OF NATIONAL INCOME BY SECTORS, SELECTED YEARS

Sector	1929	1941	1948	1949	1950	1951	1952	Average 1948–52
Entire economy	58.1	61.9	62.7	64.7	63.8	64.3	66.3	64.3
Ordinary business:								
Nonfarm corporations ...	74.1	72.6	74.2	75.3	73.3	72.9	75.2	74.2
Nonfarm proprietorships and partnerships........	48.4	47.1	49.0	49.4	49.5	50.3	51.9	50.0
Farms	16.5	13.9	14.4	17.8	16.4	15.4	16.1	16.0
All other sectors	45.2	65.9	68.9	69.7	68.5	71.0	71.4	69.9

Source: E. F. Denison, "Income Types and the Size Distribution," *Papers and Proceedings of the 66th Annual Meeting of the American Economic Association*, May 1954, p. 257.

TABLE III

ANALYSIS OF CHANGES IN EMPLOYEE SHARE IN NATIONAL INCOME,
1941–52

Year	Actual Change from 1929	Change Due to Shifts in Industry Weights	Change Due to Share Shifts Within Industries
1941	—0.8	0.8	—1.6
1948	—0.4	0.4	—0.8
1949	1.7	1.2	0.5
1950	0.8	1.6	—0.8
1951	0.8	1.8	—1.0
1952	3.1	2.3	0.8
Average 1948–52	1.2	1.5	—0.3

Source: E. F. Denison, "Income Types and the Size Distribution," *Papers and Proceedings of the 66th Annual Meeting of the American Economic Association*, May 1954, p. 258.

For the longer period, 1900–1909 to 1947–52, Johnson estimates that the (functional) share of labor in the private sector of the economy rose from 68.0 to 71.5 per cent. Part of this small increase was fictitious (because of differences in living costs in rural and urban areas), and Johnson seems to attribute the remainder to the shift of workers away from agriculture. In view of the limitations of the data, it is not stretching matters too far to say that there is general agreement between Johnson's and Denison's estimates. In any case, if we confine our attention to the private nonfarm sector, both Johnson's and Denison's data would be consistent with the hypothesis of a secularly-constant distribution of income between labor and capital during "prosperous peacetime years."

(2) Now let us turn briefly to the second question. Does labor's share, as computed from the modified Cobb-Douglas function, (6a), agree with the actual share? The available estimate of labor's functional share, Johnson's[46] places it from 68 to 71.5 per cent in the period 1900–1909 to 1947–52. Now Solow's published estimate of the exponent of L in (6a) is

$$1 - .353 = .647.$$

Unfortunately, the standard error of this coefficient is unavailable, but in a subsequent calculation Solow obtained an exponent for L of .6181 with a standard error of .0662.[47] This estimate of L, plus two standard errors,

[46] D. Gale Johnson (21).

[47] The difference between this estimate and that published is due to the fact that this estimate was made "directly"; i.e., was not computed as a residual from one minus the exponent of capital. (See footnote 34 above.)

is .7405; .6181 and .7405 comfortably span Johnson's estimate. In short, the marginal productivity theory, in this form, is not refuted by the facts.[48]

One further "advantage" of the marginal productivity theory, with the Cobb-Douglas accepted as the appropriate form of the aggregate production function, is that it explains why unionism has had little effect on labor's share. That is, the theory thus limited implies that the mechanisms of product and factor substitution have been such that whatever pressure unions have been able to bring to bear upon wage rates has been offset, insofar as any effect on relative shares is concerned.

IV

Thus, there is some merit in the marginal productivity explanation of relative shares.[49] However, let us not go overboard; the data refer only to one historical period in one country. And, even in this case, the data are not such as to guarantee that the results bear the interpretation placed upon them. An even more fundamental objection to our argument is that, unless we can relate an aggregate production function to the production functions of individual firms, our aggregate function is "floating in air." And we know very little about the production functions of individual firms, or even of industries.[50] In fact, within individual industries there is also very substantial stability (over time) of the wage share.[51] Thus, we may need an aggregate Cobb-Douglas function for individual industries, of which an economy-wide Cobb-Douglas function must be a "super-aggregate." Whether this program of constructing aggregate production functions can be carried out consistently remains to be seen.[52]

[48] It should be noted that Johnson's data refer to the private sector as a whole, and not to the nonfarm sector exclusively. However, the difference between labor's functional share in agriculture and elsewhere is not very great. Johnson (24) has estimated that labor's functional share in Agriculture is of the order of 65 per cent.

[49] A further advantage of the Cobb-Douglas function, as compared with Kaldor's theory, is that (after adjustment for unemployment of labor and underutilization of capital) it applies to all years and not merely to those of peacetime full employment.

[50] A promising beginning has been made by H. S. Houthakker (see 25).

[51] In a forthcoming paper, R. M. Solow points out that, within the manufacturing sector, the evidence for temporal stability of the share of wages within individual industries is at least as persuasive as that for stability in the aggregate.

[52] Many years ago, I criticized severely the then-current interpretation of Cobb-Douglas functions in "cross-sectional" studies. [M. W. Reder (26).] Nothing said here is in any way inconsistent with this criticism. Indeed, I think the "cross-section" studies are subject to a more serious criticism than the one made in the earlier article.

The cross-section functions imply, as does any Cobb-Douglas function, that the rewards per service unit of either factor must vary with the ratio of the factors used; i.e., partially differentiating $P = aL^kK^j$ with respect to L, we have

But what of Kaldor's theory; how does it fit together with marginal productivity, if at all. The answer is that, contrary to Kaldor's opinion,[53] the theories need not be inconsistent. Kaldor's theory "explains" the secular rise in the share of Employee Compensation, while the marginal productivity theory (as we have developed it) "explains" the secular constancy of labor's functional share. To see what it means for both theories to hold simultaneously, suppose that factor markets are cleared but the share of Employee Compensation is too big to generate enough savings to prevent inflation. Then, assuming stability, the employee share would tend to fall as wage earners became self-employed, thereby acquiring higher propensities to save.[54] Whether a dynamic mechanism such as this exists is far from obvious; but it is by no means absurd to suppose that it might.[55]

This mechanism can be visualized by means of Figure 1, on whose vertical axis we measure I/Y and S/Y (as defined in Section II), and on whose horizontal axis we measure fractions of national income. (All points in Figure 1 refer to positions of full employment of both labor and capital.) The line $(I/Y)_0$ gives the actual value of I/Y, which is determined exogenously; the SS' curve relates the aggregate saving ratio to the wage share. (The wage share and labor's functional share are measured from the vertical axis; their complements are measured from the unity line.) Equilibrium is reached where SS' cuts the $(I/Y)_0$ line; i.e., where the wage share is OW.[56] Labor's functional share is given by the vertical line, L, so that if the wage share were OW, the share of the self-employed would be WL. Disequilibrium would lead to changes in the ratio WL/OW; that is, in the ratio of Employee Compensation to the income of the self-employed. L is a vertical line because we assume arbi-

---

$$\partial P / \partial L = k(P/L).$$

As P/L obviously varies in the same direction as K (and in the opposite direction from L), the marginal productivity of labor, $\partial P / \partial L$, and hence the wage rate, must be different for differing quantities of either capital or labor. But this is inconsistent with the assumption that all units of labor (or capital) are homogeneous; hence the properties of the fitted cross-section functions mirror either the effect of qualitative differences in factor inputs or of exogenous factors that are correlated with industry size, but not the marginal productivity of (homogeneous) factors.

[53] Cf. Kaldor, pp. 592–93 in (14). Kaldor also argues that it is arbitrary to separate movements along a production function from shifts in it [see (14), pp. 595–98]; by implication, this impugns the validity of (6a). Certainly, the distinction in question is arbitrary, but its justification derives entirely from the results that it helps us obtain and charges of arbitrariness are irrelevant.

[54] This assumes that self-employed persons have a higher propensity to save than wage earners with the same income.

[55] Note that an important type of shift from self-employment to wage earning is movement from agriculture to "industry."

[56] Assume the position is stable; i.e., that if $S/Y > (I/Y)$, the wage share increases and vice versa.

trarily that labor's functional share is deduced from a Cobb-Douglas function and independent of I/Y.[57] However, if the production function were of some other form, labor's functional share might be related to I/Y by some relation such as ZZ_1. (Unity minus OL is the nonlabor share, which is also derived from a Cobb-Douglas function.) Thus it is possible that Kaldor's theory and the marginal productivity theory both hold.

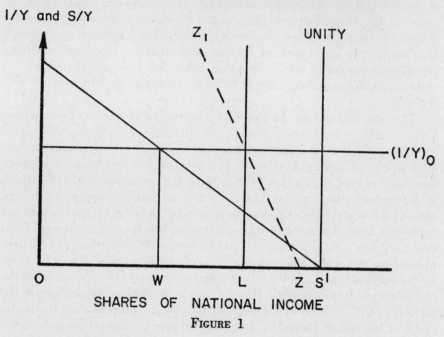

FIGURE 1

Figure 1 suggests that a satisfactory explanation either of labor's share or the share of Employee Compensation is simpler than it really is. Actually, the distribution of income is determined by the entire set of prices and quantities that the economy generates. Hence, any very large aggregates will be interrelated via the different relative weights attached to their various common components. To investigators of cautious temperament, this undeniable fact will always be adequate reason for eschewing models of the kind we have been considering. Perhaps such caution is justified, and it is foolish to take aggregative distribution theories seriously.

However, I venture the following self-serving opinion: even though

[57] It will not generally be true that the coefficients of a Cobb-Douglas function will be independent of the income share of the self-employed. I.e., a shift in the aggregate propensity to save will very likely shift the pattern of final demand and hence the coefficients, or possibly the functional form, of the aggregate production function. However, for simplicity, we confine ourselves to the special case where such independence obtains.

TABLE A

ESTIMATED COMPONENTS OF SAVINGS AND (ACTUAL) INVESTMENT,
1909–56

	(1) S_w	(2) S_p	(3) S_g	(4) Sum (1)–(3)	(5) I/Y	(6)* (5)–(4)
1909	.023	.060	.009	.092	.115	.023
1910	.023	.058	.008	.089	.138	.049
1911	.024	.057	.009	.090	.087	−.003
1912	.023	.058	.013	.094	.135	.041
1913	.024	.057	.016	.097	.100	.003
1914	.024	.056	.007	.087	.095	.008
1915	.023	.060	.009	.092	.173	.081
1916	.022	.063	.018	.103	.212	.109
1917	.021	.067	−.044	.043	.165	.122
1918	.024	.056	−.159	−.079	.022	.101
1919	.022	.061	−.071	.012	.082	.070
1920	.026	.049	.026	.101	.153	.052
1921	.028	.042	.016	.086	.055	−.031
1922	.025	.052	.014	.091	.074	−.017
1923	.025	.051	.022	.098	.120	.022
1924	.026	.051	.024	.101	.081	−.020
1925	.025	.053	.021	.099	.122	.023
1926	.025	.051	.026	.102	.113	.011
1927	.026	.049	.029	.105	.102	−.003
1928	.025	.051	.023	.099	.090	−.009
1929	.023	.051	.026	.100	.115	+.015
1930	.025	.053	−.003	.075	.041	−.034
1931	.026	.046	−.042	.030	−.048	−.078
1932	.030	.038	−.034	.034	−.143	−.177
1933	.030	.036	−.028	.038	−.135	−.173
1934	.028	.042	−.041	.029	−.078	−.107
1935	.026	.049	−.030	.045	−.013	−.058
1936	.026	.047	−.039	.038	−.004	−.042
1937	.026	.049	+.007	.082	.052	−.030
1938	.026	.046	−.020	.052	−.006	−.058
1939	.026	.048	−.026	.048	.014	−.034
1940	.026	.051	−.008	.069	.062	−.007
1941	.025	.053	−.032	.046	.084	.038
1942	.025	.053	−.211	−.133	.002	.131
1943	.026	.050	−.244	−.168	−.032	.136
1944	.026	.048	−.260	−.186	−.049	.137
1945	.027	.046	−.198	−.125	−.040	+.085
1946	.026	.049	+.021	.096	.097	−.001
1947	.026	.050	+.061	.137	.106	−.031
1948	.026	.053	+.033	.112	.119	+.007
1949	.026	.049	−.013	.062	.061	−.001

TABLE A—(*Continued*)

	(1) S_w	(2) S_p	(3) S_g	(4) Sum (1)–(3)	(5) I/Y	(6)* (5) – (4)
1950	.026	.051	+.031	.108	.107	−.001
1951	.026	.050	+.020	.096	.106	+.010
1952	.027	.047	−.010	.064	.074	+.010
1953	.027	.046	−.020	.053	.057	+.004
1954	.028	.043	−.019	.052	.052	0
1955	.027	.043	+.007	.077	.074	−.003
1956	.028	.041	+.013	.082	.083	+.001

Sources: 1909–28: *Economic Almanac, 1953–1954* (Crowell, New York, 1953), pp. 504–5 (data derived from unpublished estimates of the Department of Commerce), and Raymond Goldsmith, *Study of Saving in the United States* (Princeton University Press, Princeton, 1956). 1929–56: *Survey of Current Business*, February 1957 and July 1957.

* Components may not precisely equal total because of rounding.

1909–1929

Column 1 $.04 \times$ $\dfrac{\text{Employee Compensation}}{\text{National Income}}$ from *Economic Almanac* pp. 504–505.

Column 2 $.14 \times$ $\dfrac{1 \text{ minus Employee Compensation}}{\text{National Income}}$ *Economic Almanac op. cit.*

Column 3 $\dfrac{\text{Sum columns 7 and 8, Table T-1, Goldsmith}}{\text{Column 2, Table N-1, Goldsmith}}$

Column 5 $\dfrac{\text{Column 1, Table T-1, Goldsmith minus (Sum of Column 5,}}{\text{Column 2, Table T-1, Goldsmith}}$ Table T-8 and Column 5, Table A-3, Goldsmith)

1929–1956 (*Survey of Current Business,* February and July, 1957)

Column 1 $.04 \times$ $\dfrac{\text{Compensation of Employees}}{\text{National Income}}$

Column 2 $.14 \times$ $\dfrac{1 \text{ minus Employee Compensation}}{\text{National Income}}$

Column 3 $\dfrac{\text{Government surplus on income and product transactions}}{\text{National Income}}$

Column 5 $\dfrac{\text{Gross Investment minus (Business Depreciation Charges plus Accidental Damage to Fixed Business Capital)}}{\text{Net National Product}}$

we never succeed in creating a generally accepted aggregative distribution theory—and there is a good chance that we will not—the attempt to do so is likely to uncover a number of interrelations between different aggregates of which some will prove helpful in formulating and testing theories about other aspects of the economy. Put in another way, any theory about the whole economy will have corollaries about income distribution; Kaldor's theory and marginal productivity are two illustrations of this. To deduce and test these corollaries cannot help but improve our understanding of the operation of the economy.

APPENDIX

Table A contains the figures on which text Table I is based. Column 1 (S_w), in each year, is the share of Employee Compensation in National Income multiplied by the assumed marginal (and average) propensity to save, .04. The entries in column 2 (S_p) are found by multiplying one minus the share of Employee Compensation in National Income by the assumed marginal (and average) propensity to save, .14. This last figure is an amalgam of the appropriate propensities of households to save nonwage income and of corporations to retain (pre-tax)[1] earnings. Column 3 (S_g) is the ratio of the government surplus or deficit to National Income;[2] as S_g plays no role in Kaldor's theory it is measured directly for each year. But, though S_g plays no role in the theory, it is necessary to include it in order to satisfy the savings-investment identity.[3]

Column 5 (I/Y) is the ratio of Net Investment to National Income. Conceptually, we have aimed at getting our estimates of Y and $I \equiv S$ as close as possible to Net National Product (National Income at market prices) and net investment; i.e., Gross Investment minus (Business depreciation plus Accidental damage to fixed business capital). These definitions of saving and investment exclude purchases of durable consumer goods; this choice of concepts was made for reasons of statistical convenience only.

References

1. Joan Robinson, The Economics of Imperfect Competition. Macmillan, New York, 1933. Books VII–IX.
2. Joan Robinson, "Euler's Theorem and the Problem of Distribution," *Economic Journal*, 1934, pp. 398–414.
3. M. Kalecki, "The Distribution of the National Income," in William Fellner and B. F. Haley (eds.), Readings in the Theory of Income Distribution. Blakiston, Philadelphia, 1946, pp. 197–217.

---

[1] We are concerned with pre-tax profits because the saving propensities of the other components of S_p are defined with reference to Personal Income rather than Disposable Income.

[2] "Government" includes all government plus Government surplus on income and product transactions plus Statistical Discrepancy equals Gross Investment.

[3] I.e., Gross Private Saving plus Government surplus on income and product transactions plus Statistical Discrepancy equals Gross Investment.

4. M. Kalecki, Theory of Economic Dynamics. Rinehart, New York, 1954, Chap. I.

5. M. W. Reder, "Rehabilitation of Partial Equilibrium Theory," *American Economic Review*, May 1952, pp. 182–97.

6. M. Kalecki, "A Theory of Long-Run Distribution of the Product of Industry," *Oxford Economic Papers*, June 1941, pp. 31–41.

7. E. H. Phelps-Brown and P. E. Hart, "The Share of Wages in National Income," *Economic Journal*, June 1952, pp. 253–77.

8. Clark Kerr, "Labor's Income Share and the Labor Movement," in G. W. Taylor and F. C. Pierson (eds.), New Concepts in Wage Determination. McGraw-Hill, New York, 1957, pp. 260–98.

9. K. E. Boulding. A Reconstruction of Economics. Wiley, New York, 1950, Chap. 14.

10. K. E. Boulding, in D. M. Wright (ed.), The Impact of the Union. Harcourt, Brace, New York, 1951, Chap. VI.

11. M. Bronfenbrenner, "A Contribution to the Aggregative Theory of Wages," *Journal of Political Economy*, December 1956.

12. S. Weintraub, An Approach to the Theory of Income Distribution. Chilton, Philadelphia, 1958.

13. N. Kaldor, "Alternative Theories of Distribution," *Review of Economic Studies*, XXIII (2), No. 61 (1955–56), 83–100.

14. N. Kaldor, "A Model of Economic Growth," *Economic Journal*, December 1957, pp. 591–614.

15. Milton Friedman, A Theory of the Consumption Function. National Bureau of Economic Research. Princeton University Press, Princeton, 1957.

16. D. S. Brady, "Family Saving, 1888 to 1950," in Goldsmith, Brady, and Mendershausen, A Study of Saving in the United States. Princeton University Press, Princeton, 1957, Vol. III, Table H-9, 1957.

17. Zvi Griliches, "Specification Bias in Estimates of Production Functions," *Journal of Farm Economics*, February 1957, pp. 8–20.

18. E. H. Phelps-Brown, "The Meaning of the Fitted Cobb-Douglas Function," *Quarterly Journal of Economics*, November 1957, pp. 546–60.

19. R. M. Solow, "Technical Change and the Aggregate Production Function," *Review of Economics and Statistics*, August 1957, pp. 312–20.

20. M. W. Reder, "Wage Determination in Theory and Practice," in N.W. Chamberlain *et al.* (eds.), A Decade of Industrial Relations Research. Harper, New York, 1958, pp. 64–97.

21. D. Gale Johnson, "The Functional Distribution of Income in the United States, 1850–1952," *Review of Economics and Statistics*, May 1954, pp. 175–82.

22. E. F. Denison, "Distribution of National Income," *Survey of Current Business*, June 1952, pp. 16–23.

23. E. F. Denison, "Income Types and the Size Distribution," *American Economic Review*, May 1952, pp. 254–69.

24. D. Gale Johnson, "Allocation of Agriculture Income," *Journal of Farm Economics*, November 1948, pp. 724–49.

25. H. S. Houthakker, "The Pareto Distribution and the Cobb-Douglas Production Function in Activity Analysis," *Review of Economics and Statistics*, XXIII (1), No. 60 (1955–56), 27–31.

26. M. W. Reder, "An Alternative Interpretation of the Cobb-Douglas Function," *Econometrica*, July 1943, pp. 259–64.

Growth--Balanced or Unbalanced?

TIBOR SCITOVSKY

One of the questions most often asked by economists nowadays concerns the conditions most favorable to economic growth. This can lead one far afield, away from economics; but among the economic factors conducive to growth, two have received much attention: economic interdependence, which favors balanced growth, and economies of scale, which call for growth by large steps. Since growth by large steps often requires concentrated growth, there is something of a contradiction between these two factors. In addition, there are a number of other factors as well that also call for concentrated growth. The nature of these conflicting factors and of the conflict they involve is the subject matter of this paper.

THE EARLY ARGUMENT FOR CONCENTRATED GROWTH

Historically, and that means both in economic history and in the history of economic thought, unbalanced or concentrated growth came first. An early example of concentrated growth is England's industrial revolution; its early theory is contained in Ricardo's doctrine of comparative advantage, as becomes apparent when one restates the classical doctrine in terms of growth theory and from the point of view, not of the world as a whole, but of one country—England. The problem, in terms of growth theory, is how to organize an economy whose different industries have different productivities; and Ricardo's doctrine of comparative advantage provides a solution to this problem.

In long-run equilibrium, of course, differences in value productivity tend to disappear; but the problem must be placed in a dynamic setting and arises when technical change greatly raises the productivity and profitability of some industries but not of others. Assuming that productivity in the other industries cannot be increased, the question arises what would be better in such a situation, the balanced growth of all industries or expansion confined to the now more productive industries?

This was more or less England's problem at the time of her industrial revolution, which consisted in a tremendous increase in labor productivity and reduction in cost, but only in a relatively few industries: spinning and weaving of cotton and woolen textiles, coal mining, iron manufacture, and heavy engineering. In such a situation, the resources saved through the increase in productivity in these industries can either be used to expand the output of these selfsame industries; or they can be transferred to those other industries whose productivity has not risen and used to expand their output. It is obvious that the additional physical output will be greater in the first case than in the second—and so will be the increase in the *value* of output if relative prices do not change much. In other words, a given technological improvement, if used to expand the output of the industries in which the improvement has occurred, will lead to a very different and very much greater increase in output and, possibly, welfare than if it is used to release resources to other industries and increase their output.

The above argument, however simple, is so important for what follows that we shall illustrate it with a numerical example at the risk of boring some (we hope not all) readers with it. Assume that the industries destined to be affected by the industrial revolution employ half the economy's resources and produce half its national product. Assume further that the industrial revolution lowers costs of production in these industries to one quarter of what they used to be.[1] On these assumptions, the complete displacement of the old by the new methods of production in the industries affected would enable the economy to produce its pre-revolutionary output with the aid of only five-eighths of the resources previously needed; and the remaining three-eights could be used to produce additional output. If these freed resources were entirely reabsorbed in the now more efficient industries, the latter's output would be quadrupled and, *assuming no change in relative prices*, the national product would increase by 150 per cent. If they were used to expand the output of all industries in equal proportions, the increase in national product would be 60 per cent; if they were entirely diverted from the revolutionary industries and used to expand the output of the other industries only, the increase in national product would be a mere 37½ per cent.

These three examples were chosen for their simplicity rather than for

---

[1] This example is not as extreme and unrealistic as it might seem. Cf. the following quotation from Maurice Dobb (1), p. 303: "D. A. Wells, writing in the late '80's and speaking both of U.S.A. and of Britain, estimated that the saving in time and effort involved in production in recent years had amounted to as much as 70 or 80 per cent 'in a few' industries, 'in not a few' to more than 50 per cent and between one-third and two-fifths as a minimum average for production as a whole. It is possible that over manufacturing industry in general in this country [Great Britain] the real cost in labour of producing commodities fell by 40 per cent between 1850 and 1880." It is true that labor is not the only cost of production; on the other hand, these estimates refer to a relatively short period and purport to show the change in the overall average costs of entire industries.

their importance; and it is well to bear in mind that the first and the last are not *extreme* limiting cases. In particular, an X per cent reduction in the costs of production of an industry may well (and often does) lead to a more than X per cent expansion of demand for its output, in which case it will not only reabsorb the resources freed but divert additional resources from other industries as well. (We are now leaving open the question of what happens to prices.) As to the last case, it implies (with unchanged prices) a zero income elasticity of demand for the output of the now more efficient industries. Negative income elasticities of demand, however, are not an impossibility; and they would lead (again with unchanged prices) to a greater diversion of resources to other industries than that which would merely absorb the resources freed in the now more efficient industries. In short, the cost reduction of our example could raise the national product by any figure within an even wider range than the 37½ to 150 per cent suggested above. Here, then, is a most persuasive argument in favor of concentrating growth as much as possible in the now more efficient industries.

Concentrated growth, however, creates the problem of a changed and unbalanced composition of output; and the time-honored method of solving this problem is foreign trade. Ricardo advocated that each country concentrate its resources into its most efficient industries and use foreign trade to convert the resulting unbalanced pattern of output into a pattern of product availabilities that is more balanced in the sense of conforming more closely to the pattern of consumers' preferences and producers' needs. Concerned primarily with the point of view of the world as a whole, the classical economists showed how the unbalanced composition of two countries' national products can be mutually offsetting, and how each can, by trading with the other, convert its unbalanced pattern of output into a balanced pattern of product availabilities. From one country's—England's—point of view, the problem is how she can use world markets to convert her unbalanced pattern of output into a balanced pattern of product availabilities without turning the terms of trade against herself to such an extent as to offset the advantage of unbalanced over balanced growth. I do not know if the classical economists ever asked this question in this form; but somehow or other England solved the problem, and this may be an important reason for her rapid development and great prosperity in the nineteenth century.

The statistical picture is very striking. The expansion of Britain's industrial production was very largely based on foreign trade, the proportion of which to total national income rose from 16.6 per cent at the beginning of the nineteenth century to 66 per cent in 1910–13.[2] The proportion and rise in the proportion of exports in the total output of Britain's new and

---

[2] Cf. Werner Schlote (2).

revolutionary industries was greater still, rising in some cases to as much as 89 per cent.[3] The increased importance of Britain's foreign trade testifies to the increasing divergence between the pattern of her output and the pattern of her demand, as well as to her increasing reliance on foreign trade for converting the one into the other. One would expect this trend to have worsened Britain's terms of trade; but the statistical evidence shows that the terms of trade, while they turned against Britain, did not change very much. Schlote's index of Britain's terms of trade fell by barely a third from the 1810's to the 1880's and rose slightly thereafter. It seems, therefore, as though Britain had retained most of the benefit from her unbalanced growth; accomplishing this half by design, half by accident, through the opening up of underdeveloped countries, the construction of their transportation systems, and the export of British capital that implemented these developments; for all this must have raised the demand for Britain's exports, lowered the cost of her imports, and thus helped to prevent the terms of trade turning more sharply against her.

THE PRINCIPLES OF BALANCED GROWTH

Unbalanced growth on these principles and for these reasons is out of fashion today. For one thing, political uncertainty, balance-of-payments difficulties, and high competition in world markets have rendered export markets very precarious; for another, we live in an age of mass production, which is feasible and profitable only if it caters to a highly stable and homogeneous market. All of these factors have rendered dangerous and undesirable a great divergence between the patterns of output and consumption and the consequent great dependence on foreign trade and other countries' policies. This was first pointed out almost 100 years ago by Friedrich List, who advocated economic self-sufficiency and, in analyzing the means of achieving it, developed a rudimentary argument in favor of balanced growth. His harmony of interests could be an early statement of economic interdependence, and his general argument a precursor of the modern case for balanced growth.

Today, we take it for granted that a fair degree of self-sufficiency is desirable and base the argument for balanced growth on the recognition of economic interdependence. To analyze this, it is convenient to distinguish between interdependence in production and interdependence in consumption, and to deal with each of them in turn.

To produce a good and to invest in capacity for producing a good are the more profitable, the greater the availability (1) of the goods that serve as factors of production in its manufacture, (2) of the goods with which it is combined in the manufacture of other goods, and (3) of the capacity

---

[3] This was the percentage of exports in the total output of Britain's cotton piece goods industry in the decade before the first World War.

for producing goods in whose manufacture it serves as a factor of production. Since this statement holds true of all goods, it is generally desirable and profitable to expand simultaneously, and in the proportions determined by technological production coefficients, the production and productive capacity of all goods whose relation to each other is that of factor to product or common factors to the same product. These relations are called interdependence in production; and the effects of such interdependence on the profitability of investment are usually discussed in the literature under the name of pecuniary external economies.[4]

Very similar are the meaning and effects of interdependence in consumption. Production generates income, which gives rise to consumers' demand for an entire range of goods. Hence, an increase in output increases demand *in a given pattern* for a whole range of goods; and the profitability of output expansion will be maximized if the pattern of output expansion conforms to the pattern of demand expansion created by the additional income paid out in producing the additional output. The effects of this type of interdependence on the *aggregate volume* of income, output, and employment are discussed in Kahn's theory of the multiplier; its effects on the *pattern and geographical distribution* of demand and output are usually subsumed in discussions of pecuniary external economies, often without a clear distinction between interdependence in production and interdependence in consumption.

All of these ideas, however simple they may be, have for a long time remained alien to orthodox economic thought, even though the gist of them was already contained in List's writings. One reason for this may be that Britain's own economic development, following by and large Ricardo's doctrine, depended singularly little on these principles; another reason may be that List did not formulate his ideas very clearly and combined them with political ideas that were repugnant to the liberal and idealistic spirit of the nineteenth century British economists—and let us remember that orthodox economic theory is largely British in origin. A further reason may be that traditional economic theory deals mainly with the problems of developed economies, where these problems hardly arise. For, in the developed economy, where additions to output and income made by a single investment are usually a small fraction of the total, interdependence in production and consumption can mostly be ignored with impunity.

The situation is very different in underdeveloped economies. There, a single investment can make a big addition both to the total marketable output of a product and to total money income, and this means that considerations of interdependence and the principles of balanced growth assume great importance. For in such cases, estimates of the profitability and desirability of investment and of the optimum size of investment be-

[4] Cf. H. W. Arndt (3). See also my "Two Concepts of External Economies" (4).

come very different when interdependence is taken into account from what they are when interdependence is ignored. It is obvious that the estimates which ignore interdependence are the wrong ones; and it can be and has been shown that the private entrepreneur makes estimates close to these when he bases his judgment on market information alone. Hence the desirability in underdeveloped countries of recognizing economic interdependence and of influencing investment planning or investment decisions accordingly. This favors balanced growth, which means a simultaneous advance on all fronts, a many-sided expansion of productive capacity that maintains the product mix in conformity both with consumers' preferences (interdependence in consumption) and with the technical requirements of the productive system (interdependence in production). The advantages of such growth all have to do with effective demand. In discussions of external economies, all the stress is usually put on the greater profitability of each individual investment that balanced growth assures. Equally or even more important advantages, however, are the avoidance of bottlenecks, of special shortages, and special excess capacities; and the minimization of inflationary pressures and dangers that the avoidance of special shortages achieves. To judge by the experience of some of the countries now in the process of development, this last-mentioned may well be the main argument in favor of balanced growth.

All this has been much stressed in recent discussions of the problems of economic development; and rightly so, considering the almost complete neglect of the subject in the earlier theory of economics. There are also obstacles to and arguments against balanced growth; and they too must be expounded now that the case for balanced growth is becoming so widely known and accepted.

THE MODERN ARGUMENT FOR CONCENTRATED GROWTH

In presenting the modern argument for concentrated growth, we do not want to imply that the early argument is not valid. The gain to be had from concentrating on the production of goods in whose manufacture one has a comparative advantage is a genuine gain; and if we stressed the fact that this gain is obtained at a cost—the uncertainty that dependence on foreign trade involves—we still believe that *within limits* the gain is worth the cost. If the extent to which Britain's textile industries relied on export markets at the turn of the century seems excessive and highly precarious by today's standards, we would also regard as excessive and prohibitively expensive any attempts to render an economy completely self-contained and independent of foreign trade. In other words, the problem here is to weigh the benefits of the higher income to be had from concentrated growth against the disadvantage of the greater uncertainty that it involves, and to push the degree of concentration to the point and no further than the point at which the two are equated on the margin.

In contrast to the above, all the modern arguments in favor of concentrated growth are based on technological considerations, and they raise the problem of weighing these technological advantages of concentrated growth against the economic benefits of balanced growth. The first of these arguments has to do with economies of scale.

Economies of scale render production cheaper and investment more profitable above a certain minimum level of output and productive capacity. The desire, however, to secure these economies and to keep every investment above this minimum level may well conflict with the principles of balanced output and balanced growth. The simple and obvious reasons for such conflict are (1) insufficient effective demand to render profitable, and (2) insufficient savings to render possible, the construction of productive capacity of optimum size and design whenever total effective demand and/or total available savings are too thinly spread over a wide range of industries. One might also distinguish here between an economy that is too small to provide a market for the output even of one optimum-sized plant in every industry and an economy that is growing too slowly for the *accretion* of demand to justify or for the rate of capital accumulation to finance the simultaneous building of *additional* capacity of optimum size in every industry.

Such conflicts can be resolved by sacrificing economies of scale for the sake of balance, by sacrificing balance—at least temporarily—in order to secure the economies of scale, or by striking a compromise between the two. In the first case, investment will be less efficient, output smaller, and growth slower than they could be; whence it follows that it is always desirable to sacrifice balanced output or balanced growth, at least to some extent. This, indeed, is what usually happens.

Countries too small to secure the advantages both of large-scale production and of a balanced economy usually have much more liberal foreign-trade policies than do large countries; and this is explained not by ideological differences but by the above conflict and the small countries' willingness to resolve this conflict by accepting the uncertainties of great dependence on foreign trade for the sake of obtaining economies of large-scale production in at least some industries.[5]

Countries in the process of development face a slightly different conflict but usually resolve it in a similar way. This is certainly true of planned economies, and of economies that plan their investment; and their several-year investment plans, of which one hears so much nowadays, may be regarded as plans for unbalanced growth, extending to several years so as to restore balance by the end of the period for which the plans are made. In the interim, imbalance manifests itself by the completion of productive

[5] The conflict can be eliminated, of course, by forming larger economic units; and it is no accident that the countries most in favor of Western European integration are the small ones.

capacity before the demand for its full utilization has arisen, or by the creation of consumers' or producers' demand before the capacity to fill this demand is completed. The temporary excess capacity may have to be accepted in most cases as an inevitable cost of (temporarily) unbalanced growth for the sake of securing economies of scale; the temporary excess demand may be filled by imports, which is one reason why the availability of foreign loans or foreign exchange is so strategic a factor in investment planning.[6] Such dependence on foreign trade, however, is very different from that which accompanies unbalanced growth concentrated on industries with a comparative advantage. For one thing, this is a temporary dependence, while that is permanent; for another, the dependence here is primarily on foreign import supplies, there on foreign export markets.

This way of securing the economies of scale at the cost of a temporary imbalance comes about also in the unplanned market economy. There have been instances, especially in the smaller European countries, of productive units being built in industries new for the country but with capacities larger than the domestic market, in the hope of capturing an export market, but yet with a view to relying ultimately on the expanding domestic market. Too often, however, the economies of scale are sacrificed in the market economy because effective demand, or capital funds, or both, are insufficient for the building of efficient large-scale productive capacity. This, then, is the case where balanced growth is secured at the high cost of having less efficient investment and a slower rate of growth than the best methods of production known would have made feasible.

Indeed, something like this can happen even when the economy is large enough and its rate of growth and capital accumulation high enough to enable all industries simultaneously to add new optimum-sized plants to their already existing equipment. Technical progress may render large-scale mass production the most economical in an industry that consists of many firms, all of them smaller than the new optimum-sized plant. In such a case, and there may be many such cases, it can happen that none of the firms has access to enough capital and can capture enough of the new accretion of demand to be able to build an optimum-sized plant—with the result that traditional methods of production are retained in the industry's expansion and the new economies of scale are left unutilized. We have discussed this case in detail elsewhere, and there blamed this kind of situation on the lack—or the wrong kind—of competition.[7] For, we argued, if only competition were great enough, the firm able to lower its costs of production could also capture a substantial part of the new market, and the prospect of its doing this would enable it to obtain the requisite amount of capital.

---

[6] The other reason, of course, is that underdeveloped countries usually have to buy much of their productive equipment abroad.

[7] Cf. my "Economies of Scale, Competition, and European Integration" (5); and also my "Monopoly and Competition in Europe and America" (6).

Here too, however, there is a conflict. It is different from that discussed earlier and arises because securing the economies of scale is incompatible, not indeed with balanced growth, but with retaining the existing pattern of competition. If efficiency calls for mass production and large-scale plants in an industry hitherto composed of small firms and small plants, either the relative size of the members of the industry will become more unequal or the number of independent firms will be reduced, and competition is likely to suffer in either case. Hence, when we advocate the kind of competition that renders possible the building of bigger productive units, we may be advocating the kind of competition that will destroy itself in the long run—but this problem, however serious, is not strictly relevant to the subject matter of this paper and is mentioned here only because of its affinity to the earlier problem.

So far, all of our arguments and analyses were based on the tacit assumption that the state and rate of change of technical knowledge are given and independent of economic considerations. This assumption, however, is clearly unrealistic. The development of technical knowledge depends very much on economic factors; indeed, many of the major technical inventions have been sparked by shortages created by an unbalanced pattern of growth or resource availability in the face of rigid interdependence and complementarity in production. Hence, when we drop the assumption of given technology, we find further arguments in favor of concentrated growth.

The analysis of long-run trends in output and employment in individual U.S. industries has shown a close correlation between total output and labor productivity (output per worker).[8] The rise in an industry's labor productivity is the fastest during periods of fast rise in its total output. From this it need not follow that by promoting a rise in output one can also promote a rise in productivity; but there are independent reasons for believing that this, indeed, will happen. For one thing, the faster the rate of expansion, the higher the proportion of new as against replacement investment; and new investment provides much more scope for innovation and technical improvement than does the replacement of worn-out capacity. For another thing, the faster an industry expands, the more easily can newcomers with new ideas enter the industry, and the greater becomes the industry's general receptivity to new methods and experiments.

These are arguments in favor of fast growth, by which in this context is meant an annual expansion of from 15 to 20 per cent or more. Such fast expansion of an individual industry would be compatible with balanced growth only if the economy as a whole were expanding at a comparable rate; but outside of some of the planned economies this condition is not likely to be fulfilled. In the market economy the over-all rate of growth is always very much slower; and the fast growth therefore of some

[8] The National Bureau of Economic Research has done, and I believe is still doing, work on this subject. See, for example, their Occasional Paper 38 (7).

industries can be obtained only at the cost of no or slow growth in other industries. Unbalanced growth appears, therefore, as the price of the fast growth that in a variety of ways stimulates technical progress. In addition, however, unbalanced growth itself may also be a stimulus to technical invention and innovation, for the fast expansion of output in one field or at one stage of production is likely to create bottlenecks and shortages of specialized resources in closely related fields or at other stages of production within the same field; and the desire either to eliminate such shortages or to find new methods that economize the resources in short supply is known to be among the most powerful stimulants of technological progress.[9] An example of the former is provided by the development of England's textile industry during the industrial revolution. Kay's invention of the flying shuttle expanded weaving capacity and thus created the shortage of spinning capacity that led to the inventions of Paul and Wyatt, Hargreaves, Crompton, Kelly, and Arkwright, which revolutionized spinning. The resulting great expansion of spinning capacity, in its turn, created the shortage of weaving capacity that led to Cartwright's invention of the power-loom. An example of the latter (i.e., of the stimulating influence on invention of the need to economize resources in short supply) is the early development of mass production methods in the United States. This occurred largely in response to the shortage of skilled labor; for the idea of subdividing a complex manufacturing process into relatively simple constituent parts was conceived of primarily in order to economize skilled labor.

Having enumerated and discussed the arguments both for balanced and for unbalanced or concentrated growth, we may well ask what conclusions can be drawn from all this for practical policy. To answer this question, let us recall, first of all, that most arguments for concentrated growth are, in reality, arguments for fast growth or growth by large steps—tantamount to arguments for concentrated growth only when the economy's over-all growth rate is slow. Second, let us also recall that foreign trade, by converting an unbalanced pattern of output into a balanced pattern of availabilities, can always secure the advantages of balance for an unbalanced economy. What emerges from these considerations is an argument in favor of large size. In a large economy, mere geographical extent and diversity of climates and natural resources automatically assure some degree of self-sufficiency and balance, while allowing plenty of scope for concentrated growth on a regional or functional basis. The United States

---

[9] This seems to be generally accepted today. Most historical studies of the great inventions of the 18th and 19th centuries stress the fact that these were not fortuitous events but came about in response to an economic need. For a short summary, see Maurice Dobb's essay on "The Industrial Revolution and the Nineteenth Century" (1).

and the Soviet Union furnish examples of both types of development. The approximately 3 per cent annual rate of expansion of the American economy has in the recent past been the average of a much faster growth rate in the South and Far West and a virtual standstill in New England. Similarly, the expansion of the Soviet economy has for many years past been concentrated in its Far Eastern regions. In some cases and during some periods, such regionally concentrated growth was balanced within the region; more often it was concentrated in a few industries and the resulting unbalanced pattern of the region's output converted into a balanced pattern of availabilities through interregional trade.

The economic advantages of large size and the fact that they are compounded from the advantages of balanced and those of concentrated growth are being increasingly realized—witness the trend toward, and arguments in favor of, integration and the formation of large economic areas, not only in Western Europe but in many other parts of the world as well. In a sense, this is merely a modern and perhaps more realistic and promising attempt at realizing that old ideal of the economist: free trade; but the modern argument for this limited form of free trade has become very different from the classical (and especially from the neo-classical) argument and much closer to the arguments advanced in this paper.

References

1. Maurice Dobb, Studies in the Development of Capitalism. Routledge & Kegan Paul, London, 1946.

2. Werner Schlote, British Overseas Trade from 1700 to the 1930's. Blackwell, Oxford, 1952.

3. H. W. Arndt, "External Economies in Economic Growth," *Economic Record*, XXX (November 1955), 192–214.

4. Tibor Scitovsky, "Two Concepts of External Economies," *Journal of Political Economy*, LXII (April 1954), 143–51.

5. Tibor Scitovsky, "Economies of Scale, Competition, and European Integration," *American Economic Review*, XLVI (March 1956), 71–91.

6. Tibor Scitovsky, "Monopoly and Competition in Europe and America," *Quarterly Journal of Economics*, LXIV (November 1955), 607–18.

7. Frederick C. Mills, Productivity and Economic Progress. Occasional Paper No. 38, National Bureau of Economic Research.

Monetary Stability in a Growing Economy[1]

E. S. SHAW

Professor Haley's skills in inciting his seminars to constructively argumentative uproar are the envy of colleagues. There is reason to believe that his students, including this writer, are marked permanently by the love of parry and riposte that his pedagogy encourages.

The essay to follow is not intended to calm any intellectual sea. It is an invitation to critical perusal of the American monetary system. It takes a positive position on monetary reform, at a time when commissions for monetary reform are sprouting up in this country and elsewhere, and tacitly invites vigorous rejoinder. It is in the tradition, that Professor Haley has nurtured, of reaching for truth in intellectual give-and-take.

This essay is not explicitly concerned with allocation and distribution of economic resources. It does have a tangential bearing on the general theme of the present volume, since allocation and distribution are neither efficient nor equitable in the context of monetary instability.

My theme is that the Federal Reserve Act and its administration have retarded monetary development. The conclusion I reach is that monetary control should be automatized, with the goal of matching growth in nominal money to growth in demand for it at a price level which is in keeping with broad objectives of public policy.

There are dangling threads in my analysis. For example, no preference is stated regarding the channel through which increments in nominal money are to be introduced into the economic system. There is only a rudimentary sketch of a theory of demand for money, and no more adequate treatment of solutions to monetary disequilibrium. Such delinquencies can be blamed partly on the necessity for an efficient allocation and equitable distribution of space in this volume among its many authors.

[1] This essay is included with the consent of the American Assembly. It was presented before the 14th Assembly in October 1958, and it appears in original form as part of the Assembly's volume on *Monetary Policy: Its Contribution to Steady Economic Growth Without Inflation.*

DEFINITIONS OF MONEY

Everyone Rolls His Own

It is almost true that everyone rolls his own definition of money and has his own rules for measurement of the money supply. Federal Reserve people are noncommittal, and in the representative *Federal Reserve Bulletin* offer no tabulations headed *Money* or *Supply of Money*. Their essays about money coat the term with a film of adjectives—"active" money, "relatively active" money, "inactive" money. Our central bank cultivates uncertainty even in monetary semantics.

The rest of us have been no more incisive. Here is a list of items from which we concoct now one, now another definition of money with measurements to match. The figures apply to a date chosen at random, February 26, 1958.

TABLE I
Money or Not?

Item	Amount ($ *billions*)
Currency outside banks	$ 27.3
Demand deposits adjusted	105.5
U.S. Government balances in banks	4.2
Treasury cash holdings	0.7
Time deposits of commercial banks	57.5
Other time deposits	33.4

"Money," as the composite of some items above, increased in amount over the year before the date of measurement. "Money" comprising a different combination of these items decreased over the year. If you suspect that there was monetary expansion, you can tailor a definition to your suspicion. If you prefer to think that there was monetary contraction, you can be right again—with a different definition.

There is good fundamentalist authority for counting as money only the hard core of legal tender, the first item in Table I. There is equally reputable reformist authority for counting items that are not mentioned in the Table, for counting anything called a "deposit" in any institution called a "bank." I can cite no authority for including "shares" of savings and loan associations or credit unions, though authority may not be lacking when and if the associations win their battle of nomenclature and become "banks" owing "deposits."

A Personal Preference

The definition that strikes my own fancy begins with the *dictum*: A dollar is a dollar. A unit of money bearing the price, or face value, of $1 today bears the same price tomorrow and next year. It discharges a debt for $1 anytime, and it always buys something else with a price tag of $1. No one haggles over money's price.

My definition is not quite as rigorous as I make it seem, because I would count in money not merely legal-tender pocket money but checking balances as well. The latter do depreciate a little in price, subject as they are to service charges. And they would appreciate a little, if Congress once again permitted interest credits on demand accounts. My definition is flexible enough to admit anything that people use as money—as a means of payment: money is as money does.

Modern money is a debt, differing from other forms of debt in that its price does not vary. It is a debt of the monetary system—the commercial banks, the Federal Reserve Banks, and the Treasury monetary accounts. It is issued to other sectors of the economy in payment by the monetary system for purchases principally of nonmonetary securities and monetary metals. Textbooks classify our money as "token" money, to distinguish it from fragments of one commodity or another that people have used, in other times and places, as fixed-price means of payment.

THE SUPPLY OF MONEY

At any moment the supply or quantity of money is the monetary system's dollar aggregate of fixed-price debt. It is the sum of all legal tender in pockets and tills together with the sum of all unused credits to checking accounts. The "quantity of money" that economists talk about is this simple statistic doctored in various ways.

An observation for a moment of time does not give as accurate a "fix" as is necessary for precision in relating the supply of money to, say, national income for a year. Instead of a momentary measurement, one needs an average figure for money outstanding.

An average supply or quantity of money may be outrageously inflationary if it is spread over a small community, grossly deflationary if the community is much larger. Especially in a growth context, it is often the money supply *per capita* that one needs for analytical purposes. This is not a datum regularly accessible in official tabulations or elsewhere, possibly because most of us are preoccupied with the behavior or misbehavior of money in the short run, too few of us with monetary phenomena in periods long enough for significant change in the population of money-users.

The money I have been talking about is *nominal* money—the face value of the monetary system's debt. Economists usually suppose that it is *real* money, rather than nominal money, that affects levels and patterns of economic activity and economic welfare. Real money is the purchasing power of nominal money. The supply of real money is the supply of nominal money deflated by some one or other index of prices for things that money buys. Old hands at monetary analysis are ruefully aware that no price index is quite right for measurement of the real money supply and of changes in it.

As one puts the quantity of money into one statistical disguise after another, he can get very different impressions of its behavior. The sum of currency outside banks and demand deposits adjusted, without statistical frills, was nearly $140 billions on December 31, 1956, and nearly $138 billions on December 25, 1957. Obviously the supply of money was reduced about 1.4 per cent. But was it? In real terms, *per capita* of our noninstitutional population, the supply of money fell from $1177 to $1103. This is a decline of 6.3 per cent. In its policy of restraint for 1957, was the Federal Reserve aiming at the target of 1.4 per cent or at the target of 6.3 per cent?

The "supply of money" that central banks manipulate, that people hold most of the time and spend once in a while, that economists investigate is not, then, a simple concept. It is a figure so transformed by its visit to the statistical beauty parlor as hardly to be recognizable by its closest friends. There may be more than meets the eye in any measurement of the supply or quantity of money.

GROWTH IN THE SUPPLY OF MONEY:
FIRST THE THROTTLE, THEN THE BRAKES

It was a common complaint, before passage of the Federal Reserve Act in late 1913, that our monetary system was inelastic. The Federal Reserve Act and its amendments, and administration of the Act, have quashed that complaint. Partly out of conviction and partly to arouse discussion, I am going to argue that the Act and its administrators have put far too much elastic into our monetary system. Switching metaphors, my point will be that it was a mistake to demolish the old Model T. The juggernaut that has replaced it is not designed, nor is it driven, on principles that are compatible with money stability in a growing economy. These are fighting words that call for adequate documentation.

The Statistical Record

Table II below is a rough tracery of our monetary experience during 1896–1957. It measures growth in nominal money over the entire period and during seven subperiods. The subperiods begin with 1896–1914, when the old monetary system was running out its last miles under critical inspection by a bevy of monetary commissions, public and private. In four of the running six subperiods, policies of the new monetary system were stipulated primarily by the federal Treasury. In the other two subperiods, monetary policy was stipulated by the Federal Reserve Board, *alias* the Board of Governors of the Federal Reserve System, as an independent agency. The four "Treasury" intervals were 1914–19, 1933–41,

1941–45, and 1945–51; and the two interludes of "Board" tenure were 1919–33 and 1951–57.

The figures in Table II measure the nominal money supply as the sum of currency outside of banks and adjusted demand deposits. The first column presents absolute changes from year-end to year-end, and the second column presents compound rates of change.

TABLE II
STOP AND GO MONETARY POLICY

Period	Change in Nominal Money ($ billions)	Rate of Change (%)
1896–1914	$ 7.5	6
1914–1919	11.4	15
1919–1933	—3.5	—1
1933–1941	27.7	14
1941–1945	55.5	21
1945–1951	22.2	3
1951–1957	13.2	2
(1896–1957)	134.0	6

Six Decades in Review

In 1896 the nominal supply of money was at the near-microscopic level of $3.8 billions. At the close of 1957, the nominal supply of money was thirty-six times larger, or $137.7 billions. The average annual compound rate of growth was approximately 6 per cent. One had no need for a microscope to see the money supply at the end of last year.

For perspective, the growth rate of 6 per cent in nominal money may be compared with the more modest growth rate of about 3.75 per cent in real money. Evidently prices rose at the average annual rate of 2.25 per cent. It may come as a mild surprise that this degree of price inflation has been our method of repudiating about $100 billions of growth in nominal money: nominal money increased by $134 billions, real money by perhaps $30 to $35 billions in 1896–1957.

The Model-T Period

Consider the years 1896–1914 a little more closely. In correspondence with accelerating growth in physical production and in the nation's real income, the money stock grew at the average rate of 9 per cent in 1896–1906. From year to year there was relatively little variation in the rate of growth. After 1906 the tempo of growth slackened throughout the economy, the rate of growth in money falling to a little less than 3 per cent. The money supply declined in one year (1907), and it rose in each year of depression including the dismal year of 1908. In 1906–14 variation in annual rates of growth was narrow.

Waving aside the seasonal stresses of the old monetary system, which were amenable to treatment on the principle of the Aldrich-Vreeland Act, one is tempted to shed a nostalgic tear for our monetary experience in the two decades prior to the Federal Reserve Act. The monetary system was Model T, but it was not too much for us to handle.

Drag-racing the Monetary System

The Federal Reserve Act multiplied both horsepower and brakepower in the monetary system. Since 1914 effective control of the system has alternated between Treasury and Board. The Treasury takes out its aggressions on the throttle of the new machine. The Board reaches for the brakes. And the money supply lurches along a sawtooth course of growth.

In 1914–19 the rate of growth in nominal money was accelerated from 3 to 15 per cent. Then the brakes! Over the next fourteen years, there was a net decline in the money supply. To be sure, there was growth in money balances of 1 per cent annually to 1929, but then deceleration set in at the average annual rate of 6 per cent. This is not a profile of monetary stability.

Twice during its tenure of control in 1919–33, the Board presided over a decline of nearly 10 per cent in nominal money. In both years, 1921 and 1930, the monetary brakes were applied to an economic system that was already in the skid of deflation. In eight of the fourteen years there was net monetary contraction, and in six of these eight years monetary contraction was superimposed on other depressant circumstances. In two years of cyclic recession, 1924 and 1927, it is true that the Board followed the precedent of the old monetary system in increasing liquidity. But these were years when such a stimulus was less necessary than in four of the six years in which the Board departed from pre-1914 tradition.

The Board's license to drive the monetary system was suspended in 1933. Probation was granted in 1936–37, but once more the Board applied the brakes too hard. The monetary system slid into the recession of 1937–38, and again the Board's license to drive was lifted.

Over fourteen years, 1919–33, the Board had subjected the economy to a negligible rate of growth in money. In the next eight years, apart from the interlude of 1936–37, the Treasury chauffeur reversed policy and subjected the economic system to an absurdly high rate of monetary expansion. By 1941 the prestige of monetary policy was properly very low indeed.

In reaction to the monetary experience of 1919–33, the Congress added to the monetary system's capacity for both acceleration and deceleration in the series of reforms that appeared during 1933–45. Retrospectively it seems that the rational thing to do was to put the system on automatic pilot after 1914–33 and disengage manual controls. Important statutory restraints on monetary expansion were eased or eliminated, and powerful new discretionary restraints were added. This is the kind of reform one might have expected if the new monetary mechanism had been driven skillfully. Bad driving was rewarded with a new and still more powerful machine.

This is not the occasion to debate wartime economic controls. I simply offer the opinion that the rate of growth in money during 1941–45, on the order of 21 per cent annually, is a blemish on our record that no amount of rationalization can erase. We expanded the money supply at a rate surpassing by a wide margin even the requirements for rapid real growth in wartime, then deputized thousands of price policemen in OPA and WPB to patrol the channels of moneyflow. The money accelerator was pushed to the floorboard, and policemen were deployed in droves to keep the public out of the way of the money juggernaut. The new monetary system was not the cause but it was the instrument of our folly.

The Board's fight for repossession of the monetary system was not won until 1951. The foot shackled since 1936–37 was freed and instinctively stepped on the monetary brakes again. The ensuing screech of complaint on the security markets, in the Spring of 1953, still echoes in our ears.

Since the Board settled back on the brakeman's seat in 1951, real national income has grown at approximately 4 per cent annually, real money a little over 1 per cent annually, nominal money 2 per cent. After five years of reckless acceleration in 1914–19, fourteen years of excessive deceleration in 1919–33, eighteen years of reckless acceleration in 1933–51, we are again in the deceleration phase of our monetary drag-race. The economy's spinal column has not snapped as it has been whipped back and forth by alternating pressure on throttle and brake, but no credit is due to our "elastic" monetary system for our survival. Safety belts, sometimes known as built-in stabilizers, take up some of the strain, as OPA and WPB did in wartime. It is a pity that some of the ingenuity spent in contriving nonmonetary stabilizers has not been spent instead on stabilizing money.

In its twenty years of brakemanship, the Board has permitted an average annual increase in the money supply of $440 millions. This rate of nominal growth is almost identical with the rate of nominal growth in 1896–1914, but in real terms it can hardly be half as rapid. It is a small fraction of the economy's rate of growth in real income. In its twenty-three years the Treasury has permitted an average annual increase in the money supply of $4880 millions. It has added $11 to the money supply for every $1 permitted by the Board. Neither rate of expansion is close to an appropriate target rate.

In its twenty years the Board has presided over an absolute decrease in nominal money during nine years. There has been price deflation in eleven of its twenty years. There have been no more than six years in which the Board has permitted nominal money to increase at a rate comparable with growth in the nation's productive capacity. The Treasury team that takes over monetary control when the Board moves out has inflated money in all but three of its twenty-three years, a record that may be saluted at least for its consistency.

Neither driver of the monetary system has demonstrated sensitive reflexes to cyclical turning points along our road of growth. The old Model T was more maneuverable on the curves. With its predilection for restraint, the Board has characteristically punished a cyclical boom past its prime, aggravating ensuing depression. The notorious instances are 1919–21 and 1929–33, but the cyclical turning points of 1953 and 1957 are not exceptions to the rule.

A Robot at the Wheel

There are numerous alternative designs for a monetary system. The design that this country has hit upon builds into the monetary system an enormous capacity for both inflation and deflation. In successive trips back to the Congressional fix-it shop, the system's elasticity has been increased. As it is now put together, the system is a brilliant solution for short-period instability in some security markets. But it has financed long-period inflation on the commodity markets, interrupted by painful episodes of excessive deceleration in monetary growth. In its first half-century, the system has not created the temperate monetary environment that is most congenial to stable growth in real terms.

Now that the monetary system is undergoing revaluation, fundamental change in design should at least be discussed. My own feeling is that, on balance, there would be improvement in its performance if the monetary system were put on automatic pilot. This suggestion is not a new one. The Board had to contend thirty years ago with proposals for automatized monetary control and turned them down in favor of "judgment in matters of credit administration."

What instructions are to be fed into an automatic pilot? From the long list of alternatives that have been proposed in the history of monetary thought, one of the simplest appears most feasible. It is that, year in and year out, the nominal supply of money should increase by the average rate of growth in demand for nominal money at a stable level of commodity prices. According to usual estimates, which should be refined, the appropriate annual growth rate would be on the order of from 3 to 4 per cent.

For any good other than money, no eyebrows would rise over the premise that it is right to balance supply with demand. But "demand for money" is not a concept in popular use. There is no mention of it in the Federal Reserve Act. Only one small tabulation remotely akin to it is published in the *Federal Reserve Bulletin*. If demand for money is to be considered as the standard for regulation of supply, a moment spent in probing demand may not be amiss.

THE "DEMAND STANDARD" FOR MONETARY CONTROL

The pure gold standard is an automatic rule of monetary control. And so is pure bimetallism. The automatic rule that I am reviving for consideration may be termed the "demand standard" of monetary control. What it means can be worked out very simply with the help of a familiar expression:

$$MV = PT.$$

The Money Equation

All symbol-scarred veterans of Elementary Economists will recall that M is the average nominal supply of money during a period of time. V stands for the average frequency in turnover for a unit of money against the flow of goods and services from the community's productive facilities. P is the price level of goods and services, and T is their physical quantity—the national real income.

The money equation is a better tool for our use if it is twisted a little:

$$M = l/V \times P \times T.$$

A second twist replaces the inconvenient expression l/V with k and changes the order of terms:

$$M = P(kT).$$

Now we have the nominal supply of money M counterpoised against the community's demand for nominal money $P(kT)$. The community' demand for money in real measure—for money balances in terms of their purchasing power—is kT alone. And k is simply a proportion, a desired proportion, between the community's real balances in money and the community's real income.

With its seasonal and cyclical wrinkles ironed out, k is a remarkably stable relationship. In this country, k increased through the nineteenth century and apparently changed very little after 1900 in trend measurements. For present purposes, it may be stipulated that real money is a good, demand for which now grows at the same rate as real national income. Demand for money, of course, is motivated both by the utility of money as a means of payment and by the safety of money as a fixed-price asset.

Equality between M and $P(kT)$ is probably rare and fleeting. When it happens, there is monetary equilibrium. At all other times there is monetary disequilibrium. During most of the Treasury's tenure in monetary control, disequilibrium has been in the inflationary direction. Then M has exceeded $P(kT)$ at a stable level of prices P, so that money has been in excess supply. During approximately one-half of the Board's tenure, disequilibrium has been in the deflationary direction. Then M has been depressed below $P(kT)$ at a stable level of prices, so that money has been in excess demand.

Under the Demand Standard of monetary control, the automatic pilot would be instructed to increase M in step with "full-employment" T. On the evidence that k is disposed to stability and on the judgment that a constant P is optimal for our economy and our social structure, the automatic pilot would link growth in money to growth in output of goods and services. Better evidence may turn up that k rises a little as we produce more goods *per capita*, and the view may win out that a little price inflation is good for us. Then the automatic pilot would be instructed to be a little more generous with the supply of nominal money. In effect, the pilot would be told to aim for the spot where monetary equilibrium should be and not to worry about missing its target in the short run.

Missing the Turns in Monetary Control

Responsibility for monetary control is too heavy a cross to thrust upon a Treasury or upon a small group of men in an independent agency. A quick glance over possible disturbances to monetary equilibrium may indicate why a few technicians do conclude that automation is overdue in monetary control.

Economic systems must grow—in effective labor force, in productive capital, in output T. According to the money equation, growth in output increases demand for money. Other things being equal, it creates excess demand for money. But other things do not long remain equal. If the community has less money than it wants, it reduces demand for goods. Then growth in output implies unwanted growth in inventories. Inventories full to overflowing may be cleared by price reductions, but prices reduced in an unbalanced way cannot be relied upon to dispel excess supply of goods and excess demand for money. Price deflation is painful, and it can cumulate out of all proportion to its initial cause.

Excess demand for money is not cured by economy in demand for money k. Instead, k may rise, as deflation threatens, and accentuate excess demand for money. The sensible solution for a shortage in money balances is creation of more money balances, in nominal amount, by the monetary system.

Consider a second source of monetary instability. The k in the money equation is stable in longer periods, not seasonally and not cyclically. Business recession is initiated by an increase in k that precedes the cyclical turning point apparently by a variable interval. Demand for money rises at the expense of demand for goods. Excess demand for money eventually is satisfied, but its costs mount up in the forms of falling prices, falling output, and falling employment.

In every recession popular attention focuses on a villain. The latest villain is the "cost-price push," the rise in price that imperfectly competitive sellers force upon their markets, not in response to current demand, but in anticipation of demand. The cost-price push is characteristic of endemic inflation, but its first consequence is deflationary. It generates excess demand for money so that there is pressure brought to bear upon a monetary authority to underwrite advancing prices with increasing supplies of nominal money. If the monetary authority accedes to pressure, the cost-price push intensifies. If the monetary authority defies pressure, excess demand for money at inflated prices punishes output and employment.

Awkward manipulation of nominal money is the final source of monetary instability. Any monetary authority makes its decisions on the basis of information that it is incomplete and not altogether accurate or timely. The authority in our monetary system is handicapped by technically imperfect controls. The authority cannot see clearly the road that the monetary system should travel and, in comparison with ideal designs, the steering devices are primitive. We do not have finger-tip control of money, with the result that the best-laid plans for management of M can miscarry and widen the supply-demand gap of monetary disequilibrium.

In the light of monetary experience, it appears that many of us have romanticized monetary control. It is an illusion that the money supply can be manipulated, according to the daily flux of economic statistics and their translation by men of refined intuition, into continuous equilibrium. The limit of feasibility is to ascertain the trend rate of growth in demand for money at a given price level and to set the money supply automatically on the same course.

Money vs. Credit

The essential characteristic of a monetary system is that it produces money: it creates the money supply. The essential function of a monetary system is to adapt the money supply to the community's demand for money. The adaptation is most felicitous for real economic growth when nominal money expands along the same trend line as demand for money at a stable level of commodity prices.

Money has purchasing power. When the monetary system creates money for the rest of us to hold in money balances, the monetary system can obtain something of value in exchange. That something may be gold or silver. According to some students, that something should be composite bundles of raw materials, or foreign bills of exchange, or even bricks. The monetary authority need not be instructed to buy something with the money it creates. It could give away the purchasing power its money-creation commands, perhaps in remission of taxes.

How the monetary system does dispose of this purchasing power is incidental to the primary job of creating money. Any social benefits that result from its disposal of purchasing power are a by-product of the money industry. Any monetary system must have a technique for getting rid of the money that it produces, but there are innumerable techniques, and their relative merits should be a matter of secondary concern.

Our monetary system takes gold and silver from the community, but these purchases exhaust only a fraction of the purchasing power that creation of money puts at the system's disposal. A much larger fraction is spent on securities—in "making loans" and "granting credits." The by-product of our monetary system is credit.

I cannot emphasize too strongly that "credit" is a by-product. I cannot emphasize too strongly that it is an optional by-product. Congress willing, our monetary system need not be an investor in consumer credit, business loans, mortgages, and Treasury debt. It need not be staffed wth loan and investment committees. It could be staffed with commodity specialists who would fill warehouses with goods rather than portfolios with bonds and notes.

The Federal Reserve Act, the Board, and the Treasury have been preoccupied with the by-product of our monetary system. Their correct course would have been to prescribe and administer rules of growth in money balances, then to tackle the lesser issue of what to do with the fall-out of purchasing power. The course they have chosen, and still pursue, is to prescribe and administer rules for disposition of purchasing power on securities. As they see it, the money supply is the by-product of their operations, and the monetary system should create as much or as little as is necessary for "accommodating commerce and business" with credit and for maintaining "sound credit conditions." Our monetary management has been credit-minded, not money-minded.

The Federal Reserve Act bristles with injunctions upon the monetary system to grant this kind of credit and not that kind. Be open-handed with agriculture and starve the stockmarket. The Board concerns itself with proliferating detail of credit granted to government, business, and consumers. Quality and quantity of credit are its operating criteria. During its tenure in monetary management, the Treasury falls in line with the same tradition, fitting policy to the alleged requirements of government as borrower rather than to the requirements of the community as holders and users of money. When Board and Treasury disagree, the points of contention are the quantity, quality, and terms of credit.

The Federal Reserve Act is not the constitution of a monetary system. A new Act should be prepared, in two sections. Section I would declare the rule of growth in money balances. Section II would specify disposition of the purchasing power that growth in money balances provides to the monetary system, and its preamble would state unambiguously that Section II is subsidiary to Section I.

Laymen often suspect some perversity in monetary affairs, and rightly so. The goal of a monetary system should be, literally, to make the right amount of money. What the system does with the money is secondary. For the rest of us, coming into possession of purchasing power is presumably a means, and the end we work for is the intelligent use of purchasing power. The monetary system is on the other side of the Looking Glass.

The Demand Standard in Action

By the rule of the Demand Standard, the nominal supply of money would be increased at a constant rate compounded annually. The rate would be adjusted only with Congressional assent, since full and free debate on the matter of long-run price inflation or deflation is no less important than full and free debate on such issues as tax burdens, or labor policy, or foreign aid.

The technical procedures of adding to the stock of money should be no more difficult to establish than the procedures of extracting tax payments from the community for subsequent spending under the government budget. Monetary expansion could be a daily, weekly, or monthly "spending" by the monetary system. It could be adapted to seasonal instabilities in demand for monthly balances.

Demand for money would grow parallel with the money supply in the long run, but its growth line would rise and fall in shorter periods. In each recession, the combination of an increasing money supply and a decreasing demand for money would generate excess supply of money. In each cyclic boom, the combination of increasing money supply and still more rapidly increasing demand for money would generate a shortage in money. Both recession and boom would call forth automatically the kind of imbalance between supply of and demand for money that is cyclically corrective.

On various pretexts, each important borrower of "credit" would be able to make an eloquent case for some expansion of the money supply in his behalf. The Treasury would request support of new issues. Agriculture would expect credit accommodation for crop movements. Business, large or small, would cry out its need for "capital," and consumers would remember when banks courted their demands for loan funds to spend on cars, houses, and appliances. No sympathy should be wasted on any of these complaints, because giving in to them would mean a demonstrably inflationary acceleration in the growth rate of money.

It is no more difficult to administer orderly growth in money than disorderly growth. Every banker is more than a little proud of his ability to turn down credit applications. The automaton of the Demand Standard can be taught to say "no" to any demand upon the monetary system that would violate the basic rule of growth in means of payment.

ANOTHER BUILT-IN STABILIZER

This country takes pride in its built-in stabilizers, the economic balance-wheels that automatically limit our deviations from normal growth. The stabilizers are automatically sensitized to economic instability and go into action against it without forethought, plan, or discretion. It is not a radical proposal that monetary control should be added to the list of self-activating countermeasures against disturbances in the growth process.

Two lines of argument favor the proposal. One is that manual control of money has done badly. The other is that stable growth in money contributes to stable growth in other economic dimensions.

Management Has Had Its Day

On the evidence of our monetary experience since 1914, money management has not been a success. Over the long period, the money supply M has been inefficiently balanced against money demand $P(kT)$ at relatively stable prices. The long run casts its shadow over shorter periods. In the 1930's the long run had been deflationary, and the mood of deflation restrained short-run recoveries. As we see it now, the long run has been inflationary, and the mood of inflation permeates short-run expectations. There is an hypothesis that chronic inflation is partly to blame for one paradox of the 1957–58 recession. The paradox is that prices have run uphill against the gravity of deflation. Perhaps the gravity of long-run inflation has exerted the stronger pull.

Management has not succeeded in the cyclical short run. Students of business cycles find scarcely visible evidence that business cycles have shortened in duration since 1914. They find better evidence that cycles have become more violent, with amplitude of movement increased. I indicated earlier that monetary management has not been delicately attuned to cyclical turning points. It has missed the turns when monetary policy might have been most effective in damping instability.

Management has not sensed the need of a growing economy for stability of monetary expectations. The deeds of management have cultivated alternately expectations of inflation and expectations of deflation. As for words, the notion has developed somehow that the monetary authority is privileged to behave as a benevolent despot; that the authority may mask its plans and policies and neglect to advise the community of its intentions; that the community's prospect concerning the balance of supply and demand for money should be confused and uncertain.

If any form of policy should be explicit, out in the open for all to see, it is monetary policy. There should be certainty of price inflation or certainty of price deflation rather than doubt concerning the monetary atmosphere in which economic plans will materialize. Uncertainly is an impediment to growth. It depresses rational investment, defers gains in productivity, and contributes to the scarcities that policy is supposed to remedy.

The Positive Side of the Case

The case for automatic control does not rest solely on disillusionment with discretionary control. There are six principal ways in which continuous and stable growth in money can increase the probability of growth in output at a relatively high rate with minimal perturbations.

1. Stable growth in money lays the foundation for a solvent and efficient payments mechanism. In recurrent inflation, bank capital is sharply reduced relative to bank assets and deposits. Each deflation undermines bank capital through deterioration in asset quality. Our own banking system is propped upright, at public expense, by various devices that are presumed to be adequate substitutes for private investment in banking. Each of these devices has originated during violent movements in the money supply.

2. Stable growth in money supplied and demanded removes one hazard of private or governmental economic planning—that is uncertainty about the length of the monetary yardstick that planners use to measure prospective costs and revenues. Our own monetary system provides us with a yardstick, the value of the dollar, that has been shrinking for sixty years. Steady shrinkage at a constant rate is tolerable and certainly not as damaging to the planning process as shrinkage by fits and starts. Our yardstick has been rubberized, stretching out in each deflation and snapping back in each bout we have with inflation.

3. Stable growth in money avoids the inflations that distort the form of real capital accumulation, and it relieves the economic system of the interruptions in capital formation that result when deflation is applied as the remedy for inflation. Deflation does not undo damage done by inflation: it compounds the damage. During inflation, savings are used wastefully on capital projects that are made to seem worthwhile by advancing prices. During deflation, savings are destroyed by underemployment of men and resources. Savings misapplied or lost are never recoverable.

4. Stable growth in money and stability in the price level create a favorable environment for flexible individual prices and price relationships. General price deflation results in specific price rigidities, usually in the form of price floors. It invites combination in restraint of price adjustments downward. General price inflation produces its own crop of controlled or administered prices. The controls may be ceilings imposed by buyers or escalators dictated by sellers. Flexibility of the price level promotes rigidity of price relationships. Since a private-enterprise society relies upon flexible price relationships to allocate resources and guide demands, flexible price levels reduce its growth potential.

5. Stable growth of money and stability in the price level diminish social conflict. Deflation in the last century was politically and socially divisive. Inflation in this century has helped to cleave the population into pressure groups. Any pronounced swing in the price level incites an organized March on Washington and concessions to noisy claimants for special advantage. When price levels are on the move, rational competition of the market place loses out to passionate competition for political leverage.

6. Steady growth in money contributes to development of orderly financial arrangements throughout the community. Deflation creates its

distinctive pattern of debt, financial assets, and financial institutions. Inflation gives rise to a different pattern. Debtors are affected by a consideration that should not occur to them—the chance of windfall gain by inflation, of windfall loss by deflation. Creditors pick and choose their financial assets not solely according to debtors' real productivity but also according to debtors' vulnerability to unstable price levels. Loanable funds are allocated inefficiently among borrowers through a financial mechanism that is unduly intricate and expensive.

Stable growth in money minimizes financial distractions in the growth process. Stop-and-go growth in money, dignified as "monetary management," is a nervous tic in the economic system that diverts to finance attention and resources that should be spent on real aspects of development. Money is at its best when it is unobtrusive, its supply increasing according to a firm rule that is known to everyone.

AN INNING FOR THE OPPOSITION

It is not too partisan of me to say much less about the con's of automatic money than about the pro's. The principle of look-Ma-no-hands in money management has been debated so often that the critics have their brief well in hand. I shall tip off a few of their points simply to warn readers that there are two sides of the issue.

Objection 1

There is no one infallible rule of monetary growth. Since any single standard will not do, we must entrust our monetary fate to authority. It will deduce, in frequent conclave of its experts, the community's need for money and turn the money tap to just the right volume. Money is a mystery, and the layman should delegate its management to the expert.

Rejoinder. There is no expert in money management. Neither of our money-management teams, the Treasury or the Board, has earned the accolade of public confidence. Both teams have expertise in credit-management, but that is a different matter.

No one can measure the community's "need for money"—the quantity demanded at a stable price level in a growing economy—on a day-to-day or even a month-to-month basis. There is no clear channel of communication from public to monetary authority that reports growth in demand for money $P(kT)$ so that growth in supply can be in continuous balance with it. The balance of supply with demand for *money* is not improved when it is the practice of the authority to study demand for the wrong thing—for *credit.*

Objection 2

The first half-century of our experience with discretionary management has not been a fair test. It has been distorted by two world wars and their aftermath of crisis and disaster. The Treasury and the Board have done remarkably well under the circumstances. In a tranquil world the Federal Reserve Act would be an effective charter for sound money.

Rejoinder. Peace and tranquility are not on the horizon of the next half-century. It is just as well to take the pessimistic stand that temptations to misuse the monetary system will not diminish. There will be occasions when the Treasury will want to borrow cheaply in disregard of monetary stability. There will be occasions when the Board thinks it wise to disillusion the inflationary expectations that Treasury policy has generated.

If there were clear sailing ahead, discretionary management would be good enough. With trouble in prospect, it is more important to put monetary control on automatic pilot so that mistakes in policy will not aggravate our misfortunes. When inflationary forces are rampant, we will not want them intensified by monetary expansion in behalf of cheap credit for the Treasury. When deflation is the hazard, we will not want it accelerated by the Board's precautions against the next inflation. In rough weather the wheel of the monetary system should be lashed down.

Objection 3

A growing economy has a changing pattern of credit requirements. Legitimate demands for credit rise and fall, and they come from different sectors of the community in an unpredictable rotation. There must be a flexible program of credit control, and a central management of credit that is alert to satisfy legitimate demands while discouraging speculation, to segregate credit of high quality from credit of low quality, to smooth out discontinuities on credit markets, and to encourage development of credit facilities.

Rejoinder. The linkage of money with credit is an historical accident. Credit is one of various possible uses for the purchasing power that the monetary system commands as it increases the money supply. Whatever the use may be, disposing of the monetary system's purchasing power is incidental to the process of creating money.

The Credit Standard of money management, written into the Federal Reserve Act and administered by Treasury and Board, is a built-in destabilizer of economic activity. The community's demands upon the monetary system for credit grow quantitatively and improve qualitatively in each cyclic boom. They shrink in volume and deteriorate in quality during each cyclic relapse. The effect of linking the money supply to the cyclic yo-yo of credit demand is to intensify cycles.

Real growth is measured in terms of goods. It is not measured in terms of credit. In guiding real growth, monetary expansion should have the direct impact on markets for goods that fiscal policy has. Monetary policy is not committed by any Law of Nature to work its effects upon goods only after a detour through the markets for credit. Monetary policy yields perverse results on markets for goods when the impression develops, as it has in this country, that the credit detour is the end of the line for monetary policy.

In earlier phases of our growth, credit markets were embryonic. Then the banking system necessarily wore two hats, as supplier of money and as supplier of credit. Now the credit markets have matured, and there are efficient channels outside of the banking system for the flow of funds from saving to investment in real capital. Now the monetary system can attend to its essential function of supplying money.

Objection 4

The Demand Standard is provincial. It would isolate the American economy from world markets, raising a domestic rule of monetary growth to a pedestal above the principle of international economic cooperation. In view of this country's responsibility for stable growth internationally, self-interest in monetary policy is a luxury we cannot afford.

Rejoinder. American monetary policy has not abided by the rules of an international standard since 1914. The national gold stock has been a buffer between money here and money abroad. On the record the Credit Standard has been autarchic.

Sawtooth growth in the money supply of this country indicates our immaturity as London's successor to the role of international central bank. If a stable dollar is to be the anchor of a stable pound, peso, franc, yen, or piastre, rates of growth in the supply of dollars must vary no more between such extremes as *plus* 20 per cent and *minus* 10 per cent. Under our present rules of monetary management, we are announcing that we do not choose to run for the job that was London's for a century. Under an automatic rule, there would be less incentive for our allies to work our their own regional monetary coalitions.

CONCLUSION

Monetary economics has been dormant for two decades. Other aspects of economic analysis have left it far behind. It is so becalmed in an intellectual doldrum that no gentle breeze of inquiry can stir it. A lively storm of controversy may raise the prestige of monetary economics as an intellectual discipline, and it can do no harm to the prestige of the Federal Reserve as an instrument of social welfare if prestige is deserved. The present paper is a bid for the active interchange of views that may restore vitality to thinking about money.

Factor Inputs and International Price Comparisons[1]

LORIE TARSHIS

As Bernard Haley's essay on "Value and Distribution" in Volume I of *A Survey of Contemporary Economics* indicates, the study of the determination of price in a closed economy has passed far beyond the stage at which the explanation for the price of a certain product is sought in terms of some one variable, such as its marginal utility or its cost of production. In this area of investigation, the theorist is bound to consider both the forces of demand and those of supply, and under each of these headings he must take account of several variables; the nature of the markets for the product, and for its production factors; the technological circumstances; the conditions of factor supply; and even the kind of equilibrium (or disequilibrium) posited, all are important to the analysis. In a certain sense, we are aware of so many factors that can be expected to play a role that we are not greatly concerned when a relation between any one of them— say, the degree of market imperfection as measured by an index of industry concentration and the price level or price flexibility—finds no empirical verification. The economist can always explain away the absence of any such relation by stressing the operation of other factors, just as he has become able from constant practice to explain away almost any other observation that fails to fit his theory.

In the traditional theory of international trade, the analysis tends to be more simple-minded. Differences in the price patterns of various countries must be explained, since these differences presumably account for the existence and composition of trade. But the economist, instead of simply applying to his study of the several economies all the factors which are supposed to enter into the determination of internal prices, commonly selects from the list one specific factor—such as that one country has an

[1] Most of the research upon which this paper is based was undertaken for and financed by the RAND Corporation. A more detailed report has been prepared for this corporation.

abundance of labor, and another of capital—and rests the weight of his explanation upon it. He either disregards the other factors, or if he should allow for them explicitly, he does so by assuming they are the same in the various economies, and in this way he justifies his failure to deal with them.

I must make two reservations to my account at this point. First of all, not all international trade theorists limit their vision to the effects of one such factor; some have developed relatively general theories, though it is noticeable that these theories are usually disregarded in the formulation of policy. Secondly, the kind of question to be answered when our concern is the closed economy is so different from that when our interest is directed to the international economy that it leads to doubts as to the desirability of applying the same model to both situations. In the first instance we seek to explain why the price of a pound of butter in the United States is higher than that of a pound of bread; in the second we look for reasons to explain why the ratio of the price of butter to the price of bread in the United States is different from the corresponding ratio in another country. But although the problems are not the same, they are scarcely so dissimilar that we should expect the answers to be found along completely different lines.

The explanatory factor towards which attention is commonly directed in international trade theory is, to refer to Ohlin's well-known formulation, the differences in the various countries' endowments of productive factors. In the simplest model of two countries, two factors of production and two products, one country is taken as possessing relatively more labor; the other, more capital—in the sense that the ratio of the stock of labor to that of capital is higher in the former country than it is in the latter. The productive techniques available for producing a given product are assumed to be the same in the two countries, so that if the ratio of factor prices in both countries were the same, they would use factors in the same proportion in producing that product—this, of course, on the assumption that their producers are trying to minimize costs. Then if one product requires more of a certain factor of production (in both countries) than the other product, its price will be relatively lower in the country which possesses that factor in greater quantity; or at least this is so if, as we may normally suppose, the ratio of its price to the price of the other factor is below the corresponding ratio for the other country. From this conclusion it is supposed to follow that the country which possesses relatively more labor will export labor-intensive products; the other country will export capital-intensive products.

It seems clear that this conclusion is a very confined or restricted one. It does not allow for differences in the many other forces that are said to play a role in determining price in a closed economy. Instead, the methods of production available are assumed to be identical in the two countries; the structure of markets in the two economies is supposed to be the same; equilibrium in factor markets is taken for granted; there are only two factors of production, and no third factor, such as climate or land, specific to one or another product need be considered; an item which is intensive of a certain factor at one set of factor-price ratios is assumed to be intensive of that factor at all others; trade itself is supposed to respond to differences in product-price ratios; and so on. The list of conditions is so long and some of these conditions seem to be so improbable that we should not be greatly surprised to find that the relation between trade and factor-inputs is sometimes obscured. Bearing these conditions in mind, we are by no means bound to conclude that, if our exports are more labor-intensive than our imports, the United States must possess more labor relative to its capital than do other economies, or, instead, that the theory is wrong. It is not difficult to find several factors which could readily account for the discrepancy between theory and observation. Nevertheless, if we are to take economics as being something more than a perpetual exercise in rationalization, we are bound to be concerned with such a discrepancy, checking it carefully, and, if it must be accepted, seeing how we may most satisfactorily account for it.

The discrepancy has, of course, been noted, in two important articles (1, 2). Leontief has presented evidence on the basis of which he concludes that United States' exports are in fact more labor-intensive than are those of its imports that compete with its domestic product. His findings cannot be lightly dismissed. While one may be inclined to quarrel with details— for example, with his recording against our imports of natural rubber the labor-capital input coefficients for the synthetic product—the results are nevertheless so strikingly different from those to be expected on the basis of the simple-minded theory that we are compelled to look into the whole problem more carefully.

My purpose in this paper is, however, not to appraise Leontief's results. Instead, I shall present some data which bear upon the problems he raises from a somewhat different standpoint. The basic difference, which I will discuss more carefully later, is that, instead of utilizing United States foreign trade data, I shall make use of information on prices in various countries. But my evidence will not cover nearly so wide an area as Leontief's; for reasons that will subsequently be presented, the data that I use are necessarily fragmentary—several specific chemicals, for example, but not all the products of the chemical industry. Nevertheless, I believe that the results are significant, particularly since they suggest, unlike Leontief's, that the factor to which Heckscher and Ohlin first drew attention is indeed relatively important, even though its influence in specific instances may be offset by other factors.

The RAND Corporation in RM-1443, "A Comparison of 1950 Wholesale Prices in Soviet and American Industry" (3) has made information available on the wholesale prices in 1950 of some 2000 producers' goods

in both the Soviet Union and the United States. In the course of an enquiry that has been undertaken for the RAND Corporation, we were able
to secure information about the prices of some 200 items in Great Britain
and of about 125 items in Japan of those represented in RM-1443. Prices
for 85 items in all four countries and for 97 items in three of the countries
are available.

It must be conceded that there are difficulties about the precise comparability of some of the products for which price data from several countries have been obtained. This is to say, we are sometimes not at all confident that item X for which a U.S. price has been secured is exactly the
same thing as item Y for which a Soviet price is available. But, generally
speaking, the United States–Soviet Union comparisons are very satisfactory, and most of the United States–Great Britain comparisons are also
very good,[2] though some for which British prices were found in catalogues
are more doubtful. In contrast, the United States–Japanese comparisons
are, at best, of questionable value. For certain items—for example, chemicals, structural steel products, and nonferrous metals—the comparability
is presumably acceptable; for others, such as machinery, it is of very doubtful quality. These problems of product comparability are, of course, no
different from those that must be faced in preparing time-series of price
indices for a single country, and our own results are frequently more acceptable. Still, the difficulties must be admitted.

With price information from three or four countries, it is possible to
isolate instances in which the price of a certain product in one country
is especially high or low, compared to its price in the others. Our procedures for making this determination can be easily illustrated.

First, price ratios for all products were computed. The price of copper
sulphate in the United States was $154.35 a metric ton, and in the Soviet
Union was 2380 rubles for the same amount; accordingly, the ruble-dollar
ratio for this product stood at 15.4 (=2380/154.35). In the same way,
ruble-sterling, ruble-yen, sterling-dollar, yen-dollar, and yen-sterling ratios
for all possible products were determined. Median values were then established for each of these ratios; the median of the ruble-dollar ratios coming to 11.5, that of the sterling-dollar ratios to .268 (corresponding to
£1 = $3.73), and so on. Now if, for a certain product, the ruble-dollar,
ruble-sterling, and ruble-yen ratios stand well above the median values of
each of these series, we can conclude that the price in rubles of that product
is unusually high compared to its price in dollars, sterling and yen.[3] To

[2] These were obtained through the courtesy of officials of the Board of Trade
who had access to RM-1443 [see (3)] and its descriptions.

[3] More precisely, it means that the relation between the ruble price of that
product and other ruble prices is quite different from (higher than) the corresponding relation involving prices in dollars, sterling, and yen.

illustrate: the ruble-dollar ratio for titanium dioxide was 39.1 or 3.4 times the median value of this series, the ruble-sterling ratio for the same product is 2.9 times the median value of its series, and the ruble-yen ratio is 1.7 times the median value of its series. This obviously means that the ruble price is high compared to its prices in the other three countries. For some products, we can identify the price in one country as very high, while the price in another is very low. Thus the ruble-dollar, ruble-sterling, and ruble-yen ratios for Glauber's salt are all well below the respective median values, implying a low price in rubles; while the sterling-dollar, and yen-dollar ratios are also very low, implying, with the low ruble-dollar ratio for this product, a high price in dollars. Naturally, too, there are certain products for which the price in no single country stands out as exceptionally high or low.

The next step consists in setting down the appropriate factor inputs as ratios of labor (in man-years) to capital (in units of $10,000) against each item represented as having an unusually high or low price in any country. Unfortunately, it is rarely possible to determine this for the specific product. Input-output tables which provide the basic data are prepared in terms that are far more aggregative in character and, to take a relatively unfavorable example, we do not have data for copper sulphate, but rather for "industrial chemicals," of which copper sulphate is only one out of many hundreds and quite possibly an unrepresentative one at that. Nevertheless, no better data on factor inputs are available, and for all their defects[4] they have been used in our study, just as they were in Leontief's. However, we have made use of an unpublished RAND study of factor-inputs instead of employing the data used by Leontief; a superficial check showed that this made no significant difference to the results. Illustrating the procedure more concretely: Glauber's salt is a product which has an unusually low price in one country and an unusually high price in another. The factor inputs for the class of industrial chemicals to which Glauber's salt belongs are shown as 133.2 man-years of labor and $2.171 million dollars of capital for every million dollars' worth of output; the ratio of labor to capital comes, therefore, to 0.613. It is this ratio which is set down against Glauber's salt with the appropriate figure determined in the same way against each of the other products. Incidentally, on the basis of these data, industrial chemicals are found to be one of the least labor-intensive products in our list; petroleum refining (where the ratio is 0.314), cement (0.546), primary aluminum (0.387), and the products of aluminum rolling and drawing (0.491) rank also as especially capital-intensive. At the other extreme are such products as machine tools and metal-working ma-

---

[4] Among others is the fact that the "capital" item is measured not as the amount of capital *used up* in production, but rather as the amount of capital investment required to permit an expansion in capacity by one unit of output. It then does not allow for the difference in the length of life of capital assets in the various industries.

chinery (for which the ratio is 2.352); spinning, weaving and dyeing (2.172); fabricated wood products (2.453); and plywood (2.155).

The unweighted arithmetic means of the various entries for the ratio of factor inputs for all the products in each separate category—viz., for items that are high in price in the United States, for those that are low in price in the United States, and so on—were then determined. The results are shown in the following table:

Average value of ratio	$\dfrac{\text{labor (in man-years)}}{\text{capital (in dollars 10,000)}}$	for items:	
High in price in U.S.	1.416		
Low in price in U.S.	.842	Ratio of ratios	1.682
High in price in U.K.	1.426		
Low in price in U.K.	1.026	Ratio of ratios	1.390
High in price in Soviet Union	0.889		
Low in price in Soviet Union	1.070	Ratio of ratios	.831
High in price in Japan	0.844		
Low in price in Japan	1.477	Ratio of ratios	.571

These results are what we should expect on the basis of the Heckscher-Ohlin theorem, although, considering the many other factors that we could expect to be operative, they are perhaps too good. In the United States, which presumably possesses more capital per unit of labor than the others, items that are especially high in price are on the average almost 70 per cent more labor-intensive than are those that are especially low in price; in the United Kingdom, the high-priced items are 39 per cent more labor-intensive. In the Soviet Union, which must possess far less capital per unit of labor than does the United States, and somewhat less than does the United Kingdom, the high-priced items were 17 per cent more capital-intensive than were the low-priced items. Finally, the high-priced items in Japan—the most labor-rich and capital-poor country of the four—were decidedly capital-intensive (43 per cent more) compared to the low-priced items.

These results are further confirmed in the following comparisons, which involve pairs of countries. The average value of the labor-to-capital ratio for all items for which the ruble-dollar ratio stood above its median value was 0.87; the corresponding figure for items for which the ruble-dollar ratio was below its median value was 1.31.[5] Hence, once again, the United States, an economy with a much higher stock of capital relative to its labor

---

[5] These comparisons involve far more commodities than those made above. Many items for which the ruble-dollar price ratio stands above the median value of that series may not qualify as items for which the price in one country (or two) is especially high or low.

force than is the Soviet Union, appears to have its comparative advantage
in terms of price in respect to items that are relatively capital-intensive.
The complete results involving each pair of countries follow:

Average value of labor-capital ratio for items for which

	Above Median	Below Median
Ruble-dollar ratio was:	0.87	1.31
Ruble-sterling ratio was:	0.855	1.30
Ruble-yen ratio was:	1.18	0.81
Sterling-dollar ratio was:	1.02	1.215
Yen-dollar ratio was:	0.82	1.385
Yen-sterling ratio was:	0.76	1.26

Thus, the evidence is surprisingly clear that, on the average, a country
can be expected to enjoy a price advantage in respect to products that are
intensive of its relatively more abundant factor.

In the space remaining we shall discuss a few of the many issues that
these findings raise.

First of all, it is important to realize that the factor-input data we have
used refer to the United States, but that they have nevertheless been applied
to items produced in the other countries. In some circumstances this does
not matter; or, at any rate, in the model that is commonly assumed in discussions of international trade, it does not matter. In such models if one
product is, say, labor-intensive compared to another product at a certain
set of factor price ratios, it is supposed that it will continue to be so at all
other ratios; there are no crossovers of factor intensities with which we
must be concerned. Whether this assumption correctly portrays reality or
not is something that can be determined only empirically. In any case, if
it can be accepted, the order of commodities ranked in accordance with the
ratio of their factor-inputs will be the same in all countries, and the use of
United States data in place of the appropriate information from the other
countries will not determine the general nature of the findings, though it
will influence their quantitative aspect. In other words, if British, Japanese,
and Soviet factor-input data were used appropriately, we should still find
that items that were much higher in price in, say, Britain than in the United
States, were items which, even in British terms, were relatively capital-
intensive, just as they are on the basis of United States data, and so on.

However, if the assumption cannot be granted and crossovers of factor
intensities do occur, there is no special presumption for expecting that a
country will specialize, or display a comparative price advantage, in products that are intensive (in *that* country) of its relatively more plentiful
resource. The United States may be able to sell a certain product which
is capital-intensive on the basis of United States factor-inputs at a very
low price. But this product may be labor-intensive in another country in
which the ratio of labor-to-capital resources is much higher; yet it will sell
at a relatively high price in that country, despite the fact that it is the labor-

intensive product of an economy which possesses a relatively large labor force. To put this somewhat differently: if factor intensities do cross, then it is not possible on the basis of *our* data to assert that an item that is low (or high) in price in another country is intensive, *in terms of its production technique*, of its relatively abundant (or scarce) factor. However, the fact that such a result appears to hold for the United States perhaps establishes a presumption that it would hold for other countries as well on the basis of their factor-input data.

A second matter to be raised has to do with the inclusion of prices from the Soviet Union in the study. Something is known, or at least we pretend it is, about pricing practices in capitalist economies. Scarcely as much can be claimed for our understanding of the determination of price in the Soviet Union. If in that country prices do not correspond to costs in about the way they do in the other countries, if costs are computed quite differently, if costs are not minimized, or if equilibrium in factor markets does not exist,[6] we should not expect the conventional international trade theory to apply. Our main excuse for including the Soviet data is that they were available, and very little else was. Whether the results in which these other figures are used are meaningful or not is a different matter. They may be the result, not of the applicability of conventional international trade theory, but instead of the chaotic nature of Soviet pricing practices. Or possibly, the fact that the results are quite consistent with those for the other countries suggests that Soviet pricing practices are not significantly more chaotic than our own. But this is a different matter.

Certainly, as we have already noted, there are very many reasons for expecting results far less systematic than those we seem to have found. Fortunately, when we look at our results more closely, we can detect a satisfying degree of irregularity. Thus, while the average value of the ratio of the input of labor to capital in items that are high in price in the United States is well above the corresponding figure for items that are unusually low in price, there are many exceptions. Thus, a number of industrial chemicals (eight in all) are found to be high in price in the United States, in the sense in which we have used this term, yet the factor input ratio for industrial chemicals shows that the class as a whole is relatively capital-intensive. Or again, the price, in the United States, of an oil pressure gage is decidedly low; but the gage is a member of a class "Instruments, both Scientific and Mechanical Measuring" which is relatively labor-intensive. To illustrate this still further: there are 28 items which are classified as having an unusually high price in Japan. Two of them—the oil pressure gage and felt sheets—are produced with a ratio of labor to capital inputs greater than 1.477 which is the average value of the ratio for Japan's 33 low-priced items. And of these latter items, five chemicals, cement, ferrotungsten, and one steel product are produced with a ratio of labor-to-

---

[6] At least in the sense that relative factor scarcities are reflected in the ratio of factor prices as these prices are employed in the determination of costs.

capital inputs lower than 0.844 which is the average value of the corresponding ratios for the 28 items that are unusually high in price. We must, however, once again warn the reader that the factor inputs for the class may not be representative of the factor inputs for the specific item.

These results appear to be at variance with those secured by Leontief, and some consideration of the differences is in order. In the first place, our study is partial, being restricted to items for which price data could readily be obtained. Second, it is restricted to a study of items for which exact counterparts are produced, or at least are available, in at least three of the four countries. Third, our attention is directed to differences in patterns of prices rather than to trade flows. In this connection it is worth while to point out that, insofar as it is possible to locate trade figures for items for which prices in the United States are unusually high or low, there is no evidence for the relation between prices and trade that we should normally expect. Instead, a number of high-priced items are exported—commonly to Canada, Latin America, Japan, and the Philippines, while a number of distinctly low-priced items are imported. Several explanations suggest themselves, but the finding itself should be kept in mind in any consideration of Leontief's results.

Our empirical results are clearly of limited significance.[7] Nevertheless, they are, I believe, the first that directly bear upon a central aspect of international price theory, and, though they can scarcely claim to be conclusive, they do establish a reasonably convincing case for the view that the proportions of productive factors in various countries play an important role in determining their patterns of prices. As we stressed at the beginning of this paper, there are certainly other determining factors and possibly some that are more important. But it still seems to be true that an economy which possesses a relative abundance of capital will enjoy comparatively low prices for its capital-intensive products and will be compelled, unless it wants to tap foreign sources of supply, to pay decidedly high prices for items which require an especially large amount of labor in production. Here, at least, is a classical view that we need not reject.

References

1. Wassily Leontief, "Domestic Production and Foreign Trade: the American Capital Position Re-examined," *Proceedings of the American Philosophical Society*, XCVII, No. 4 (September 1953).

2. Wassily Leontief, "Factor Proportions and the Structure of American Trade: Further Theoretical and Empirical Analysis," *Review of Economics and Statistics*, XXXVIII, No. 4 (November 1956).

3. Norman Kaplan and William L. White, A Comparison of 1950 Wholesale Prices in Soviet and American Industry. The RAND Corporation, RM-1443, Santa Monica, California, 1955.

---

[7] In the study which is being prepared for the RAND Corporation, a further substantial body of information will be presented. On the whole, this additional data confirms our own conclusions.